EDUCATION IN A
NEW ERA

ASCD YEARBOOK 2000

Edited by **Ronald S. Brandt**

ASSOCIATION FOR SUPERVISION AND CURRICULUM DEVELOPMENT
ALEXANDRIA, VIRGINIA USA

Association for Supervision and Curriculum Development
1703 N. Beauregard St. • Alexandria, VA 22311-1714 USA
Telephone: 1-800-933-2723 or 703-578-9600 • Fax: 703-575-5400
Web site: http://www.ascd.org • E-mail: member@ascd.org

Gene R. Carter, *Executive Director*
Michelle Terry, *Associate Executive Director, Program Development*
Nancy Modrak, *Director, Publishing*
John O'Neil, *Director of Acquisitions*
Julie Houtz, *Managing Editor of Books*
Margaret Oosterman, *Associate Editor*
Carol Rawleigh, *Proofreader*
Charles D. Halverson, *Project Assistant*
Gary Bloom, *Director, Design and Production Services*
Karen Monaco, *Senior Designer*
Tracey A. Smith, *Production Manager*
Dina Murray, *Production Coordinator*
John Franklin, *Production Coordinator*
Valerie Sprague, *Desktop Publisher*
M. L. Coughlin Editorial Services, *Indexer*

Copyright © 2000 by the Association for Supervision and Curriculum Development. All rights reserved. No part of this publication may be reproduced or transmitted in any form or by any means, electronic or mechanical, including photocopy, recording, or any information storage and retrieval system, without permission from ASCD. Readers who wish to duplicate material copyrighted by ASCD may do so for a small fee by contacting the Copyright Clearance Center (CCC), 222 Rosewood Dr., Danvers, MA 01923, USA (telephone: 978-750-8400; fax: 978-750-4470). ASCD has authorized the CCC to collect such fees on its behalf. Requests to reprint rather than photocopy should be directed to ASCD's permissions office at 703-578-9600. James A. Banks holds the copyright to his chapter, "The Social Construction of Difference and the Quest for Educational Equality." Deborah Meier holds the copyright to her chapter, "Progressive Education in the 21st Century: A Work in Progress." These chapters may not be reproduced in any form without the consent of the authors.

ASCD publications present a variety of viewpoints. The views expressed or implied in this book should not be interpreted as official positions of the Association.

Printed in the United States of America.

January 2000 member book (pc). ASCD Premium, Comprehensive, and Regular members periodically receive ASCD books as part of their membership benefits. No. FY00-4.

ASCD Stock No. 100000
ASCD member price: $20.95   nonmember price: $24.95

ISSN: 1042-9018
ISBN: 0-87120-363-4

04 03 02 01 00   10 9 8 7 6 5 4 3 2 1

MVFOL

Education in a New Era

Introduction: A New Century

RONALD S. BRANDT, EDITOR

For decades, we have used "21st century" as convenient shorthand for an exciting future, a world very different from the present. Urging radical change in schools, reformers have warned that we should begin preparing students for life in an ultramodern era that was almost upon us. Not just a new century but a whole new millennium was about to begin. Educators, more than most, had to be aware of the forthcoming revolution. Our profession, we were reminded, has the awesome responsibility of equipping young people with the knowledge and skills needed in an ever more complex society. Our business *is* the future.

Now that the new century is here (or almost here, depending on how one counts), we are reminded that the calendar is a convenient but arbitrary symbol of passing time. Today is pretty much like yesterday, regardless of how we number it. Things are indeed changing, but in most cases incrementally, not overnight. Making a fuss about the brand-new year each January 1 can be fun, even motivating, but nothing in nature relates that event directly to the material world.

Of course, our observance of these occasions is not so much about nature as about ourselves. Both for individuals and organizations, pausing now and then to look back on past achievements and ponder future possibilities pays dividends. Alert businesses, school systems, and other institutions do it under the banner of strategic planning. No one can say for sure what *will* be, but reviewing their problems, capabilities, and opportunities, people decide what they *want* to happen, then create plans to improve chances that their aspirations will become reality.

This book is like that. Published as we enter an age that stirs our imaginations, it looks back to also look ahead. Its purpose is to divine

1

what may happen—as well as what should happen—in the education of children and youth, after thoughtfully reviewing what has happened so far.

The authors, chosen for their expertise in the topics they write about, were invited to highlight a few 20th century ideas, events, or developments they considered especially notable. Then, after considering the elements of experience that seemed most enduring, they were asked to envision what educators could expect, and commit to, in the years ahead.

Most authors found that making such projections was difficult. Mindful of spectacularly erroneous predictions about airplanes, television, and computers made by experts in the past, they were hesitant to go out on the proverbial limb. Nevertheless, each has made a conscientious effort to peer into the mist-enshrouded vistas of days to come.

With or without soothsayers, we can safely make two broad generalizations about the future: (1) Technological change will continue at a rate difficult for people to keep pace with; and (2) Technological changes will produce social, political, and economic changes that will demand responses from educational institutions. These statements may be obvious, but they are laden with implications.

The challenge of technological change is sometimes portrayed as the need to keep abreast of technology itself. Science classes need access to the sophisticated equipment used in universities and industrial laboratories. Mathematics classes need graphing calculators. Automotive repair is no longer a matter of replacing spark plugs and points but requires systems for computer analysis. In fact, computers are now considered a basic tool for learning almost any subject. But computers become obsolete in a few years. Paying for, as well as making wise use of, all the improvements in tools that our society routinely generates is indeed a challenge, especially for schools, where such tools do not pay for themselves in increased productivity.

But in the long run, technological change has more significant indirect than direct effects in education. Nearly everyone recognizes that invention of the automobile led to the building of suburbs. Mass commuting has contributed to many problems, including deterioration of large cities. For education, these problems have translated into issues associated with *urban education*.

Other examples abound. Modern forms of transportation, along with other technological developments such as radio and television, have enabled people to migrate from developing nations to more developed areas, producing educational responses such as *multicultural education* and *bilingual education*. Advances in medicine have saved children with severe disabilities—children who might not have survived in former times—and educators are now required to educate these children regardless of cost. With machines performing physical tasks, most work no longer requires muscle power. Such a change led to an expanded work force that includes more men and women who previously had not worked outside the home. The changing work force has meant that children's lives are different from those of earlier generations, creating new challenges for educators.

These examples are grossly oversimplified, of course. Each phenomenon has many causes, not just one. I cite them only to make a point: The technological changes going on around us, along with those to come, will produce effects beyond their immediate terrain.

If we were to survey the many ways evolving technology is changing the world, we would come up with a long list, ranging from exploration of space and ocean depths to investigation of the human brain. Surely, though, the aspect of technology that we are most aware of these days—and the one that contributes to all the other advances—is the information revolution. Looking back centuries from now, people will undoubtedly see the computer as a major milestone in human history, comparable to invention of the printing press and the harnessing of fossil fuels.

At this point, we have only glimpses of how life will eventually be different because of computers. Personally, I enjoy the convenience of banks, bookstores, and travel agencies online; I routinely use e-mail; and I frequently search for information on the Web. Equally important, I note that every agency I deal with—even my church—has begun to inquire about communicating electronically instead of on paper.

As for educators, most of us have not yet grasped the enormities of how the information revolution will affect education in the long run. We struggle to buy more machines, connect them to one another and the world, and use them within the existing system. But the rest of society is undergoing a transformation inconceivable at this point to all but the most visionary, and education will slowly but surely change along with everything else.

We wish we could provide a blueprint for the ways society will change, and what those changes will mean for curriculum, instruction, assessment, and other aspects of our profession. Such predictions, unfortunately, are impossible. All we can do is offer informed speculation, trusting that what we have written will encourage our colleagues not only to ponder future prospects but also to work for the possibilities they value the most.

From the Editor: Please note that throughout the yearbook, phrases such as "America," "our country," and "our nation" refer to the United States.

1

Governing the American Dream of Universal Public Education

CHRIS PIPHO

When the 20th century began 100 years ago, public education in the United States was already moving toward a more centralized system of governance than our forefathers had envisioned. Early legislation adopted by the Massachusetts Bay Colony, although it emphasized family responsibility, also established the principle of publicly supported universal education (Good, 1963). The state's interest in education, which can be traced back to this era, has gradually turned into state control.

The major reason for expansion of state dominance is growth of the New World, both economically and geographically, which—with its waves of new immigrants—presented great challenges to the American dream of universal public education. Families remained the central focus, but these were families who had already bid farewell to ancestral ways. They were eager to learn the English language and the basic skills needed for new jobs. And they were quick to adopt democratic principles, which meant that all citizens could control, through voting and representative government, how even their neighborhood school was to be run. No central government and no central religious order controlled the curriculum; families were free to choose parochial schools or private academies. Most important, all children had access to a public school, where they quickly learned a new culture and language, often brought home to parents and grandparents to be shared around the evening dinner table.

Although these immigrants recognized the need for education, they were often forced to put family survival needs ahead of it. School attendance in rural areas was seen as secondary to harvesting the crops. In cities, child labor was often needed to put food on the table. To address these varying levels of education compliance, states developed a uniform set of educational offerings and expected all citizens to comply with them. Laws for compulsory attendance and length of the school year followed; next came more consistency in teacher training through certification laws.

Each succeeding generation and national group brought new problems and new state demands. The story of governance in American public education, then, is one of meeting these challenges and producing new solutions. Ironically, the solutions that one generation of policymakers adopted often became problems for the next generation to fix. Today, some see states so deeply involved in education rule making that they possess a monopolistic stranglehold on education. To advocates of free enterprise, the obvious solution is a market approach: charter schools, vouchers, and choice. This chapter traces some reasons for our current situation and considers how governance may change in the years ahead.

STATEHOOD AND CONSTITUTIONAL CONTROL

By the time Arizona and New Mexico became the 47th and 48th territories to enter statehood in 1912, state constitutions generally contained a clause on public education. Except for Iowa, all states use a constitutional clause to describe their governance needs; Iowa uses an education code (Ziebarth, 1998).

Governance—who makes what decisions and how—was a key part of state constitutions and centralized control over education.

6

Families were considered a part of this mix through provisions for state and local boards of education and for local superintendents of education. The most central provision in state constitutions is the clause calling for each state to maintain a free system of public schools open to all children of the state. Also included is a funding or finance clause and a separation of church and state clause. The latter forbids appropriating or using public funds to support sectarian schools and requires public schools to be free from sectarian control (Ziebarth, 1998).

Because the constitutional provisions are so central to managing education, public dissatisfaction with education eventually finds its way back, through governance questions and court action, to state constitutional concerns. In the last two decades, advocates pushing for vouchers for students in public and private schools have seen the constitutional provisions for separation of church and state as a major roadblock. The existence of charter schools has likewise raised many questions about the legal duties of state and local boards.

The basic constitutional provisions have stood the test of time for almost a century. But some experts see the steady incursion of vouchers, charters, and parent choice, especially when court decisions support them, as bringing about fundamental state constitutional changes in the future.

THE MOVE TO CENTRALIZATION

Nowhere is the move to centralization more evident than in the reduced number of school districts since the turn of the century. The United States now has 15,000 districts, compared to 150,000 in 1900. With vast rural lands homesteaded at a time when transportation was difficult, thousands of one-room schools were built, each with its own school board. Such small, locally governed schools met the education demands of large families and the need for schools to be within two miles walking distance from homes.

The one-room school reached its zenith in the 1920s and '30s. Teacher training was often hurried and superficial. Faculty members at the teachers colleges (former normal schools) talked about "60-day wonders": Students who had graduated from high school in May took courses for 60 days in the summer, and were given responsibility for an entire school in September. The county superintendent supervised them, they had one-day workshops on some Saturdays during the year, and they returned for annual summer sessions until they were awarded a two-year degree.

In the years following World War I, conditions began to change. As cities expanded, high schools, junior high schools, and kindergartens became commonplace. Demands for higher-quality education prompted state legislatures and local school boards to respond to their constituents' needs. Both compulsory attendance ages and length of school year were expanded significantly. By midcentury, the collection of dropout statistics was added as another measure of quality.

PROFESSIONALIZATION AND BUREAUCRACY

The chicken-and-egg dilemma of what caused educational governance to become more centralized is an interesting question. Schools have always been asked to serve the changing needs of society and families. But did family demands bring about higher levels of teacher-administrative training and state certification regulations, or did the advent of larger schools (with a decline in the rural economy and growth of the urban economy) bring on a need for better-trained principals, superintendents, and teachers? Above all, when the cycle of certification, job specialization, and unionization got under way, did it feed the call for more bureaucratization in the name of serving families and the state? Sprinkled in was the proliferation of national commissions, professional organizations, and university-based education "experts" like John Dewey and James B. Conant. All these contributed to the gradual professionalization of teaching, the growth of colleges and laboratory schools, and the governance "omelette" that we have learned to live with.

Adding to the mix were families and communities who wanted to control the teachers' and administrators' lives (with rules on smoking, alcohol, and marriage), plus many other issues that often brought warring parties to the state board of education, the legislature, or even the courts. Each ruling contributed to the growing centralization of control.

Some interesting collections of people, organizations, and ideas shaped the history of education governance. The state of Oregon produces one of these stories. In 1925, a landmark school court case, *Pierce v. Society of Sisters,* pitted the Ku Klux Klan against parochial and private education. The Klan wanted compulsory education restricted to public schools, because private schools taught private ideas to defenseless children. The court decision upheld the right of parents to control and direct their children's education. The court, however, also upheld the right of the state to reasonably regulate, inspect, supervise, and examine schools, including teachers, and to require compulsory attendance (Tyack, James, & Benavot, 1987). The ruling confirmed not only the rights of parents but also the prerogatives of the state.

THE FEDERAL GOVERNMENT'S IMPACT ON LOCAL GOVERNANCE

States are responsible for education, and the federal government is relegated to a supporting role. But throughout our history, the federal government, using money and pork barrel politics—sometimes led by prominent congressional members—has dramatically influenced education. These efforts were not always aimed specifically at education but rather at supporting agencies that could improve life for large populations in our society. Creation of the land grant colleges is one example. As their mission—to supply scientific research and practical education to a growing agriculture and manufacturing segment of society—was expanded through the Smith-Lever Act of 1914, extension teaching directed to rural families became one of the largest adult education efforts ever undertaken by a country. Schools became vehicles for some of these education programs. When the Smith-Hughes Act of 1917 added vocational education to the mission of land grant colleges, high schools became the agency to deliver such programs. Teachers were prepared, curriculums were written, and local and state boards administered combined federal, state, and local programs. During the 1920s, these programs and 4-H clubs expanded rapidly, and county and state fairs were added to improve society. Vocational education, including home economics, influenced city schools, so school boards everywhere found themselves governing a wider variety of programs, each with broad public support. School board meetings were probably rarely if ever devoted to discussing the federal intrusion into education governance. Instead, local boards accepted federal initiatives along with federal dollars because these initiatives met local needs.

ECONOMIC AND TECHNOLOGICAL INFLUENCES

Societal needs, pushed along by technological changes in transportation and communication, have probably affected the governance of education more than most people realize. A farm-to-market road system and a state highway system were not designed to change education, but paved roads and school buses made consolidating school districts possible in the 1930s. A better-educated populace, produced in part by the land grant colleges and the normal schools (established to produce more qualified teachers), changed the fabric of American families. The first college graduate in a family provided a new goal for younger siblings and extended family members to emulate. The benefits of further education became more widely accepted—leading to identification of more education needs.

The Great Depression of the 1930s slowed down some expectations, but also added many new opportunities for realizing the ideal of universal education. Because of the depression, families could no longer take care of their own needs and increasingly had to turn to state and federal governments for assistance. The funding of education, which to a large extent had rested on local property taxes, took a severe hit as land values plummeted and businesses failed. More than 5,000 rural schools closed in 1932. Many never opened again, and town and city schools were called upon to absorb the rural students.

Professor John K. Norton of Columbia University said in 1935 that the early years of the depression "had been the most disastrous in education history" (Norton, in Good, 1963, p. 513). Student enrollments were increasing, but teachers were being laid off or were working unpaid. Taxpayer groups were growing, which in turn probably forced the growth of professional education organizations and teacher groups to fight tax cutbacks. New state funding mechanisms replaced some of the lost local tax revenues. Even the federal government got into the local funding picture in 1934 when President Roosevelt's Reconstruction Finance Corporation loaned the city of Chicago $22 million so it could pay salaries owed to teachers for the previous three years (Good, 1963).

A HIDDEN GOVERNANCE STRUCTURE

New education programs were affected, but little thought was given to who was going to make decisions about education and who was to be accountable for these decisions—key elements in a visible governance structure.

While the average citizen was struggling to move out of the Great Depression, the education establishment gained visibility and influence in universities, colleges, and urban school districts. Many factors contributed to this increased visibility: new federal programs, expanded teacher education and educational research, growth of professional education organizations, and the academic specialization needed to support the increasing number of high schools and junior high schools.

A symbiotic governance structure around public education gradually evolved, a relationship that most parents or other citizens had not envisioned. It was led by well-known education professors who depended on an expanding state education system, like John Dewey at the University of Chicago and a bevy of similar professors at Columbia Teachers College and other major universities. Their students replicated and expanded their influence and became leaders in the model urban school districts in positions such as curriculum coordinators, supervisors, department chairs, superintendents, and principals. They exercised great control over public schools in the name of improving education for families and students. They authored the college and high school textbooks, conducted research, devised organizational improvement strategies such as the Dalton and Winnetka plans,[1] and advised state education agencies that were also growing in importance.

Partly because of their efforts, states strengthened teacher certification rules, and as rural schools faded from the scene, the two-year elementary teaching certificate became the norm and the four-year B.A. or B.S. degree the goal. Teacher organizations persuaded local districts to establish salary schedules based on length of service and degrees earned, replacing personally negotiating with the local board of education. Education started to look more like a profession.

These successes, however, may have planted the seeds of discontent for later generations to handle. One can argue that this hidden governance structure was needed, that the populace supported it, and that it produced good education results. True, but as the goal of profession-alization moved forward, the original goal of free and universal educa-tion for all children may in some respects have been moved to the background. Did the profession get overprofessionalized? Good question, but who should answer it? And in what decade might the true answer be found?

WORLD WAR II BRINGS BIG CHANGES

Had World War II not occurred, the directions taken by the "pro-fessionalization" gurus of the 1930s might have produced lasting results. Unfortunately for them, the events following Pearl Harbor put education in a holding pattern.

It was an unusual time in education. Everyone focused on the war effort. Schools closed when the federal government issued ration books to all citizens. Elementary school students used school time to collect metal for scrap drives and milkweed pods for navy life vests. In high schools and colleges, men teachers were drafted or enlisted midyear. Senior classes in some high schools finished the year with only girls because the boys had enlisted on their 17th birthday. In my one-room school, an emergency teacher was found whose husband had been drafted. Because she had no car, a senior citizen was hired to drive her to school each day. If governance concerns existed during these years, they were not evident.

Near the end of the war and in the years that followed, the federal government offered discharged veterans and those still in the service opportunities to further their education and receive credit for service-related training. Most notable was the Serviceman's Readjustment Act (G.I. Bill), which gave monetary assistance to those who wanted to attend college. Large numbers of veterans swelled enrollments and in turn changed the maturity level of student bodies. The military services created the United States Armed Forces Institute (USAFI) to formally give college credit for training and college courses taken while people were in the military.

High school dropouts and others who had never attended high school were also included in these programs. The University of Iowa (developers of the Iowa Test of Basic Skills) was contracted to develop the General Educational Development (GED) High School Equivalency Examination. Veterans and young adults could receive a high school diploma by passing a battery of five tests.

These programs created nontraditional ways to enter higher education or complete high school. All states currently use the GED program; it awards thousands of diplomas yearly in each state. In some ways, the seeds for nontraditional entry and exit from education programs evident today in distance learning and Internet college programs were planted in the 1940s and 1950s.

RURAL SCHOOLS ON THE DEFENSIVE

After the war, state agencies and national groups like the National Education Association (NEA) and its Department of Rural Education took up the cause of school district consolidation in earnest. The National Commission on School District Reorganization issued a report in 1948 showing that the United States had 104,000 local school districts. Nine years later, when President Eisenhower called a White House Conference on Education, the number of districts was down to 59,000 (Cooper, Dawson, & Isenberg, 1957). The NEA played an important role in this reduction by preparing model state legislation.

As this major governance shift took place, many states abolished the county superintendent's role. The nearest town district took over supervising rural schools that remained open. In a few states, the county superintendent structure was phased into an intermediate education agency, such as the Board of Cooperative Education Services in New York State. In others, all schools in a county became a single school district. For example, in 1950, 39 districts in Jefferson County, Colorado, were reorganized into a new single school district under one superintendent and board, forming what continues to be the district with the largest student population in Colorado.

Of course, these changes were not made without opposition. In many parts of the country, people questioned the efficiency of consolidating school districts. State law usually required a formal vote of taxpayers before a new larger district could be established. The job of orchestrating this vote, drawing up the new boundaries, and finding new board members who would run and old board members who

13

would step aside was tough. It was usually assigned to someone in the state agency who had rural credentials and good diplomatic skills.

While some experts were writing off small rural schools, others were trying to keep them in business. Frank Cyr, a professor at Columbia Teachers College, started the Catskill project in upstate New York to assist small schools by providing models of instructional improvement. One of his students, Elbie Gann, working in the Colorado Department of Education, took Cyr's ideas and with a colleague, Frank Anderson, wrote a large Ford Foundation proposal that created the Western States Small Schools project. At its height, it involved state agencies in Colorado, New Mexico, Arizona, Nevada, and Utah. Their goal was to help schools that were necessarily small: the ones that, because of geographic isolation, consolidation could not reach. These efforts helped state boards and commissioners of education counter the charge they heard at so many irate community meetings: "You're only interested in closing rural schools."

PROBLEMS FROM THE POSTWAR BOOM

The postwar era, with its baby boom and shortage of buildings and teachers, created governance shocks and waves that have continued to the end of this century. The federal office of education reported that between 1955 and 1965, student enrollment increased from 36 million to 50 million. The average annual increase of 700,000 students produced a need for over 25,000 additional teachers a year (Good, 1963).

This overall increase, along with consolidation of small school districts, suburban growth in formerly rural districts, and the general shift of population from industrial areas to the Sunbelt states, produced a period of rapid expansion unforeseen in U.S. education. Between 1950 and 1960, Nevada and Florida experienced more than a 100 percent increase in student populations. Many forces were at work, and some management and governance decisions made in these years created problems that have surfaced in the 1980s and 1990s. Here are examples:

• School construction for the postwar boom gave this country many cinder block, flat-roof buildings that are now part of the current crumbling infrastructure problem.

• The new teachers who entered the work force in the 1950s and 1960s have retired or are approaching retirement.

• A perceived decline in educational quality influenced by rapid student growth produced critical books such as Flesch's (1955) *Why Johnny Can't Read* and conservatives such as Arthur Bestor, author of *The Restoration of Learning* (Bestor, 1955) and *Educational Wastelands* (Bestor, 1953), the intellectual forebears of today's school critics.

• Court decisions on topics such as desegregation and finance equity have had a stronger impact on education than research studies.

• Beginning in the 1960s and continuing to the present, foundations such as the Ford Foundation's Educational Facilities Laboratory began to invest in education by encouraging reforms or promoting promising practices, such as team teaching, open classrooms, and modular scheduling. Although most of these efforts were not focused directly on governance, they helped create fads and movements that brought public backlash against open classrooms and team teaching (Trump & Baynham, 1961).

CHARTERS, CHOICE, AND VOUCHERS

Since 1985, when former Governor Rudy Perpich of Minnesota got the first open enrollment law passed, and six years later when the state enacted the first charter school law, other state legislatures have created an alternative governance structure that in many ways replaces or ignores state and local boards of education. Governor Perpich often described how the idea for choice grew out of his own family situation. When he wanted to enroll his children in a district other than the one where he rented a home for the legislative session, he was told that the law demanded that his children attend the school in the district where he lived. So he changed the law.

Most parents, of course, can't change the law, and quite often, they can find no policymaker sympathetic to their complaints. But enough such concerns have been expressed and responded to that most states now have broadened the options available to parents to include home schooling, inter- and intradistrict open enrollment, and charter schools, with growing support for vouchers. Should personal needs force changes in the governance structure, or should the governance

15

structure force individuals to change their demands? Because we live in a representative democracy, the scales, over time, are probably weighted in favor of public demands.

So far, the growth of charter schools, open enrollment, and provisions for home schooling has been slow but steady. There does not appear to be any move to stop or slow this growth, and a safe prediction is that these new structures are here to stay. Vouchers may be a different story because of state constitutional provisions for separation of church and state. Florida's enactment of a statewide voucher program in 1999 may hasten court activity on this issue.

GETTING TO THE FUTURE

What can we learn about education governance by looking back? What events had lasting impact, and what elements, if any, did those events have in common? More to the point, did the people involved at the time know that their decisions would be so influential?

Our looking back in this chapter, where we examined education governance over the last century, leads one to conclude that the major social and economic shifts that accompanied the move from an agricultural to a manufacturing society were more responsible for governance changes than what resulted from educational research or the views of enlightened gurus. Although the latter may have helped smooth the way for governance shifts with new administrative structures, new training methods, and new ideas for reform, these shifts were what prompted major changes in governance.

PROBABLE DEVELOPMENTS IN THE 21ST CENTURY

Governance changes have tended to come from outside education, driven by events or people who saw unmet needs from families or individuals. A few educators may have lent quick support for a change in governance, but most have defended the status quo. If this pattern continues—as it probably will—how might the future look? This section offers some possibilities.

MORE CHOICES

Parents and students will have more choices for selecting an education provider. Public schools will increasingly have to accommodate these changes by forming alliances with private and for-profit providers. Governance changes will follow by removing obstacles such as compulsory attendance laws and substituting uniform achievement standards for all education providers.

CHANGES IN STATE CONSTITUTIONS

State constitutional provisions for education will be amended to address uniform standards and compulsory assessment requirements for all providers. When these modifications occur, state dollars, through some mechanism, will find their way to these providers. If the modifications are fought out state by state in the courts, change will come slowly, but if a voucher-type change can be successfully pushed through the U.S. Supreme Court, change will be swift.

BROADER PROVISIONS FOR TEACHER PREPARATION AND SUPPLY

Teacher training and state certification laws will have to change to meet new market demands. Higher-education institutions will not be able to keep a monopolistic hold on teacher training as private for-profit groups enter to help provide teachers for multiple providers. Boards of education for K–12, if they respond quickly, might be able to replace some of the control factors dealing with teacher certification and recertification.

BLURRING OF STATE AND DISTRICT DIFFERENCES

Technology will erase state lines and school district jurisdictions. Governance changes will have to carve out a new role for states. If the delivery of education services for K–12 and higher education becomes too contentious, the federal government could use "interstate commerce" as a reason to substitute federal governance controls.

PROVISIONS FOR EARLY CHILDHOOD AND COMPETITION WITH SENIOR CITIZENS

Changing family demographics and economic needs could force states or the federal government to take a stronger role in providing early childhood education and day care for all families. Competition could come from a growing senior citizens population that will demand its share of state and federal resources. Day care and senior centers may combine their services out of fiscal necessity.

NEW ROLES FOR PROFESSIONAL ASSOCIATIONS

National education organizations and their state affiliates will be hit hard in the shift to recognize the multiple-provider phenomenon. Old membership bases will dissolve, protecting the status quo will no longer be a viable way to survive, and only those who can provide a needed service will remain. As in business, expect mergers, buyouts by private for-profit groups, and surprises.

SUMMARY

The United States' system of universal public education has undergone many changes in the last 100 years. The task of interpreting and reinterpreting this American dream is new work for each succeeding generation as it sets out to educate its children and ask the public schools for assistance. Each generation contended with changing social and economic needs that produced a new climate in which families had to respond. Often these changes were cyclic: Rural one-room schools created in abundance by one generation were closed or consolidated by the next. Urban model districts, which served as sources for new ideas, have in many cities now become a blight on the American dream. Some see the push for stronger state control and funding of education as a monopolistic stranglehold, bringing on calls for choice, charters, and vouchers.

In reality, the governance of U.S. education is propelled by many international, national, and personal problems, all demanding to be heard and fixed. Underneath are the state constitutional provisions for education. They will continue to serve as the touchstone for governance

18

changes—which surely the new century will bring. Some of these changes will be economically driven, and some will be motivated by personal gain. In the end, families will respond and select what seems best for their children. If anything can be learned from studying the history of public school governance changes, it is that the public has a low tolerance for the status quo if it isn't serving their needs.

Interpreting and reinterpreting the American dream of universal public education will continue alive and well into the next century.

Endnote

1. The Dalton and Winnetka plans were nongraded plans that differentiated academic from nonacademic courses and allowed students to move through the academic courses at their own rate. Each plan was named after its city of origin: Dalton, Massachusetts, and Winnetka, Illinois.

References

Bestor, A. (1953). *Educational wastelands.* Urbana: University of Illinois Press.

Bestor, A. (1955). *The restoration of learning.* New York: Knopf.

Cooper, S., Dawson, H. A., & Isenberg, R. M. (1957). School district organization. *Encyclopedia of Educational Research* (3rd ed.). New York: Macmillan.

Flesch, R. (1955). *Why Johnny can't read.* New York: Harper and Row.

Good, H. G. (1963). *A history of American education.* New York: Macmillan.

Trump, L. J., & Baynham, D. (1961). *Focus on change: Guide to better schools.* Chicago: Rand McNally.

Tyack, D., James, T., & Benavot, A. (1987). *Law and the shaping of public education 1785–1954.* Madison, WI: University of Wisconsin Press.

Ziebarth, T. (1998). State constitutions and public education governance. Clearinghouse Notes. Denver: The Education Commission of the States.

2

The Social Construction of Difference and the Quest for Educational Equality

JAMES A. BANKS

Je est un autre (I am an other).

—Rimbaud, in Todorov, 1987, p. 3

istorical, political, and social developments within the last half
century were a watershed in the quest for educational equality in
the United States. Racial segregation within the nation's educational institutions and within the larger society received a major
blow when the Supreme Court, in *Brown v. the Board of Education
of Topeka* (1954), declared separate but equal schools unconstitutional.
The Brown decision paved the way for the Civil Rights movement of
the 1960s and 1970s.

Note: I am grateful to the following colleagues for their perceptive and helpful
comments on an earlier draft of this chapter: Cherry A. McGee Banks, Ron
Brandt, Eugene B. Edgar, Sonia Nieto, and Christine E. Sleeter.

Copyright © 2000 by James A. Banks.

In education, developments aimed at increasing educational equality emerged, including school desegregation, affirmative action, bilingual education, and multicultural education. Each has been contested and has stimulated acid debates, and each has changed the nation and its educational institutions in ways that will have profound consequences in the new century. Equality will be an essential component of educational discourse in the 21st century.

School desegregation, affirmative action, bilingual education, and multicultural education have brought the nation closer to the democratic values of its founding documents—the Declaration of Independence, the Constitution, and the Bill of Rights. Progress toward democratic ideals during the last half century, however, has been cyclic and uneven rather than linear and straightforward. Progress during the new century will continue, but will also be cyclic and uneven. Periods of progress will be followed by periods of retrogression. But during retrogressive periods, some progress attained in previous periods will be maintained. Regression and progress will often occur at the same time. Today, for example, some communities are strongly contesting bilingual education, while throughout the nation, multicultural content is becoming institutionalized in school textbooks and in college and university courses.

During the last 30 years, such educational developments have revealed the inconsistency between America's democratic ideals and its educational practices, a gap that has been called the "American dilemma" (Myrdal, 1944). Uncovering this dilemma is an essential step in the march toward educational equality. Positive steps have included identifying the issues related to educational equality, discussing them in public forums, and implementing programs and practices that create greater educational equality for groups on society's margins.

The quest for educational equality resulted in the participation of more women, people of color, language minority groups, and people with disabilities in shaping educational research, policy, and practice. Their efforts uncovered—as well as contested—established paradigms, canons, categories, and concepts that they believed justified their marginalized status, defined them as the "other," and played a role in denying them equal educational opportunities.

The most powerful groups in a society largely determine what knowledge is produced and becomes institutionalized in schools, colleges, and universities. The battle over whose knowledge should be institutionalized was an important consequence of the pursuit for educational equality in the closing decades of the 20th century (Schlesinger, 1991; Sleeter, 1995); that battle will continue until marginalized groups become equal-status participants in mainstream U.S. society.

Grounded in the sociology of knowledge (Mannheim, 1936/1985; Berger & Luckmann, 1966), this chapter examines how race, mental retardation, and giftedness are socially constructed categories that have been used to reinforce the privileged positions of powerful groups, established practices, and institutions. It also discusses how marginalized groups have contested these concepts and created oppositional knowledge aimed at increasing their educational opportunities and possibilities. Emerging issues related to these concepts will continue to manifest themselves in the new century.

In my examination, I do not intend to obscure the concepts' distinct histories, purposes, and aims. I realize that most special and gifted educators believe that their work helps actualize educational equality by providing essential resources and support for targeted groups of students. Some educational programs with humanitarian goals, however, have latent functions that contradict those goals and promote inequality (Tomlinson, 1982). For example, classes for mentally retarded students—whose public aim is to provide special instruction for students who need it—are overpopulated by males, low-income students, and students of color. My sociological analysis focuses on the *latent* rather than the *manifest* function of knowledge and the institutions it supports (Merton, 1968).

Any body of knowledge can be socially established as reality (Berger & Luckmann, 1966). Varenne and McDermott (1998) call socially constructed knowledge "cultural facts." The cultural facts about race, mental retardation, and giftedness have often been used to justify and legitimize educational practices limiting the academic achievement of students of color, language minority students, students with disabilities, and students from lower socioeconomic groups.

I encourage readers to consider these questions as they read this chapter:

- Who has the power to define groups and institutionalize their concepts within schools, colleges, and universities?

• What is the relationship between knowledge and power?

• Who benefits from how race, mental retardation, and giftedness are defined and conceptualized in the larger society and within educational institutions? Who loses?

• How can race, mental retardation, and giftedness be reconstructed so that they can empower marginalized groups and create greater educational equality?

To provide a historical context for discussing the construction of categories and the quest for educational equality, I begin by describing the state of race relations as we enter the new century.

RACE RELATIONS AT THE DAWN OF A NEW CENTURY

Race relations and racial equality in the United States are at a turning point. The nation made notable progress toward eliminating racial, ethnic, and gender discrimination from the 1960s to the early 1980s. Significant advances in racial equality continued from the Brown decision (1954) to the Reagan presidential years (1981–1989), when progress was slowed. Even during the Reagan and Bush years, however, people of color and women made substantial progress toward educational equality and inroads toward full inclusion into mainstream society. Because they were already a part of mainstream society and had substantial educational, financial, and cultural capital, middle- and upper-class white women progressed further than ethnic groups of color within the last 25 years. But they still face intractable glass ceilings in some of the most coveted jobs and in the world of business and finance.

Although racial and ethnic groups and women made considerable progress in the decades between 1960 and 1980, the gap between the rich and the poor widened considerably within the last several decades (Wilson, 1996). After declining for 40 years, the share of the nation's wealth held by the wealthiest households (0.5 percent) rose sharply in the 1980s. In 1976, this segment of the population held 14 percent of the nation's wealth. In 1983, it held 26.9 percent (Phillips, 1990). In 1992, the top 20 percent of American households received 11 times as much income as the bottom 2 percent. In 1997, 35.6 percent of Americans were living in poverty, which included a high concentration of African Americans and Hispanics (U.S. Bureau of the Census, 1998a). In 1997, the poverty rate for non-Hispanic whites was 8.6 percent, compared to 25.5 percent and 27.1 percent for African Americans and Hispanics, respectively.

Although groups of color such as African Americans, Puerto Ricans in the United States, and Mexican Americans have disproportionately high poverty rates, many individuals of color joined the middle class. Class divisions increased within both ethnic minority and majority groups during the last three decades.

The nation's student population reflects the widening social class gap. In 1990, about one in five students lived below the official government poverty line (U.S. Bureau of the Census, 1998a). The class divide between teachers and students, and between middle-class and low-income students, will be a major influence on the quest for educational equality in the 21st century.

The nation seems exhausted in its struggle for racial equality. Some conservative leaders and scholars argue that the playing field is now even and that people of color must join the race for progress without governmental intervention or help (Thernstrom & Thernstrom, 1997; Steele, 1998). These individuals appear to ignore the long history of institutionalized discrimination in the United States and have not acknowledged that we cannot correct problems in several decades that have been in the making for nearly four centuries (Franklin, 1993; Lawrence & Matsuda, 1997).

We begin the new century with the problems of institutional discrimination still with us and with a nationally organized and effective conservative backlash. The backlash is not only stemming governmental intervention to create a more just society but is also eroding gains that ethnic minorities have made within the last three decades. The actions of conservative groups and institutions, which include federal court actions, have been both ominous and effective. For example, the decision in the *Hopwood v. State of Texas* case ended affirmative action at the University of Texas Law School; Initiative 209 in California and Initiative 200 in Washington State prohibit affirmative action in government employment and university admissions (Orfield & Miller, 1998).

That affirmative action is being dismantled at the same time that the first data-based study reveals its success is ironic: It has enabled more African Americans to gain admission to college and graduate school, enter mainstream society, and contribute substantially to their communities and society (Bowen & Bok, 1998). Institutions of higher education in California and in Washington State are faced with finding new ways to achieve student and faculty diversity now that established practices are illegal. Success in California and Washington will most likely encourage affirmative action opponents to take their campaign to other states. Affirmative action policies within several schools have also been challenged, a trend that is likely to continue into the foreseeable future.

An antibilingual movement has emerged in response to the significant increase in the percentage of students who speak a first language other than English. U.S. English, formed in the 1980s, is a group that lobbies to make English the nation's official language and the only language used in public places. By 1998, 25 states had made English their official language, either by amending their state constitutions or by enacting new legislation (U.S. English, 1999). Arizona's law, enacted in 1988, was declared unconstitutional by the Arizona Supreme Court in 1998.

Another indication of antibilingual sentiment is the large number of California residents who voted for Proposition 227 (also known as the Unz Amendment, after the millionaire Ron Unz, who led the campaign for it). Proposition 227, which essentially eliminates bilingual education, was approved overwhelmingly at the polls. This vote is ironic because research indicates that the best way for students to learn a second language, such as English, is to strengthen—not eradicate—their first language (August & Hakuta, 1997).

The Challenge of Fostering Diversity and Equity

Two somewhat contradictory developments make it imperative for U.S. educators to set a high priority on diversity and equity. One is the challenge from individuals and groups opposed to affirmative action and other diversity initiatives. The other is the growth of ethnic, cultural, and language diversity in the nation. Educators need to be a counterforce and help students acquire a strong commitment to democratic values and become reflective citizens. Students should also be helped to understand that a gap between ideals and realities always exists in a democratic society and that their roles as citizens is to take actions to help close that gap (Banks, 1997a).

I call the significant changes in the racial, ethnic, and language groups that make up the nation's population the "demographic imperative" (Banks, 1997a). The United States is experiencing its largest influx of immigrants since the beginning of the 20th century. Between 1980 and 1990, 80 percent of the documented immigrants came from nations in Latin America and Asia (U.S. Bureau of the Census, 1994). In contrast, only 9 percent came from Europe. The U.S. Bureau of the Census projects that people of color will make up 47.5 percent of the nation's population by 2050.

Increases in racial, ethnic, and linguistic diversity in the general population are reflected in the student population. It is projected that students of color will make up about 48 percent of school-age youths by 2020 (Pallas, Natriello, & McDill, 1989). In 1990, 14 percent of school-age youths spoke a first language at home other than English (U.S. Bureau of the Census, 1994). A document from the Teachers of English to Speakers of Other Languages (1997) states, "Current projections estimate that by the year 2000, the majority of the school-age population in 50 or more major U.S. cities will be from language minority backgrounds" (p. 1). A research synthesis published by the National Research Council highlights the nation's growing language minority population and describes its instructional needs as an important priority for its schools (August & Hakuta, 1997).

Increased diversification in the school population has produced serious academic and social problems needing urgent and thoughtful attention. Despite gains within the last decade, African American and Latino youths are still substantially behind Anglo mainstream youths on many indexes of academic achievement. They also have lower high school graduation rates and higher retention, suspension, and dropout rates (Gay, 1997).

School-based reforms are needed to help students learn how to live together in civic, moral, and just communities that respect and value all students' rights and cultural characteristics. Such efforts are made more difficult because an increasing percentage of students of color attend racially segregated schools (Orfield, Eaton, & The Harvard Project on School Desegregation, 1996), and because segregation often exists within racially and ethnically mixed schools using tracking and special programs.

A FOCUS ON DIFFERENCE

Increasing diversity, the widening gap between the rich and the poor, and renewed efforts by marginalized groups to gain recognition and legitimacy have focused attention on issues related to difference within the last three decades. Because such issues are unresolved—for example, backlashes against affirmative action and bilingual education—this focus is likely to increase and intensify in the new century.

A major problem facing the nation-state is how to recognize and legitimize difference and yet construct an overarching national identity that incorporates the voices, experiences, and hopes of the diverse groups that compose it. What groups will participate in constructing a new national identity, and what factors will be used to motivate powerful groups to share power with marginalized groups, are also issues that have to be addressed. Power sharing is an essential characteristic of a nation-state that reflects the cultures of its diverse population.

NEW CONCEPTIONS OF DIFFERENCE

Traditional categories used to differentiate and define human population groups will become more contested as marginalized racial, ethnic, cultural, and language groups grow in size, power, and legitimacy. Uncovering and deconstructing these institutionalized conceptions that deny human population groups equal educational opportunities, and replacing them with liberatory concepts, paradigms, and theories, are important agenda items for the new century. These new conceptions should view human potential as unlimited and describe ways in which group boundaries are flexible and interactive, rather than limited and distinct. Schools, colleges, and universities should integrate these ideas into programs to educate teachers and educational leaders.

THE SOCIAL CONSTRUCTION OF RACE

Race is one of the main categories used to construct differences in the United States and in other societies (Montagu, 1997). Racialization is a characteristic of both past and present societies (Hannaford, 1996). Groups holding political and economic power construct racial categories to privilege members of their groups and marginalize outside groups. Jacobson (1998) calls races "invented categories" (p. 4). Omi and Winant (1994) state that the "determination of racial categories is . . . an intensely political process" (p. 3). Their theory of racial formation "emphasizes the social nature of race, the absence of any essential racial characteristics, the historical flexibility of racial meanings and categories, . . . and the irreducible political aspect of racial dynamics" (p. 4).

Racial categories have shifted over time, established racial categories have been deconstructed, and new ones have been formed. The large influx of immigrants from Ireland in the 1840s and from eastern, southern, and central Europe in the late 1800s challenged the category of whiteness. White ethnic groups who were already established in the United States and who had social, economic, and political power defined the "huddled masses" of new immigrants as peoples from different races. Writes Jacobson (1998), "Upon the arrival of the massive waves of Irish immigrants in the 1840s, whiteness itself would become newly problematic, and in some quarters, would begin to lose its monolithic character" (pp. 37–38).

Jacobson describes these developments as "the fracturing of whiteness" (p. 38). Various groups of whites became distinct races that were ranked, such as the Celtic, Slav, Hebrew, Iberic, Mediterranean, and Anglo-Saxon. Anglo-Saxon was classified as the superior race. One writer stated that because of their "Celtic blood," the Irish threatened the American republic (Jacobson, 1998, p. 49). A newspaper described the Irish as a "savage mob," "a pack of savages," and "incarnate devils" (Jacobson, 1998, p. 55). The Irish became defined as the other and consequently were denied opportunities that the Anglo-Saxons enjoyed.

Italians and Jews were also defined as the other near the turn of the century and experienced racial discrimination and hostility. Italians were often called disparaging terms, such as "dagos" and "white niggers." In some parts of the South, Italians were forced to attend all-black schools (Waters, 1990). In 1891, during the height of American nativism, 11 Italians were lynched after being accused of murdering the police chief of New Orleans.

Leo Frank, a Jewish northerner, became a victim of anti-Semitism and racial hostility when he was accused of murdering a white girl who worked in a pencil factory he co-owned. In 1915, he was found guilty in an unfair trial. When the governor of Georgia commuted his sentence, a white mob forcibly removed him from jail and lynched him.

Multiple categories that had described the races among white ethnic groups in the mid-19th century became one racial category in the 20th century (Alba, 1990; Ignatiev, 1995; Jacobson, 1998). A single white racial category formed when the various white ethnic groups assimilated culturally, racially identified as one group, and defined themselves in opposition to African Americans (Morrison, 1992).

LESSONS FROM THE PAST

The past has taught us that racial categories and their meanings will keep changing, that groups with power will construct race to benefit themselves and disadvantage powerless groups, and that race is a powerful variable in the American conscience and society. Politicians are keenly aware of race's power. This savviness became evident when George Bush, who was lagging in the presidential polls in 1988, used a commercial that featured a black escaped criminal (Willie Horton) to solicit support from white voters.

History has also taught us that once groups attain sufficient power, they will challenge existing conceptions of race if necessary and push for redefining the meaning of racial categories. Such opposition will most likely come from biracial individuals and from Latino groups who are expected to outnumber African Americans by 2020 if their current birthrates and immigration rates continue.

In 1990, biracial individuals challenged the racial categories that the Census Bureau used. After reviewing the results of tests and hearings, the Office of Management and Budget changed a 2000 Census question so that an individual may check one or more racial categories. The bureau expects this change to affect its results only slightly because "fewer than 2 percent of respondents in recent tests used this option"

(U.S. Bureau of the Census, 1998b).

Many biracial individuals who have one African American and one white parent do not believe that they should be forced to belong to one racial category, but rather should be able to indicate that they are both African American and white. Ironically, the push by biracial individuals to create new racial categories reifies the concept of race itself, which many scholars think is a bogus and unscientific concept (Montagu, 1997).

Biracial marriages and births in the United States have increased significantly within the last several decades and are likely to continue increasing in the 21st century. Between 1970 and 1992, the number of African American–white couples quadrupled, to 246,000 (Kalish, 1995). Interracial births more than doubled between 1978 and 1992, while total births increased 22 percent (Kalish, 1995). Interracial marriages are also increasing.

The biracial and multiracial student population is increasing, creating a greater need for educators to help students realize that interracial relationships and biracial children from these unions have a long history in the United States. That history is evidenced by the relationship between Sally Hemings and Thomas Jefferson (Gordon-Reed, 1997; Murray & Duffy, 1998), the often silenced and denied black heritages within white families (Ball, 1998), and the mixed racial heritage of many eminent African Americans. Both Booker T. Washington and Frederick Douglass had white fathers and enslaved mothers.

Whites and African Americans, Native Americans and whites, and Native Americans and African Americans have produced offspring with mixed heritages since these groups first interacted in the Americas (Nash, 1982). The dominant racial and ethnic group in Mexico and throughout most of Latin America is racially mixed. The Mexican people were created when the Spaniards colonized Mexico and produced offspring (known as mestizos) with Native American women. The Africans who were brought to Mexico added to its ethnic mix. Legitimizing interracial mixtures in the United States is a recent phenomenon, although interracial mixture itself is historic. This is an important distinction that teachers and students need to understand.

Existing racial categories are also challenged by how some students perceive their racial and ethnic identification. Research in inner-city communities found that many youths of color refused to identify with a particular ethnic group (Heath & McLaughlin, 1993). They said that they were simply "ethnic." According to Heath (1995), "Contrary to general perceptions, within the daily lives of young people in many (not all) inner cities, racial or ethnic identities are always situated and multiple" (p. 48).

Ethnic identities are not fixed but are constantly changing, in part because of group interactions within a society characterized by racial, ethnic, language, and religious diversity (Nieto, 1998). Both mainstream white students and students of color are changed in these interactions.

The complex and changing nature of ethnic groups within U.S. society challenges the idea that educators can accurately identify a student's racial or ethnic group membership by physical characteristics or behaviors. The significant number of African American and Latino students entering the middle and upper classes also defies static classification.

THE CONTINUING SIGNIFICANCE OF RACE

In a nation such as the United States, where racism is embedded within the societal structure, how individuals identify themselves racially can be at odds with how outside groups and institutions view and respond to them. For example, schools may treat biracial students who have an African American parent as African American, even though the students identify with two races. The difference in classification indicates that self-identification of race is insufficient to establish one's racial identification within a racially stratified society.

THE CONTINUING SIGNIFICANCE OF CULTURE

Cultural issues will likely continue to be important in educating students from diverse groups because culture and social class interact in complex ways. Plus, many students of color are socialized in low-income, predominantly minority communities, where they learn cultural behaviors, communication styles, and values that do not always integrate smoothly into the mainstream culture of schools (Anyon, 1997; Wilson, 1996).

A number of researchers have described the cultures of various ethnic groups, argued that cultural conflicts exist between the schools and the cultures of ethnic minority students, and explained ways that teachers can adapt their teaching to make it culturally congruent. Among the most significant are Philip's (1983) study of the participation structures that Native American students use; Au's (1980) study of participation structures that native Hawaiian students use; Heath's (1983) study of language socialization patterns in an African American and a white community; and Lee's (1993) study of African American language usage. Another influential and informative study profiles eight teachers who implement culturally congruent teaching in their classrooms (Ladson-Billings, 1994).

It is important to remember that work on the cultural differences of students is not static; practitioners should view it within the context of students' changing ethnic identities and cultural characteristics.

EXPANSION OF EDUCATIONAL EQUALITY FOR STUDENTS WITH DISABILITIES

Before the Civil Rights movement, many students with disabilities were isolated in special schools and classes, stigmatized, viewed as the other, and sometimes denied the opportunity to attend their local public schools. The Supreme Court decision in the *Brown* case in 1954 established the principle that segregated schooling on the basis of race was inherently unequal and denied students equal educational opportunities. Advocates for students with disabilities reasoned that if segregating students on the basis of race were unconstitutional, segregating students with disabilities could also be challenged. Encouraged by the opportunities that African Americans attained as a result of their leadership and work in the Civil Rights movement, they contested the segregation of students with disabilities within schools and classrooms. The enactment of Public Law 94-142 in 1975, the Education for All Handicapped Children Act, was a major victory.

INTELLECTUAL HIERARCHIES

Psychology's historic and strong influence on educational theory, research, and practice has entrenched the bell curve and its implications

33

in schools. The bell curve assumes that only small percentages of the population will have high or low levels of intellectual ability. It does not focus on ways to create and nurture intellectual ability. This institutionalized hierarchical notion of mental ability is reflected in practices such as academic tracking—students are given differential access to high-status knowledge and skills (Oakes, 1985; Darling-Hammond, 1995)—and in programs for mentally retarded students and for gifted students.

Hierarchical conceptions of intellectual ability have also led to a focus on the *individual* characteristics of students rather than on ways that *social systems* structure academic norms and expectations (Brookover, Beady, Flood, Schweitzer, & Wisenbaker, 1979). Schools have done little to change norms and expectations to create intellectual ability (Levine & Lezotte, 1995).

DISABILITY AND RACE

One of the most contested aspects of special education programs is the disproportionate percentage of African American and Latino students who are categorized as mildly mentally retarded and as having emotional/behavior disorders (Artiles & Trent, 1994). Special education programs for students with speech and language problems tend to have a disproportionate percentage of Latino students (Artiles & Trent, 1994).

Parents and other student advocates have legally challenged the disproportionate percentage of students of color in special education programs. Several courts have ruled in favor of the plaintiffs, including verdicts in *Diana v. California State Board of Education* (1970) and *Larry P. v. Wilson Riles* (1986). In the *Diana* case, the plaintiffs alleged that the California State Board of Education used biased tests in the procedures that assigned Mexican American and Chinese American students to special education classes. The state of California agreed to develop tests that reflect its diverse cultures. In the *Larry P.* case, the U.S. District Court for the Northern District of California prohibited the use of IQ tests to place African Americans in special education programs (Mercer, 1989).

THE SOCIAL CONSTRUCTION OF MENTAL RETARDATION

In her pioneering work, Mercer (1973) proposes that mental retardation is a social construction and describes it from both a *clinical* and a *social system* perspective. From a clinical perspective, mental retardation is viewed as a handicapping condition because individuals' attributes prevent them from functioning effectively within the mainstream society. This individual condition "can be diagnosed by clinically trained professionals using properly standardized assessment techniques" (Mercer, 1973, p. 2). Mercer states that the clinical perspective uses a pathological or medical model that classifies individuals as mentally retarded when they deviate from the mean or norm of the mainstream population.

Mercer (1973) describes how the clinical perspective is problematic in a society where many individuals are socialized within socioeconomic and ethnic cultures that differ substantially from the mainstream culture. Their behaviors and cultural characteristics are functional and sanctioned within their ethnic and socioeconomic subsocieties but are considered deviant and are devalued within the mainstream society. Consequently, students who are judged competent in their ethnic subsocieties may be labeled mentally retarded in the mainstream society and thus in schools. Mercer states that the core mainstream society consists primarily of cultural patterns of middle- and upper-class Anglo-Protestant Americans.

From a social system perspective, normal behavior is determined by examining how an individual functions within that individual's specific cultural community (Mercer, 1973). Behavior is judged deviant when it varies greatly from behavior expected by the ethnic group or community. The point of reference is the cultural or ethnic community, not the mainstream society.

When a social system perspective is used to determine mental retardation, individuals who are considered normal in their families or neighborhoods might be considered mentally retarded in a school setting. Mercer found that Mexican American youths who were considered normal in their families and communities and who functioned effectively in those settings were labeled mentally retarded in school. She writes, "Mental retardation is not a characteristic of individuals, nor a meaning inherent in behavior, but a *socially determined status*, which he [or she] may occupy in some social systems and not in others, depending on their norms" (p. 31) (emphasis added).

THE SOCIAL CONSTRUCTION OF GIFTEDNESS

The socioeconomic groups and groups of color that are overrepresented in programs and classes for mentally retarded students and for students with emotional/behavior disorders are underrepresented in classes and programs for gifted and talented students. In 1984, whites made up 71 percent of the general student population and 81.4 percent of the students enrolled in programs for gifted and talented students (Fisher, 1998). In contrast, Latinos and African Americans made up 9.1 percent and 16.2 percent of the general student population and 4.7 percent and 8.4 percent, respectively, of the students enrolled in programs for gifted and talented students.

Sapon-Shevin (1994) describes giftedness "as a social construct, a way of thinking and describing that exists in the eyes of the definers" (p. 16). Individuals and groups who are defined as gifted vary with the times, state and school district guidelines and procedures, assessment measures used to identify gifted students, and opportunities to learn that have been available to the students being considered for gifted programs. Giftedness is contextual and situational: "The particular criteria are constantly changing and vary from place to place. What all programs share is their attempt to identify children they think are especially deserving of extra opportunities" (Oakes & Lipton, 1994, p. xi).

Political factors also influence which students become categorized as gifted. A number of school districts in large cities have lost many middle-class white students to suburban school districts and to private schools within the last two decades. Special programs, magnet schools, and gifted programs are sometimes used in these districts—which have declining enrollments and an eroding tax base—to lure white middle-class parents back to city schools.

Middle-class white parents also have more political and cultural capital than most lower socioeconomic parents and parents of color; they use their cultural know-how and political clout to pressure school districts to admit their children to programs for gifted and talented students. Parents compete to get their children admitted to programs for gifted and talented students because they view the benefits of these programs as a limited resource.

Programs for gifted and talented students tend to have better qualified teachers, lower teacher-pupil ratios, and more intellectually engaging teaching than classes for lower-track students (Oakes, 1985). Classes for lower-track students tend to be characterized by low-level instruction, drill exercises, and a lack of higher-level content. Schools that are racially desegregated often have gifted, special education, and bilingual programs and classes—a type of segregation.

The factors that result in higher enrollment levels of African Americans and Latinos in classes for mentally retarded students are probably the same ones that account for their low enrollment in classes for gifted and talented students. These factors include their lower scores on standardized tests often used to determine placement in both type of classes; fewer opportunities to learn the content and skills that the standardized tests measure; and cultural and language characteristics that are inconsistent with those valued by the schools and test-makers.

USING POWER TO DEFINE CATEGORIES

People and groups who have power exercise authority over others and influence their perceptions, beliefs, and behaviors. Shafritz (1988) states that *expert power* "is based on the perception that the leader possesses some special knowledge or expertise." Leaders exercise *legitimate power* when followers believe that the leaders have "the legitimate right or authority to exercise influence" (p. 427). Bourdieu (in Swartz, 1997) argues that power cannot be exercised unless it is legitimate.

One way that powerful groups legitimize their power is through the construction of knowledge, which includes concepts and propositions that justify their privileged position and explain why marginalized groups deserve a low status in society. When Columbus arrived in the Caribbean, he knew that the Indians called the islands Guanahani, yet he renamed them when he claimed ownership. Writes Todorov (1987), "Columbus knows perfectly well that these islands already have names. . . . however, he seeks to rename places in terms of the rank they occupy in his discovery, to give them the right names; moreover nomination [naming] is equivalent to taking possession" (p. 27).

When establishing categories for race, mental retardation, and giftedness, individuals and groups with power construct categories and characteristics and distribute rewards and privileges that benefit the existing hierarchies (Sleeter, 1986; Sapon-Shevin, 1994). Ford (1996) describes the problems and limitations of such categories:

> No group has a monopoly on giftedness. . . . It is illogical and statistically impossible for giftedness to be the prerogative of one racial, gender, or socioeconomic group. Nonetheless, gifted programs represent the most segregated programs in public schools; they are disproportionately white and middle class (pp. ix–x).

Just as groups with power and hegemony construct knowledge and categories that benefit entrenched institutions, marginalized individuals and groups create *oppositional knowledge* that challenges established knowledge, ideologies, practices, behaviors, and institutions (Banks, 1996). These groups also demand that hegemonic knowledge structures be dismantled and that more democratic forms of knowledge be created and implemented in institutions, including schools, colleges, and universities. In another publication (Banks, 1998), I describe case studies of researchers' lives and the ways in which their community cultures, biographical journeys, and status within the social structure influence the knowledge they construct. I also explain how mainstream researchers construct concepts and paradigms that reinforce their privilege positions, and how researchers on the margins of society contest knowledge systems and canons that privilege established groups and contribute to the victimization of marginalized groups.

To create democratic schools, colleges, and universities, the established concepts and knowledge systems must not privilege any particular racial, ethnic, social class, or gender group, but rather reflect the experiences of all groups that make up the nation-state. Consequently, educators must reform the cultures of the nation's schools, as well as the curriculum, to institutionalize and legitimize the knowledge systems, perspectives, ideologies, and behaviors of diverse ethnic, racial, cultural, social class, and language groups. This reform requires that more liberatory and multicultural paradigms and canons be constructed and institutionalized. In the last two decades, work in ethnic

38

studies (Banks, 1997b), women's studies (Schmitz, Butler, Rosenfelt, & Guy-Sheftall, 1995), and multicultural education (Banks & Banks, 1995) has provided an important foundation for such efforts. Much of this work is reviewed and discussed in the *Handbook of Research on Multicultural Education* (Banks & Banks, 1995).

REFORMING SCHOOLS

In the 21st century, schools, colleges, and universities can help teachers and students uncover old conceptions of difference and construct and institutionalize new conceptions of marginalized groups. Teachers and students need to rethink, re-imagine, and reconstruct their images and representations of groups of color and of American exceptionalism as presented in textbooks and in the popular culture (Appleby, 1992; Banks, 1996).

Students bring to the school community a set of values, commitments, ideologies, assumptions, and knowledge that influences their interactions with teachers, other students, and the school curriculum. These kinds of knowledge are becoming increasingly varied as student diversity increases, which will continue in the new century. Teachers should help students critically examine their cultural and community knowledge, understand how it relates to institutionalized knowledge systems, and construct new paradigms and conceptions about human diversity.

Teacher education needs to be reformed so that teachers can examine their own personal knowledge and values. They also need to uncover and examine the knowledge and values that underlie, justify, and legitimize practices in schools—such as the classification of racial and ethnic groups, special education programs, and programs for gifted and talented students—and the knowledge related to institutionalized beliefs—such as knowledge about skill grouping (Mosteller, Light, & Sachs, 1996), characteristics of black English or Ebonics (Baugh, 1983), and the effects of loss of first language on learning English as a second language (August & Hakuta, 1997).

Concepts such as race, mental retardation, and giftedness are undergirded by strong normative claims and assumptions. Race assumes that human groups can be divided on the basis of their biological and physical characteristics, a highly contested claim (Omi & Wanant, 1994; Montagu, 1997). Mental retardation focuses on the characteristics of individuals rather than on the social systems in which they are required to function (Mercer, 1973; Tomlinson, 1982; Mehan, Hertweck, & Meihls, 1986; Varenne & McDermott, 1998). Giftedness is rarely defined in a way that indicates that all individuals have gifts as well as disabilities (Sapon-Shevin, 1994).

Other concepts in the school curriculum and teacher education that are often used without deep reflection to uncover their implicit meanings carry strong value claims and assumptions, such as the westward movement, at-risk students, and busing. In U.S. history, the term *westward movement* implies that a group foreign to a land can name as well as claim it. The term also suggests that the West was a wilderness before it was settled by European pioneers, another value-loaded concept. *At-risk students* suggests that some groups of students are at-risk, and others are not, and that at-risk students can be identified (Cuban, 1989). Missing from this concept is the idea that every student and individual, including every educator, is at-risk on some variable. *Busing* is not used to describe transporting students from their homes in predominantly white neighborhoods to predominantly white schools. Rather, *busing* is a term that contains specific value judgments about race and racial mixing in schools.

THE ROAD AHEAD

The new century poses challenges but also offers opportunities in the continuing quest for educational equality. Challenges include the widening gap between the rich and the poor; the growing isolation of low-income, inner-city students within the nation's aging cities; and the conservative backlashes against affirmative action and bilingual education.

The growing percentage of racial, ethnic, and language groups poses challenges to established institutions but are a potential source of hope and renewal. As Okihiro (1994) points out in his thoughtful and empowering book, *Margins and Mainstreams*, groups on the margins of American society have forced it to live up to its democratic ideals. A salient example is the Civil Rights movement, which forced the United

States to eradicate apartheid. As groups who are victimized by established concepts and practices challenge and reconstruct them—and therefore acquire more freedom and liberation—all of us will become more humanized and free, because all Americans are "caught in an inescapable network of mutuality" and "tied in a single garment of destiny" (King, 1994, p. 3). We are the other, and the other is us.

References

Alba, R. D. (1990). *Ethnic identity: The transformation of white America*. New Haven, CT: Yale University Press.

Anyon, J. (1997). *Ghetto schooling: A political economy of urban educational reform*. New York: Teachers College Press.

Appleby, J. (1992). Recovering America's historic diversity: Beyond exceptionalism. *Journal of American History, 79,* 413–431.

Artiles, A. J., & Trent, S. C. (1994). Overrepresentation of minority students in special education: A continuing debate. *Journal of Special Education, 27,* 410–437.

Au, K. (1980). Participation structures in a reading lesson with Hawaiian children. *Anthropology and Education Quarterly, 11*(2), 91–115.

August, D., & Hakuta, K. (1997). *Improving schooling for language-minority children: A research agenda*. Washington, DC: National Academy Press.

Ball, E. (1998). *Slaves in the family*. New York: Farr, Straus, and Giroux.

Banks, J. A. (Ed.). (1996). *Multicultural education, transformative knowledge, and action: Historical and contemporary perspectives*. New York: Teachers College Press.

Banks, J. A. (1997a). *Educating citizens in a multicultural society*. New York: Teachers College Press.

Banks, J. A. (1997b). *Teaching strategies for ethnic studies* (6th ed.). Boston: Allyn and Bacon.

Banks, J. A. (1998). The lives and values of researchers: Implications for educating citizens in a multicultural society. *Educational Researcher, 29,* 4–17.

Banks, J. A., & Banks, C. A. M. (Eds.). (1995). *Handbook of research on multicultural education*. New York: Macmillan.

Baugh, J. (1983). *Black street speech: Its history, structure, and survival*. Austin, TX: University of Texas Press.

Berger, P. L., & Luckmann, T. (1966). *The social construction of reality: A treatise in the sociology of knowledge*. New York: Anchor.

Bowen, W. G., & Bok, D. (1998). *The shape of the river: Long-term consequences of considering race in college and university admissions.* Princeton, NJ: Princeton University Press.

Brookover, W. B., Beady, C., Flood, P., Schweitzer, J., & Wisenbaker, J. (1979). *School social systems and student achievement: Schools can make a difference.* New York: Praeger.

Cuban, L. (1989). The "at risk" label and the problem of urban school reform. *Phi Delta Kappan, 70,* 780–801.

Darling-Hammond, L. (1995). Inequality and access to knowledge. In J. A. Banks & C. A. M. Banks (Eds.), *Handbook of research on multicultural education* (pp. 465–497). New York: Macmillan.

Fisher, M. (with Perez, S. M., Gonzalez, B., Njus, J., & Kamasaki, C.). (1998). *Latino education: Status and prospects: State of Hispanic America 1998.* Washington, DC: National Council of La Raza.

Ford, D. Y. (1996). *Reversing underachievement among gifted black students: Promising practices and programs.* New York: Teachers College Press.

Franklin, J. H. (1993). *The color line: Legacy for the twenty-first century.* Columbia, MO: University of Missouri Press.

Gay, G. (1997). Educational equality for students of color. In J. A. Banks & C. A. M. Banks (Eds.), *Multicultural education: Issues and perspectives* (3rd ed., pp. 195–228). Boston: Allyn and Bacon.

Gordon-Reed, A. (1997). *Thomas Jefferson and Sally Hemings: An American controversy.* Charlottesville, VA: University Press of Virginia.

Hannaford, I. (1996). *Race: The history of an idea in the West.* Baltimore: The Johns Hopkins University Press.

Heath, S. B. (1983). *Ways with words: Language, life, and work in communities and classrooms.* New York: Cambridge University Press.

Heath, S. B. (1995). Race, ethnicity, and the defiance of categories. In W. D. Hawley & A. W. Jackson (Eds.), *Toward a common destiny: Improving race and ethnic relations in America* (pp. 39–70). San Francisco: Jossey-Bass.

Heath, S. B., & McLaughlin, M. W. (Eds.). (1993). *Identity and inner-city youth: Beyond ethnicity and gender.* New York: Teachers College Press.

Ignatiev, N. (1995). *How the Irish became white.* New York: Routledge and Kegan Paul.

Jacobson, M. F. (1998). *Whiteness of a different color: European immigrants and the alchemy of race.* Cambridge, MA: Harvard University Press.

Kalish, S. (1995). Multiracial birth increases as U.S. ponders racial definitions. *Population Today, 23*(4), 1–2.

King, M. L. (1994). *Letter from the Birmingham jail.* New York: HarperCollins.

Ladson-Billings, G. (1994). *The dreamkeepers: Successful teachers of African American children.* San Francisco: Jossey-Bass.

Lawrence, C. R., III, & Matsuda, M. J. (1997). *We won't go back: Making the case for affirmative action.* Boston: Houghton Mifflin.

Lee, C. E. (1993). *Signifying as a scaffold for literary interpretation: The pedagogical implications of an African American discourse.* Urbana, IL: National Council of Teachers of English.

Levine, D. U., & Lezotte, L. W. (1995). Effective schools research. In J. A. Banks &. C. A. M. Banks (Eds.), *Handbook of research on multicultural education* (pp. 525–547). New York: Macmillan.

Mannheim, K. (1936/1985*). Ideology and utopia: An introduction to the sociology of knowledge.* San Diego, CA: Harcourt Brace Jovanovich. (Original work published 1936)

Mehan, H., Hertweck, A., & Meihls, J. L. (1986). *Handicapping the handicapped: Decision making in students' educational careers.* Stanford, CA: Stanford University Press.

Mercer, J. R. (1973). *Labeling the mentally retarded.* Berkeley, CA: University of California Press.

Mercer, J. R. (1989). Alternative paradigms for assessment in a pluralistic society. In J. A. Banks & C. A. M. Banks (Eds.), *Multicultural education: Issues and perspectives* (1st ed., pp. 289–304). Boston: Allyn and Bacon.

Merton, R. K. (1968). Manifest and latent functions. In R. K. Merton, *Social theory and social structure* (Enlarged ed., pp. 73–138). New York: The Free Press.

Montagu, A. (1997). *Man's most dangerous myth: The fallacy of race* (6th ed.). Walnut Creek, CA: AltaMira Press.

Morrison, T. (1992*). Playing in the dark: Whiteness and the literary imagination.* Cambridge, MA: Harvard University Press.

Mosteller, F., Light, R. J., & Sachs, J. A. (1996). Sustained inquiry in education: Lessons from skill grouping and class size. *Harvard Educational Review, 66,* 797–828.

Murray, B., & Duffy, B. (1998, November 9). Did the author of the Declaration of Independence take a slave for his mistress? DNA tests say yes. *U.S. News and World Report, 125,* 59–63.

Myrdal, G. (with Sterner, R., & Rose, A.). (1944). *An American dilemma: The Negro problem and modern democracy.* New York: Harper.

Nash, G. B. (1982). *Red, white, and black: The peoples of early America* (2nd ed.). Englewood Cliffs, NJ: Prentice-Hall.

Nieto, S. (1998). On becoming American: An exploratory essay. In W. Ayers & J. L. Miller (Eds.), *A light in dark times: Maxine Greene and the unfinished conver-*

sation (pp. 45–57). New York: Teachers College Press.

Oakes, J. (1985). *Keeping track: How schools structure inequality.* New Haven, CT: Yale University Press.

Oakes, J., & Lipton, M. (1994). Foreword. In M. Sapon-Shevin, *Playing favorites: Gifted education and the disruption of community* (pp. ix–xvi). Albany: State University of New York Press.

Okihiro, G. Y. (1994). *Margins and mainstreams: Asians in American history and culture.* Seattle, WA: University of Washington Press.

Omi, M., & Winant, H. (1994*). Racial formation in the United States: From the 1960s to the 1990s* (2nd ed.). New York: Routledge and Kegan Paul.

Orfield, G., Eaton, S. E., & The Harvard Project on School Desegregation. (1996). *Dismantling desegregation: The quiet reversal of* Brown v. Board of Education. New York: New Press.

Orfield, G., & Miller, E. (1998). *Chilling admissions: The affirmative action crisis and the search for alternatives.* Cambridge, MA: Harvard Education Publishing Group.

Pallas, A. M., Natriello, G., & McDill, E. L. (1989). The changing nature of the disadvantaged population: Current dimensions and future trends. *Educational Researcher, 18*(5), 16–22.

Philips, S. (1983). *The invisible culture: Communication in classroom and community on the Warm Springs Indian Reservation.* New York: Longman.

Phillips, K. (1990). *The politics of rich and poor: Wealth and the American electorate in the Reagan aftermath.* New York: Random House.

Sapon-Shevin, M. (1994). *Playing favorites: Gifted education and the disruption of community.* Albany: State University of New York Press.

Schlesinger, A. M. (1991). *The disuniting of America: Reflections on a multicultural society.* Knoxville, TN: Whittle Direct Books.

Schmitz, B., Butler, J. E., Rosenfelt, D., & Guy-Sheftall, B. (1995). Women's studies and curriculum transformation. In J. A. Banks & C. A. M. Banks (Eds.), *Handbook of research on multicultural education* (pp. 708–728). New York: Macmillan.

Shafritz, J. M. (1988). *The Dorsey dictionary of American government and politics.* Chicago: Dorsey Press.

Sleeter, C. E. (1986). Learning disabilities: The social construction of a special education category. *Exceptional Children, 53*(1), 46–54.

Sleeter, C. E. (1995). An analysis of the critiques of multicultural education. In J. A. Banks & C. A. M. Banks (Eds.), *Handbook of research on multicultural education* (pp. 81–96). New York: Macmillan.

Steele, S. (1998). *A dream deferred: The second betrayal of black freedom in America.* New York: HarperCollins.

Swartz, D. (1997). *Culture and power: The sociology of Pierre Bourdieu.* Chicago: University of Chicago Press.

Teachers of English to Speakers of Other Languages. (1997). *ESL standards for pre-k–12 students.* Alexandria, VA: Author.

Thernstrom, S., & Thernstrom, A. (1997). *America in black and white: One nation, indivisible.* New York: Simon and Schuster.

Todorov, T. (1987). *The conquest of America: The question of the other.* New York: HarperCollins.

Tomlinson, S. (1982). *A sociology of special education.* London: Routledge and Kegan Paul.

U.S. Bureau of the Census. (1994). *Statistical abstract of the United States* (114th ed.). Washington, DC: U.S. Government Printing Office.

U.S. Bureau of the Census. (1998a). *Statistical abstract of the United States* (118th ed.). Washington, DC: U.S. Government Printing Office.

U.S. Bureau of the Census. (1998b). Questions and answers about Census 2000 [On-line]. Available: http://www.census.gov/dmd/www/advisory.html

U.S. English. (1999, June 10). States with official English laws [On-line]. Available: http://us-english.org

Varenne, H., & McDermott, R. (1998). *Successful failure: The school America builds.* Boulder: Westview Press.

Waters, M. C. (1990). *Ethnic options: Choosing identities in America.* Berkeley, CA: University of California Press.

Wilson, W. J. (1996). *When work disappears: The world of the new urban poor.* New York: Alfred A. Knopf.

3

Teaching and Teacher Development: A New Synthesis for a New Century

ANN LIEBERMAN AND LYNNE MILLER

What is there about teachers and schools that make them so open to critique and everyone's counsel? Why is it that strong ideological claims get attached to particular ways of organizing and teaching subject matter content? How can schools and teachers continue to grow and deepen their work in a society that is rapidly changing the rules? These questions have been at the center of the debate about educational change and improvement perhaps as long as schools have been around, especially in the last half of the 20th century. As we begin to shape a future for teachers and teaching in the new century, we need to take the time to assess our history. We can then come to understand the connections between the issues and concerns of the past and the demands and needs of the decades to come.

THE CHANGING CONTEXT OF TEACHING

The context of teaching has changed in the past two decades, and it promises to change even more dramatically in the coming century. Our democratic society is being transformed as we rapidly move toward an information society and a global economy. The changes are happening more quickly than schools seem able to accommodate. From cognitive theorists to business executives, people outside schools are pressing people inside to teach students how to frame and solve problems, to think critically, to develop a multicultural awareness, and to demonstrate mastery of basic skills. All these demands have strong implications for teaching. This section highlights some conditions that currently affect teaching and the challenges they raise for the next century.

NEW DEMOGRAPHICS, NEW TECHNOLOGIES

Emerging demographics contribute significantly to the press for change. In the last two decades, although prosperity has been increasing and the unemployment rate is the lowest in history, the number of poor families has risen dramatically. The gap between those who participate fully in society and those who do not has widened, creating what many view as a threat to democracy (Glickman, 1998). Although students with social, physical, or educational problems have always been a challenge to teachers, their increased numbers in recent years have made individual accommodations more difficult to deliver. Legislation, which guarantees more school services without the funding to support them, depletes local resources and forces schools and teachers to make tough decisions about whom they can serve and how well. While student populations are becoming more diverse ethnically and linguistically, the teaching population remains the same and continues to disproportionately represent the white middle class.

The technological revolution has also added to the challenges teachers face. Although many more teachers have access to computers, schools have been slow to use technology as a tool for enhanced student engagement and learning. The reasons are complex and have to do with the unequal distribution of technology in rich and poor districts, stockpiling of hardware without seriously involving teachers in its use, and difficulties in organizing institutional and individual changes that might use the technologies on the market. At a time when demands on teachers for accountability are increasing, technology-rich schools have a clear advantage.

COMPETING STRATEGIES FOR SCHOOL REFORM

Many educators, who have come of age in the profession within the past 40 years, have developed a skeptical view of school reform. Weary of the agendas for change that regularly appear almost every 10 years, they tend to distrust innovations offered by researchers who purport to have found the "one best way" to solve an enduring problem. Teachers have found that generalizations guided by empiricism don't attend to issues faced in *my* classroom with *my* students. They tend to discount the belief that policies and practices rooted in research can be disseminated to schools and adopted whole.

This rational-linear, empirically driven perspective has dominated the educational landscape for almost a century. But an alternative, albeit minority, view about how to effect change in classrooms has also been around a long time. This position holds that contexts are critical and that organizational and personal change has to do with the meaning and enactment of changes in schools. In this approach, developing new ways of working and thinking, and creating new roles and relationships, are important. This work requires a fundamental rethinking of the organization and practice of teaching.

Teachers have been receivers of both sets of formulations: that there is knowledge created by research that needs to be implemented; and that there is knowledge that is created in the process of action and reflection on practice (Rorty, 1979; Schon, 1991; Cochran-Smith & Lytle, 1993). From a historical perspective, these two ways of thinking about knowledge and improvement have been coupled with America's continuous and contentious quest to provide excellence and equity in its schools (Lazerson, 1987). They represent growth differences in the research community; the way policymaking occurs at the district, state, and federal levels; and the ways that the public learns about and expresses its opinions on schools and teachers (Bruner, 1985; Darling-Hammond, 1998; Cochran-Smith & Lytle, 1999). Neither approach has led to far-reaching, deep-seated school reform. Part of education's task in the 21st century is to reconcile the two approaches, borrowing what is best and worthy from each, to move the school reform agenda forward.

THE PRESS FOR STANDARDS

Schools are feeling a tremendous press to improve student achievement levels and the quality of the teaching force. This pressure is not new; it has its roots in three reports that were issued in the years between 1983 and 1996. A small volume, *A Nation at Risk* (National Commission on Excellence in Education, 1983), rallied the country around the need for greater accountability for student learning. It was based on the proposition that American schools were not meeting desired outcomes in terms of student achievement, and that externally generated, empirically based knowledge would make things better. To increase student achievement on standardized measures, policymakers were encouraged to add to the curriculum in the areas of science, math, and technology; lengthen the time students spend in school; increase requirements for high school graduation; and develop and implement more rigorous assessments of student learning. In this document, we can see the seeds of the student accountability initiatives that are now taking hold at the local, state, and federal levels as evidenced by state assessments, high school exit examinations, and talk of developing a federal examination of student achievement.

A second report was issued just three years later. *A Nation Prepared: Teachers for the 21st Century* (Carnegie Corporation of New York, 1986) provided the impetus for another round of national discussions, this time about teachers and teaching. While giving a nod to higher standards for students, the report looked to teachers as the key to school reform. It made the claim that if teachers became engaged as leaders in curriculum, instruction, and assessment, they would successfully implement what was necessary for student success. Rather than rely on external knowledge as the starting point for improvement, the report placed its trust in teachers as the major transformative agents. In many cases, teacher-led efforts to restructure schools, and in some instances to create new ones, were implemented as a result of this report.

A decade later, a document issued by the National Commission on Teaching and America's Future (1996) reenforced and extended the focus on teaching. Entitled *What Matters Most: Teaching and America's Future,* it describes a systemic reform strategy that complemented the development of standards for students by proposing a system of standards and rewards for teaching. By connecting standards for teachers with standards for students, the commission provided a blueprint of what is required to take teaching into the 21st century. Included in the blueprint are higher requirements for teacher licensure and renewal; rigorous testing of teacher knowledge; an overhaul of preservice teacher preparation programs and the closing of programs that don't meet national standards; incentives and rewards for accomplished teaching; provisions for peer assistance to help teachers needing improvement, and for the dismissal of teachers who do not respond to assistance; enhanced professional development throughout a teaching career; and improved working and learning environments for teachers and students.

THE NEW SOCIAL REALITIES OF TEACHING

The growing pressure on teachers necessitates rethinking their job description and what the teaching role entails. The old norms of individualism, isolationism, and privatism (Lortie, 1975) no longer suffice; teachers need to develop new ways of doing business and of viewing themselves and their profession. We call these necessary changes "the new social realities of teaching" (Lieberman & Miller, 1999) because they represent major shifts in both perspective and practice. We have identified seven transitions that teachers need to make:

• *From individualism to professional community.* By forgoing individual work for joint work, teachers can build a strong school culture that values collegiality, openness, and trust over detachment and territoriality (Little, 1981; McLaughlin & Talbert, 1993; Rosenholtz, 1989). This new culture supports the experimentation, risk taking, and feedback that is necessary for reflecting and improving teaching practice.

• *From teaching at the center to learning at the center.* When teachers direct their attention away from the technology of teaching and toward the construction of learning, they approach their charge in a very different way. They situate student work at the center of the educational enterprise, and they craft learning opportunities that respond to particular contexts. Such an approach leads to "authentic instruction" (Newmann & Wehlage, 1995) that ultimately connects in-school learning to life beyond school.

• *From technical work to inquiry.* The emphasis on student work leads to a broader formulation of the teaching task. Teachers can no longer think of themselves as mere technicians who can only be held responsible for the mastery of a prescribed set of skills and techniques. Rather, they see themselves as intellectuals engaged in the process of discovery and reflection. As researchers, meaning-makers, scholars, and inventors, they establish a firm professional identity as they model the lifelong learning they hope to infuse in their students.

• *From control to accountability.* As the notion of teacher work expands, so does the concept of accountability. Long identified with controlling student behavior, accountability has changed in definition to focus on the public responsibility for student performance. This new definition encourages teachers to establish expectations that include all students. Teachers acknowledge that they control the conditions for student learning in their individual classrooms and in the whole school. The realities of students' lives are not denied, but neither are they accepted as excuses for students not to achieve in school.

• *From managed work to leadership.* As teachers redefine and augment their roles, they become leaders in curriculum, instruction, and teaching. They simultaneously complement a principal's administrative leadership and contribute to a school's management and well-being. Teacher leadership is no longer appointed or anointed by the principal; it is considered a necessary part of being a teacher.

• *From classroom concerns to whole school concerns.* Teacher leadership is but one example of how the new realities of teaching expand the boundaries and perspectives of teaching. As teachers move from individuality to collaboration and from control to accountability, they make a transition from exclusive concerns about *my* classroom and *my* students to more inclusive concerns about *our* school and *our* students. Teachers become members of vibrant professional communities that challenge and support their continued development.

• *From a weak knowledge base to a stronger, broader one.* New research in human cognition and intelligence has helped considerably teachers' efforts to professionalize their work and to assume a greater role in decision making and leadership. Long criticized as having a weak knowledge base, teaching is now able to draw on a wealth of information and basic research that can guide practice. Though teaching will never lose its intuitive and speculative dimensions, it can now rely on a firm knowledge base that not only provides more tools for work but also earns the profession more credibility.

BROADENING CONCEPTIONS OF INTELLIGENCE

An important source of new knowledge is the research of cognitive psychologists and others who have been investigating the nature of intelligence. Since the publication of Howard Gardner's *Frames of Mind* (1983), debate about what intelligence is and how it is measured has been ongoing. Gardner posits that there is not one general intelligence (called "g" by psychologists), but rather a plurality of intelligences (Checkley, 1997). Gardner identifies eight distinct intelligences, with their own symbol systems and sets of core operations. The eight intelligences are (1) linguistic: the ability to use words effectively, to manipulate language and syntax, and to express meaning; (2) logical-mathematical: the ability to use numbers well and to reason effectively; (3) spatial: the ability to perceive the visual-spacial world accurately and to form mental images; (4) bodily kinesthetic: the ability to use one's body to express feelings and ideas, to solve problems, and to transform things; (5) musical: the ability to recognize, produce, and transform musical forms; (6) interpersonal: the ability to understand the moods, feelings, intentions, and motivations of other people; (7) intrapersonal: the ability to know oneself; to understand one's own moods, feelings, intentions, and motivations; and to act based on that knowledge; and (8) naturalist: the ability to discriminate among and value phenomena of the natural world. Gardner proposes that each person has all eight intelligences and, at the same time, is dominant in one or two; that the eight intelligences interact in complex ways; and that all people can develop all eight intelligences to adequate levels of competence.

Although schools have become adept at measuring linguistic and logical-mathematical intelligences, they have not yet developed the tools to assess the others adequately. David Perkins (1985), Gardner's colleague at Harvard, has conducted research that indicates that all intelligences can be learned. Such an assertion leads to reconsidering schools' function. In this view, a school's job is to help all children develop intelligences, and a school's energies need to be directed toward assessing the ways that each student is smart and can become smarter.

In a similar reframing of intelligence, Sternberg (1985) has developed a triarchic theory that speculates there are three fundamental kinds of intelligence: analytic, creative, and practical. He makes a case for balancing analytic or academic intelligence, which is valued in school, with an appreciation for the other two. Sternberg defines analytic intelligence as the ability to solve problems that have been clearly defined by other people who provide all the necessary information to reach a single and correct solution. Analytic problems are not embedded in ordinary experience and have little or no intrinsic interest.

In contrast, Sternberg views practical intelligence as the ability to solve poorly defined problems that require reformulation and the search for more information. Practical problems have a variety of solutions and are embedded in everyday experiences that are motivating. He considers this intelligence to be a "tacit intelligence" that is valued in the workplace and is tied to job performance.

Sternberg's conception of intelligence provides the basis for educational practices that develop what have been called "authentic" (Newmann & Wehlage, 1995) learning tasks, assessment strategies, and pedagogies. These tasks move beyond rote memorization and encourage complex thinking skills.

Finally, biological approaches that study the brain are adding to the knowledge base about the nature of intelligence and how to measure it. Using new forms of brain imaging, neuroscientists are developing hypotheses about how the brain organizes itself; how it interacts with the environment; how it learns, remembers, and forgets; and how it solves problems (Sylwester, 1995). Thus far, a connection between the anatomy and physiology of the brain and applications to the classroom is purely speculative. Although many are eager to make the translation to classroom practice, others caution that "the mind is not an isolated thing like the brain inside its skull" (Egan, 1997), and that context-specific studies of learning and teaching may be more useful avenues of knowledge to pursue.

NEW KNOWLEDGE ABOUT LEARNING AND TEACHING

As indicated earlier, forces in the wider culture are calling for a new kind of citizen, worker, and thinker. Even though basic skills are still deemed necessary, they are no longer considered sufficient. Schools are being asked to produce students who can demonstrate *understanding* as well as knowledge and skill. Darling-Hammond (1997) describes these students as having the capacity to

> Test and apply ideas . . . look at concepts from many points of view . . . develop proficient performances . . . evaluate and defend ideas with careful reasoning and evidence . . . inquire into a problem using a productive research strategy . . . produce a high-quality piece of work and understand the standards that indicate good performance . . . solve problems they have not encountered before (p. 96).

Agreement is growing within the research community about the premises that underlie this kind of learning and the instructional practices that move students beyond recall, recognition, and reproduction and toward evaluation, analysis, synthesis, and production. Here are the premises:

• Student learning is based on the construction of knowledge. Students need to make sense of what they learn—in a sense, to re-invent it for themselves. Such work requires that they connect new learning to prior knowledge and see for themselves the link between what the curriculum is teaching and their own experiences and frames of reference.

• Students learn to make the connection through guided practice and interaction with others. Talking is a vehicle for learning; relationships enable students to move to deeper levels of understanding.

• Students learn according to their own developmental dispositions. Generalizations about what is developmentally appropriate at different ages and stages have been established, but students still have unique paths that must be acknowledged and attended to. By teaching to each student's "zone of proximal development" (Vygotsky, 1978), educators can help them move along a continuum and not remain stuck.

Applying these premises to classrooms requires a significant shift in practice. These shifts represent an "unrecognized consensus" (Zemelman, Daniels, & Hyde, 1998) about what needs to happen more and what needs to happen less in instruction (see Figure 3.1).

Such shifts do not mean that old practices are abandoned and replaced by new ones. Rather, the shifts require that teachers "add new alternatives to a wider repertoire of choices, allowing them to alternate among a rich array of activities, creating a richer and more complex balance" (Zemelman, Daniels, & Hyde, 1998, p. 213).

FIGURE 3.1
SHIFTS IN PRACTICE TO HELP STUDENTS DEMONSTRATE UNDERSTANDING

DESCRIPTION OF INSTRUCTIONAL PRACTICE	
Less	**More**
Whole class, teacher-directed.	Experiential, hands-on.
Worksheets, seatwork.	Active learning.
Transmission of information.	Demonstration, coaching, mentoring.
Coverage of curriculum.	Deep study of a few topics.
Textbooks and basal readers.	Real texts, primary sources.
Rote memorization of facts.	Higher-order thinking.
Tracking and leveling.	Heterogeneously grouped classes.
Reliance on standardized measures.	Reliance on teacher descriptions.

Source: Adapted from Zemelman, Daniels, & Hyde, 1998.

HOW TO GET THERE FROM HERE:
NEW MODES OF TEACHER DEVELOPMENT

As stated earlier, the face of teaching has to change to meet the challenges that public expectations and new information demand. If schools commit to the attainment of high standards of knowledge, skills, and understanding for an increasingly diverse and needy population, then teachers will have to wed new technologies to an expanded instructional repertoire. Education in the new century will require that teachers know more about their students, their subject matter, and the context of their work. The question is, How do we get there from here? Of course, there is no single answer to the question, no magic bullet that will prepare teachers for the 21st century. We believe, however, that educators have collected enough experience and wisdom over the past two decades to chart a course for change that places teacher preparation and ongoing professional development at the center of reform efforts for the next century.

The case for high-quality preservice education has been effectively made, given the urgency of filling over two million teacher vacancies within the next 10 years. Equally important, and much less acknowledged, is the need for high-quality professional development for experienced teachers. As expectations for students continue to increase, so will expectations for teachers. Even the best prepared and most accomplished of the profession will, over the course of their teaching careers, need the time and opportunity to update their professional knowledge, increase their teaching repertoire, and talk to each other about how to solve emergent problems.

The issue of professional development is rapidly becoming an object of concern for the research, practice, and policy communities. Recent scholarly work indicates that effective professional development has these basic premises:

- Teachers' prior beliefs and experiences affect what they learn.
- Learning to teach to the new standards is hard and takes time.
- Content knowledge is key to learning how to teach subject matter so that students understand it.
- Knowledge of children, their ideas, and their ways of thinking is crucial to teaching for understanding.
- Opportunities for analysis and reflection are central to learning to teach (Darling-Hammond & Ball, n.d.).

Most educators admit that these premises are rarely, if ever, found in current professional development programs. Effective development programs of the future will break from the traditional mold because the new century requires new forms (Cochran-Smith & Lytle, 1993, 1999; Darling-Hammond & McLaughlin, 1995; Hargreaves, 1994; Lieberman,

1995a; Little, 1993). Skill development should be only a part of teachers' overall professional development:

> The well-tested models of skill development, built on the staff development and implementation-of-innovations literature, will work reasonably well to introduce teachers to a repertoire of classroom practices. However, much of what we anticipate in the current reforms does not lend itself to skill training because it is not readily expressed in terms of specific, transferable skills and practices (Little, 1993, p. 5).

PROMISING TRENDS

This section explores trends in teacher learning and professional development that hold the greatest promise for maintaining a teaching force equipped for the task of educating the next generation of Americans.

PROFESSIONAL COMMUNITIES

A growing body of literature and experience has documented the importance of teachers' growth and development when they work together in communities teaching each other, learning together, and focusing on the successes and challenges of educating their students (Little, 1996; McLaughlin & Talbert, 1993; Shaps, Watson, & Lewis, 1996). This idea of belonging to a community changes the way we think about teacher learning. Its importance lies in the fact that it changes the relationship of teachers to their peers, breaking the isolation that most teachers have found so devastating. In supportive communities, teachers reinforce each other in a climate that encourages observing students, sharing teaching strategies, trying out new ways of teaching, getting feedback, and redesigning curriculum and methods of instruction. Teachers' professional communities serve as important mediators for teachers' interpretations and analyses of student learning. In communities where reform, restructuring, and school transformation are the vision, teachers learn to make public their challenges as well as their successes. Teachers receive support, learn from one another, and gain confidence for changing their practice to better meet their student's needs (Newmann & Wehlage, 1995; Lieberman, 1995a).

USING BOTH INSIDE AND OUTSIDE KNOWLEDGE

Teachers' growth and development come about in many ways. Teachers learn from outside knowledge (e.g., research, reform ideas, conferences, workshops, speakers, books, and consultants); they also learn from each other, from looking at student work, from helping shape assessment tools, and from examining their own practice (Ayers, 1993; Cochran-Smith & Lytle, 1993; Lieberman, 1995b; Schon, 1995). Schon (1995) phrases it well:

> Perhaps there is an epistemology of practice that takes fuller account of the competence practitioners display in situations of uncertainty, complexity, uniqueness, and conflict. Perhaps there is a way of looking at problem setting and intuitive artistry that presents these activities as describable (p. 29).

This kind of knowledge is passed on to teachers in primarily informal ways and has become part of teaching lore. Educators have yet to build a body of knowledge that could be accepted as a scholarship of teaching (Shulman, 1986). Yet, a number of efforts are looking carefully at how teachers produce knowledge by documenting their own practice. This form of professional development is becoming more important; it is one way that teachers not only look at their own practice and gather evidence of its effect, but also build "teacher knowledge" to be put alongside "researcher knowledge" (Cochran-Smith & Lytle, 1999; Richert, 1996; Zeichner, 1998).

A notable example of the recognition of inside knowledge is the success of the National Writing Project. In this professional development effort, teachers themselves not only write and receive feedback from their colleagues, but they also teach each other lessons they have learned with their own students. This type of local knowledge sharing is receiving more attention as professional development becomes the linchpin for improving teachers' practice. This kind of professional development—recognizing that teachers' knowledge may be as important as research knowledge—changes the way we think about what counts for professional development as well as how we think of the organizational arrangements that support it.

NETWORKS, COALITIONS, AND PARTNERSHIPS

Perhaps as interesting as the debate on what (and how) teachers learn and how they implement new knowledge is the discussion on reform networks, coalitions, partnerships, and their role in teacher learning. For many years, educators have assumed that a fixed process produces and disseminates research knowledge for teachers. Such a view has been consonant with how professional development has been organized as well. Teachers, it is assumed, will use research knowledge to better their practice. But this view ignores what we now know about the realities of teachers' worklives. Teachers are fundamentally affected by "multiple, embedded contexts," including their grade level; subject matter; department; school; principal; district policies; community; and, most importantly, their students' academic abilities, needs, interests, and backgrounds (McLaughlin, 1998, p. 74). State-level efforts to create standards and assessments as well as rewards and sanctions add yet another context.

Rather than a linear, deficit approach, staff development is expanding to include networks, coalitions, and partnerships that provide a new model of teacher involvement and learning—one that not only encourages teacher knowledge, but also is far more sensitive to the contexts that help shape teacher practice. We are learning that professional development that increases teacher knowledge is more likely to occur when such development provides teachers with opportunities to be members of a community; respects local knowledge (i.e., problems and practices that attend to the particulars of a context); and uses inside and outside knowledge as sources for teacher learning.

These reform networks and partnerships have been organized nationally, regionally, and locally. Although they differ in purpose, they share common characteristics:

• Authentic problems of practice are central to professional development. Research and reform ideas are often catalysts for helping teachers invent strategies that fit their particular local situations. Teachers' knowledge is developed through inquiry into their own practice, providing opportunities for teachers to make their assumptions, intuitions, and prejudices public and accessible for reflection and change.

• Structures and mechanisms for teacher learning are collaborative. A variety of roles for teachers are provided, including participant, learner, leader, liaison, developer, teacher, researcher, and scholar.

• Professional communities—school-university partnerships, networks, and coalitions— are organized around such concerns as subject matter lines, school reform issues, problems of pedagogy, and standards.

• Inside and outside a school system, these learning communities are evolutionary and flexible, rather than permanent and rigid.

• These collaborative arrangements—whether national, regional, or local—are characterized by a tight-loose structure: Values are tightly held, while the work is flexibly organized.

• Supportive communities find ways to provide time for sharing, evaluating, choosing among alternative ideas, reading, studying, taking action, reflecting, changing, and improving.

• Collaborative rather than bureaucratic structures involve teachers, administrators, and university educators as equals in the decision-making process.

A PROFESSIONAL CONTINUUM FOR TEACHER DEVELOPMENT

Preparation of new teachers cannot be isolated from the ongoing professional development of experienced teachers. Until recently, pre-service education has been de-coupled from ongoing professional development. A continuum that cuts across the teacher career needs to be developed. As suggested by the National Commission on Teaching and America's Future (1996), such a continuum begins with the recruitment of students into a teacher education program, segues into solid preprofessional grounding in a validated setting, and results in initial certification as a teacher. After initial licensure, new teachers continue to develop in a supportive teacher induction program that involves early career mentoring and evaluation for the first two years in the classroom. Following the induction period, teachers have available a wide array of professional development activities that occur in and out of classrooms and incorporate the principles and practices of effective teacher learning. Along the way, teachers have opportunities to exhibit their knowledge and skills to an audience outside their classroom, receive feedback, and remain connected to professional communities. To address their personal and professional needs, some teachers elect to pursue advanced degrees, while others choose to qualify for advanced certification through the National Board for Professional Teaching Standards. Teachers also have the opportunity to become engaged in educating preservice teachers.

This last opportunity connects the preparation of new teachers with the continuing learning of experienced teachers. Teacher education becomes a vibrant partnership among universities, colleges, and local schools, providing for the "rub between theory and practice" that is essential in educating professionals. Like teaching hospitals, schools become sites for extended internships and residencies that are jointly overseen by practicing professionals in the field and institutions of higher education. A professional continuum joins inside and outside knowledge, establishes professional communities, and solidifies networks and partnerships. Such an approach guarantees a superior clinical preparation for people entering the field as well as significant opportunities for inquiry, reflection, and professional learning for experienced educators.

A NEW SYNTHESIS

Changing contexts place enormous demands on teachers and teaching as the 21st century approaches. Too often in the past, practicing educators as well as policymakers have responded to public exhortations to change with an *either/or* mentality. They have supported reform strategies that are *either* rational-linear *or* developmentally responsive; they have trusted in a knowledge base that is *either* external *or* internal; they have pressed for standards that are designed *either* for students *or* for teachers; they have depended on practices that are *either* teacher-directed *or* student-centered. If this kind of dichotomous thinking continues, we can imagine two possible scenarios.

One scenario is a continuation of the current push toward greater centralization and control from the top. Driven by an urgency to make social change, federal and state interventions will make demands and press for reform through mandates to the bottom. We can envision increased emphasis on standards and testing and tightened curricular

62

controls. An assumption that people can be shamed into changing may well dominate, and we will see an adherence to principles on one side of the either/or division.

The second scenario is a bottom-up effort led by reform groups, networks, collaborations, and partnerships who abandon the current wave of centralized approaches. These ventures, however, will have a hard time becoming institutionalized. Adhering to the other side of the either/or dichotomy, they will receive scant support from public policy, and change will be uneven, scattered, and idiosyncratic.

We suggest a third view based on our work in educational theory and practice over the past three decades. This perspective tries to make sense of the past dualities and combines them into a new synthesis for the future. It joins the centralization of standards and assessments with the localism of means and methods. It recognizes accountability not only at the level of policy but also at the level of practice. It supports a broader variety of focused learning opportunities for teachers and principals both in and out of school, and it legitimizes structural and organizational supports that promote best practices without mandating what is and is not politically correct. Such an approach requires that serious money be put into the professional development of teachers and that adequate time be allocated for school-embedded learning. It also calls for a willingness to assume an attitude of both/and rather than either/or as we approach the new century.

References

Ayers, W. (1993). *To teach: The journey of a teacher.* New York: Teachers College Press.

Bruner, J. (1985). Narrative and paradigmatic modes. In E. Eisner (Ed.), *Learning and teaching the ways of knowing: Eighty-fourth yearbook of the National Society for the Study of Education, Part II.* Chicago: University of Chicago Press.

Carnegie Corporation of New York. (1986). *A nation prepared: Teachers for the 21st century.* New York: Author.

Checkley, K. (1997, September). The First Seven . . . and the Eighth: A Conversation with Howard Gardner. *Educational Leadership, (55)*1, 8–13.

Cochran-Smith, M., & Lytle, S. (1993). *Inside/outside: Teacher research and knowledge.* New York: Teachers College Press.

Cochran-Smith, M., & Lytle, S. (1999). Teacher learning in communities. In A. Iran-Nejad & D. Pearson (Eds.), *Review of research in education.* Washington, DC: American Educational Research Association.

Darling-Hammond, L. (1997). *The right to learn: A blueprint for creating schools that work.* San Francisco: Jossey-Bass.

Darling-Hammond, L. (1998). Policy and change: Getting beyond bureaucracy. In A. Hargreaves, A. Lieberman, M. Fullan, & D. Hopkins (Eds.), *International handbook of educational change. Part one.* Boston: Kluwer Academic Publishers.

Darling-Hammond, L., & Ball, D. L. (n.d.). *Teaching for high standards: What policymakers need to know and be able to do.* New York: National Commission on Teaching and America's Future and Consortium for Policy Research in Education.

Darling-Hammond, L., & McLaughlin, M. W. (1995). Policies that support professional development in an era of reform. *Phi Delta Kappan, 76,* 597–604.

Egan, K. (1997). *The educated mind: How cognitive tools shape our understanding.* Chicago: University of Chicago Press.

Gardner, H. (1983). *Frames of mind: The theory of multiple intelligences.* New York: BasicBooks.

Glickman, C. (1998). *Democracy in education: Revolution, change, and the real renewal of America's schools.* San Francisco: Jossey-Bass.

Hargreaves, A. (1994). *Changing teachers, changing times: Teachers' work and culture in the postmodern age.* New York: Teachers College Press.

Lazerson, M. (Ed.). (1987). *American education in the twentieth century: A documentary history.* New York: Teachers College Press.

Lieberman, A. (1995a). Practices that support teacher development: Transforming conceptions of professional learning. *Phi Delta Kappan, 76,* 591–596.

Lieberman, A. (Ed.). (1995b). *The work of restructuring schools: Building from the ground up.* New York: Teachers College Press.

Lieberman, A., & Miller, L. (1999). *Teachers—transforming their world and their work.* New York: Teachers College Press.

Little, J. W. (1981). *School success in staff development: The role of staff development in urban desegregated schools.* Boulder, CO: Center for Action Research.

Little, J. W. (1993). Teachers' professional development in a climate of educational reform. *Educational Evaluation and Policy Analysis, 15*(2), 129–151.

Little, J. W. (1996, January). *Organizing schools for teacher learning.* Paper presented at the American Educational Research Association Invitational Conference on Teacher Development and Reform, Washington, DC.

Lortie, D. (1975). *Schoolteacher.* Chicago: University of Chicago Press.

McLaughlin, M. (1998). Listening and learning from the field: Tales of policy implementation and situated practice. In A. Hargreaves, A. Lieberman, M. Fullan, & D. Hopkins (Eds.), *International handbook of educational change. Part one.* Boston: Kluwer Academic Publishers.

McLaughlin, M. W., & Talbert, J. (1993). *Contexts that matter for teaching and learning.* Stanford, CA: Stanford University, Context Center on Secondary School Teaching.

National Commission on Excellence in Education. (1983). *A nation at risk: The imperative for educational reform.* Washington, DC: U.S. Government Printing Office.

National Commission on Teaching and America's Future. (1996). *What matters most: Teaching and America's Future.* New York: Teachers College Press.

Newmann, F., & Wehlage, G. (1995). *Successful school restructuring.* Board of Regents, University of Wisconsin System.

Perkins, D. (1985). Creativity by design. In A. L. Costa (Ed.), *Developing minds: Vol. 2. A resource book for teaching thinking* (pp. 295–297). Alexandria, VA: Association for Supervision and Curriculum Development.

Richert, A. (1996). Teacher research on school change: What teachers learn and why that matters. In K. Kent (Ed.), *Breaking new ground: Teacher action research, a wealth of new learning* (pp. 9–18). Redwood City, CA: Bay Area IV Professional Development Consortium.

Rorty, R. (1979). *Philosophy and the mirror of nature.* Princeton, NJ: Princeton University Press.

Rosenholtz, S. (1989). *Teachers' workplace: The social organization of schools.* New York: Longman.

Schon, D. (1991). *The reflective turn: Case studies in and on educational practice.* New York: Teachers College Press.

Schon, D. (1995, November/December). The new scholarship requires a new epistemology. *Change, 27*(6), 27–34.

Shaps, E., Watson, M., & Lewis, C. (1996). A sense of community is key to effectiveness in fostering character education. *Journal of Staff Development, 17*(2), 42–47.

Shulman, L. (1986, February). Those who understand: Knowledge growth in teaching. *Educational Researcher, 15*(2), 4–14.

Sternberg, R. J. (1985). *Beyond IQ: A triarchic theory of human intelligence.* New York: Cambridge University Press.

Sylwester, R. (1995). *A celebration of neurons: An educator's guide to the human brain.* Alexandria, VA: Association for Supervision and Curriculum Development.

Vygotsky, L. S. (1978). *Mind in society: The development of higher psychological processes.* Cambridge, MA: Harvard University Press.

Zeichner, K. (1998). *The nature and impact of teacher research as a professional development activity for P–12 educators.* Paper written for the Office of Educational Research and Improvement. Madison, WI: University of Wisconsin.

Zemelman, S., Daniels, H., & Hyde, A. (1998). *Best practices: New standards for teaching and learning in America's schools.* Portsmouth, NH: Heinemann.

4

20th Century Advances in Instruction

Robert J. Marzano

One can probably safely say that before the 20th century, the topic of effective instruction was not often a focus of scientific inquiry. This is not to say that effective and innovative instructional techniques had not been employed. Indeed, Socratic inquiry, designed over 2,000 years ago, was certainly a well-articulated, highly effective pedagogy that is still widely used today. Pedagogy, however, did not emerge as a legitimate emphasis of study until the 20th century. This chapter reviews this century's major advances in classroom pedagogy, particularly in grades K–12, and projects possible advances for the 21st century.

Note: This publication is based on work sponsored wholly or in part by the Office of Educational Research and Improvement (OERI), Department of Education, under Contract Number RJ96006101. The content of this publication does not necessarily reflect the views of OERI or any other U.S. Government agency.

THE FIRST HALF OF THE CENTURY:
INDIRECT ATTENTION TO INSTRUCTION

The 20th century in American education began with a firm commitment to content and little regard for pedagogy. Specifically, as reported by Unruh and Unruh (1984), the 1893 report by the National Education Association's Committee of Ten affirmed that the purpose of high school education was to enhance "mental discipline" and that the best way to realize this goal was a curricular emphasis on language, the humanities, and the sciences. Within this context, the act of teaching was either not questioned or assumed to consist primarily of presenting information. In 1895, the National Education Association appointed a Committee of Fifteen and solidified the emphasis on mental discipline as the purpose of schooling. It defined a six-year course of study for grades 7–12 (see Unruh & Unruh, 1984), which specified the content students should master to ensure mental discipline. Again, a discussion of pedagogy was virtually nonexistent.

In 1906, the Carnegie Foundation for the Advancement of Teaching further emphasized the role of content when its president, Henry S. Prichett, defined a "unit" as "a course of five periods weekly throughout an academic year" (Prichett, in Tyack & Tobin, 1994, p. 460). By convention, these periods came to be thought of as 55 minutes long. The Carnegie Foundation reaffirmed the central role of content, again heavily emphasizing the acquisition of knowledge and de-emphasizing, or at least not commenting on, the role of instruction.

Somewhat ironically, a discussion of the content that should be emphasized in schools was what began the first focused consideration of pedagogy. The exhortations of political reformers such as Jane Addams, Jacob Riis, William Jennings Bryan, and Theodore Roosevelt began to focus social consciousness on the unequal distribution of wealth, the personal misery brought about by industrialization, and corruption in politics. Reformers began to view schools as a vehicle for correcting these social injustices. In this atmosphere, Dewey's (1916) classic book, *Democracy and Education*, was published; it not only underscored the imperative that American education become the breeding ground for a powerful democracy, but also provided explicit guidance on how this goal might be accomplished. Dewey explained that the classroom should be an arena where ideas are shared and the basic principles of community living developed. This approach was a significant departure from the previous emphasis on the acquisition of knowledge. Dewey emphasized the role of the scientific method in the learning process, and he viewed group inquiry as the cure for elitism. Although Dewey did not identify an explicit pedagogy that one would employ to implement his general principles, the implied Deweyan pedagogy placed the teacher in the role of facilitator of discovery as opposed to presenter of knowledge.

Establishment of the Progressive Education Association in 1919, under the influence of John Dewey, William Kilpatrick, George Counts, and Boyd H. Bode, led to formalizing the instructional principles underlying progressive education. According to Schaefer (1971), those principles included

- Instruction must take into account a learner's developmental needs.
- Knowledge cannot be imposed on a learner, but must be actively constructed by the learner.
- Participation in social life is central to learning.
- The scientific method is one of the primary tools for learning.
- Development of the individual is one of the primary purposes of education.

Although not a tight pedagogy, these principles began to provide strong guidance for classroom practice. A teacher following the tenets of progressive education would attempt to engage students in long-term, group projects that students designed and controlled as much as possible.

The instructional tenets of progressive education had the potential to change the presentation-oriented pedagogy followed in most schools. This potential was almost realized after the Eight-Year Study, conducted from 1932 to 1940 (Aiken, 1942) and sponsored by the Commission on the Relation to School and College of the Progressive Education Association. Thirty public and private schools were involved in the study, with each school planning its own curriculum using the general tenets of the progressive movement. In general, this study shows that those students attending schools following the progressive education curriculum attained greater competence than students from schools following a traditional curriculum in areas such as problem solving, intellectual curiosity, drive, and resourcefulness in meeting new situations. Had World War II not intervened, the implied pedagogy of progressive education might have spread throughout the country. As Unruh and Unruh (1984) note, however,

> Unfortunately, the impact of the eight-year study on curriculum development was minimal in its day. The five volumes of the report were released in 1942, at a time when our nation's interests were absorbed in World War II (p. 14).

A discussion of the influences on pedagogy during the first half of the 20th century would not be complete without mentioning Ralph Tyler's work. Tyler's career began about 1930 and lasted to the 1970s. His contributions to education were many and varied. Probably one of his major ones was to point out the importance of identifying specific learning outcomes both from a teaching perspective and a learning perspective. A mandate to set and communicate clear objectives not only introduced a specific element into the instructional practices of classroom teachers, but also created an awareness that different types of content might involve different types of learning and, consequently, different types of instruction. For example, as a by-product of one study, Tyler identified 20 behaviors that must be mastered to effectively use a microscope (Tyler, in Madaus & Stufflebeam, 1989). Perhaps for the first time, educators recognized a relationship between the types of knowledge that were the focus of instruction and the type of instruction that should be utilized—a theme picked up later in the century.

THE SECOND HALF OF THE CENTURY: STEPS BACKWARD, THEN FORWARD

Emerging interest in instructional practices changed direction midcentury when public interest returned to a 19th century emphasis on content. As with the first half of the century, a world event changed what the American public focused on.

THE 1960S

The 1960s began with a return to strongly reaffirming the importance of subject matter knowledge. Shocked by the launch of Sputnik in 1957, the American public began to question the rigor of the content addressed in schools. Indeed, influential figures such as Admiral Hyman Rickover (1959) forwarded the position that public educators, with their anti-subject matter curriculum, were weakening the intellectual strengths of American students. Rickover's book, *Education and Freedom*, even made direct links between the security of the nation and the quality of education. The initial concern was with mathematics and science but soon spread to other disciplines.

Had a few significant events not occurred, emphasis on content coverage and a de-emphasis on instruction would probably have remained. Perhaps the most influential was the 1959 Woods Hole Conference. As reported by Unruh and Unruh (1984):

> In 1959, the Woods Hole Conference was called, and psychologists ranging from Freudian to behaviorist in approach engaged with representatives of the various curriculum projects in an examination of the learning process, motivation, and the nature of intelligence as these related to problems of curriculum content (p. 16).

Jerome Bruner's (1960) report on the conference was highly influential in promulgating its conclusions. One of the most important was that the act of teaching could profoundly affect what and how students learn. Although Woods Hole certainly emphasized the importance of subject matter, it also placed instruction, perhaps for the first time, center stage in education.

The work of Hilda Taba also strongly influenced promoting a focus on classroom pedagogy. Taba popularized methods of inquiry and advocated using different instructional techniques for different types of knowledge—a theme Tyler had first emphasized. For example, Taba noted that instructional techniques that optimize students' learning of concepts are somewhat different from those that optimize students' learning of facts.

Although the works of Bruner and Taba significantly advanced an understanding of sound pedagogy, curriculum was still the focus of attention. To illustrate, the book that contained Taba's (1962) seminal ideas on instruction was entitled *Curriculum Development: Theory and Practice.* Instruction did not become a legitimate focus of study in itself until the 1970s.

THE 1970S AND EARLY 1980S

Before the 1970s, "an emphasis on the curriculum over the teacher" (Brophy & Good, 1986, p. 330) characterized research on classroom practice. In the early 1970s, educators began discussing if generalizable teaching behaviors could be identified. But reports by Rosenshine (1970) and Popham (1971) advanced the position that the teaching/learning process was so "situated" that generalized instructional strategies were invalid. Despite these warnings, studies of teaching abounded in the 1970s, dramatically increasing research on instruction as a phenomenon in its own right instead of as a component of curriculum. Brophy and Good (1986) and Rosenshine and Stevens (1986) named those studies they considered the most influential:

- The *Study of Teaching* (Dunkin & Biddle, 1974).
- The Canterbury Studies (Wright & Nuthall, 1970).
- Flanders Interaction Analysis (Flanders, 1970).
- The Follow-Through Evaluation Study (Stallings & Kaskowitz, 1974).

This body of work became loosely referred to as the "teacher effectiveness" literature. Although this research disagreed on certain points, it did agree on generalized teaching practices. For example, Figure 4.1 contrasts the differences between effective and ineffective praise.

Here are some other categories of teacher behavior for which specific guidelines emerged within the teacher effectiveness literature:

- Questioning students.
- Organizing groups.
- Introducing lessons and activities.
- Ensuring student participation.
- Assigning homework.
- Assigning seatwork.
- Introducing and reviewing content.

Figure 4.1
Guidelines for Effective Praise

Effective Praise	Ineffective Praise
Is delivered contingently.	Is delivered randomly or unsystematically.
Specifies the particulars of the accomplishment.	Is restricted to global positive reactions.
Shows spontaneity, variety, and other signs of credibility; suggests clear attention to the student's accomplishment.	Shows a bland uniformity that suggests a conditioned response made with minimal attention.
Rewards attainment of specified performance criteria (which can include effort criteria, however).	Rewards mere participation, without consideration of performance processes or outcomes.
Provides information to students about their competence or the value of their accomplishments.	Provides no information or gives students no information about their status.
Orients students toward better appreciation of their own task-related behavior and thinking about problem solving.	Orients students toward comparing themselves with others and thinking about competing.
Uses students' prior accomplishments as the context for describing present accomplishments.	Uses the accomplishments of peers as the context for describing students' present accomplishments.
Is given to recognize noteworthy effort or success at difficult (for *this* student) tasks.	Is given without regard to the effort expended or the meaning of the accomplishment.
Attributes success to effort and ability, implying that similar successes can be expected in the future.	Attributes success to ability alone or to external factors such as luck or low-task difficulty.
Fosters endogenous attributions: Students believe that they expend effort on the task because they enjoy the task or want to develop task-relevant skills.	Fosters exogenous attributions: Students believe that they expend effort on the task for external reasons, such as to please the teacher or win a competition or reward.
Focuses students' attention on their own task-relevant behavior.	Focuses students' attention on the teacher as an external authority figure who is manipulating them.
Fosters appreciation of, and desirable attributions about, task-relevant behavior after the process is completed.	Intrudes into the ongoing process, distracting attention from task-relevant behavior.

Source: Adapted from Brophy, 1981.

META-ANALYTIC EFFORTS

One group of studies that attempted to synthesize the research on instruction can be thought of as representing a unique genre of studies in itself. These studies share the common characteristic of using the methodology of meta-analysis. Meta-analysis translates the effects that a given intervention produces into an expectation about achievement gain or loss.

When conducting a meta-analysis, a researcher translates the results of a given study into a unit of measurement, referred to as an effect size. An effect size expresses the increase or decrease in achievement of the experimental group—that is, the group of students who are exposed to a specific instructional technique—in standard deviation units. To illustrate, in a meta-analysis involving 20 studies, Redfield and Rousseau (1981) found the average effect size for using higher-level questions was 0.73. One of the most useful aspects of effect sizes is that they can be interpreted in terms of percentile gain. This interpretation is depicted for the Redfield and Rousseau findings in Figure 4.2.

Given that effect sizes are expressed in standard deviation units, an effect size of 1.0 means that the average student in the experimental group (shown by the broken line in Figure 4.2) would be one standard deviation higher than the average student in the control group (shown by the solid line). We know that 34 percent of students in a normal distribution fall within one standard deviation above the mean. Therefore, an effect size of 1.0 would indicate an achievement gain of 34 percentile points.

Redfield and Rousseau found that the average score of students in the experimental group (those exposed to higher-level questions) was 0.73 standard deviations above the mean score of subjects in the control group (those not exposed to higher-level questions). This effect size is slightly less than 1.0. By consulting statistical tables, we find that an effect size of 0.73 indicates a percentile gain of about 27 points.

Given its synthetic power, meta-analysis is a perfect methodology for summarizing the findings from hundreds of studies. A number of meta-analyses that shed a great deal of light on classroom pedagogy have been conducted (see Hattie, 1992; Lipsey & Wilson, 1993; Crismore, 1985; Athappilly, Smidchens, & Kofel, 1983; Bredderman, 1983; Hansford & Hattie, 1982; Haller, Child, & Walberg, 1988; Ross, 1988).

FIGURE 4.2
EFFECT SIZE INTERPRETATION

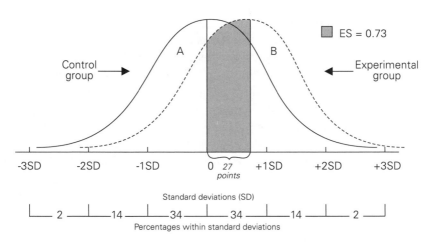

A = Control group mean   B = Experimental group mean

Perhaps the most ambitious was conducted by Fraser, Walberg, Welch, and Hattie (1987). Their meta-analyses addressed 22,000 studies that involved 5 to 15 million students; their findings identified certain classroom instructional interventions as among the most powerful in terms of achievement gains (see Figure 4.3).

SPECIFIC LEARNING STRATEGIES

An emphasis on learning strategies began in the 1970s, indicating a shift in focus from what is taught to how instruction should occur. The term "learning strategy" generally refers to a set of steps or heuristics a student can use to accomplish a specific task. Learning strategies, then, are tools for students to become more effective learners. According to Weinstein and Mayer (1986), "These techniques, referred to as learning strategies, can be defined as behaviors and thoughts that a learner engages in during learning" (p. 315).

For example, a popular learning strategy is K-W-L (Ogle, 1986). Each letter stands for a specific mental action that a learner can take to improve the comprehension and understanding of written information.

The letter *K* stands for asking oneself, What do I already *know* about the topic? The letter *W* stands for, *What* do I want to learn? The letter *L* stands for, What did I *learn*?

Since the 1970s, learning strategies have been identified for different types of knowledge and situations in virtually every subject area. (For comprehensive reviews see Jones, Palincsar, Ogle, & Carr, 1987; Pressley & Levin, 1983a, 1983b; Hattie, Biggs, & Purdie, 1996.) The role of classroom teachers shifted from teaching content to teaching students how to learn. This shift coincided with a rapidly developing theory that some psychologists promoted: Competence in any given domain—even general intelligence—is a malleable characteristic that can be taught and reinforced (see Sternberg, 1979, 1986a, 1986b; Perkins, 1986, 1992).

FIGURE 4.3
CLASSROOM STRATEGIES EXPECTED TO PRODUCE
HIGH ACHIEVEMENT GAINS

Strategy	Effect Size	Percentile Gain in Points
Reinforcement	1.13	37
Use of advanced organizers	0.37	15
Homework	0.43	17
Use of simulations	0.37	15
Remediation	0.64	24

Source: Derived from Fraser et al., 1987, pp. 194–197.

INSTRUCTIONAL MODELS

The latter part of the 20th century saw the proliferation of what might be referred to as instructional models. Here the term "model" refers to an organized set of generalizations about the nature of the interaction between the teacher, student, and the knowledge to be learned. Using this definition, a model goes beyond specific instructional techniques, such as asking students higher-level questions. Rather, models commonly include a wide variety of instructional techniques that ideally address the totality of the teaching-learning process, or at least some key aspects of the process.

Although these models drew from the research and theory on instruction—in other words, they offered relatively little in new instructional techniques—they did mark the beginning of systematic attempts to improve the quality of instruction in a robust, comprehensive way. Because research literature had identified generalizable teaching behaviors, educators assumed that effective teaching skills could also be taught. The act of teaching, perhaps for the first time, was viewed as a learnable set of attitudes and actions.

Mastery Learning

Mastery learning is one of the most well-researched instructional models of this century. According to Guskey (1995), the basic tenets of mastery learning can be traced to such early educators as Camenius, Pestalozzi, and Herbart. Modern applications, however, are derived primarily from the writings of Benjamin Bloom. In his book, *Human Characteristics and School Learning*, Bloom (1976) synthesizes over 20 years of research on instruction using a meta-analytic technique. He formulated a relatively tight pedagogical model, with feedback, correctives, and enrichments as the main features. Bloom notes that most teachers tended to divide instruction into units and give a test at the end to determine the extent of student learning. He believes, however, that these tests did little more than identify those students for whom the initial instruction was or was not appropriate. If these tests were used as *feedback* to students, to identify and use *corrective* procedures, then learning would be enhanced. If the feedback indicates that a student had an acceptable understanding of the content, then *enrichment* activities allowing the student to elaborate on and deepen understanding would be prescribed. Reviews of the research on mastery learning by Guskey and Gates (1986) indicate that it produces impressive achievement gains, although Slavin (1987) challenged some of their conclusions.

Madeline Hunter's generalizations about classroom pedagogy had great popular appeal and were the basis of staff development efforts across the country, even though they did not have the level of supporting research enjoyed by mastery learning. Hunter (1995) refers to her model as mastery teaching. Here is her description:

> [Mastery teaching] is a way of thinking about and organizing the decisions that all teachers must make before, during, and after teaching. These decisions are based on research but should be implemented with artistry (p. 181).

Before the phrase "mastery teaching" was coined, Hunter communicated her techniques in a series of popular, teacher-friendly books on classroom pedagogy. Titles included *Reinforcement* (Hunter, 1967); *Teach More Faster* (Hunter, 1969); *Teach for Transfer* (Hunter, 1971); and *Rx: Improved Instruction* (Hunter, 1976). These books explain and exemplify generalizations about classroom practice.

Perhaps the best-known aspect of Hunter's model is her approach to lesson design, which includes the elements shown in Figure 4.4.

Cooperative Learning

Cooperative learning is another model with a long history (see Johnson & Johnson, 1995) and a strong research base (see Johnson, Maruyama, Johnson, Nelson, & Skon, 1981). It is best described as "the instructional use of small groups through which students work together to maximize their own and each other's learning" (Johnson, Johnson, & Holubec, 1994, p. 4). The basic elements of cooperative learning include the following (Johnson & Johnson, 1995):

- Positive interdependence. Students link together so one cannot succeed unless the other members of the group succeed.
- Face-to-face promotive interaction. Students help, encourage, and support each other's efforts to learn.
- Individual accountability. Each student's performance is assessed and the results given to the group and the individual.
- Social skills development. Group members improve skills in leadership, decision making, trust building, communication, and conflict management.
- Group processing. Group members evaluate the strengths and weaknesses of their interactions.

Cooperative learning is widely used in almost every subject area and grade level. It provides a central shift in how instruction is viewed

---

Figure 4.4
Elements of Lesson Design

Anticipatory set. A mental set that causes students to focus on what will be learned. It may also give practice in helping students achieve the learning and yield diagnostic data for the teacher. *Example:* "Look at the paragraph on the board. What do you think might be the most important part to remember?"

Objective and purpose. Not only do students *learn* more effectively when they know what they're supposed to be learning and why that learning is important to them, but teachers *teach* more effectively when they have that same information. *Example:* "Frequently people have difficulty in remembering things that are important to them. Sometimes you feel you have studied hard and yet you don't remember some of the important parts. Today, we're going to learn ways to identify what's important, and then we'll practice ways we can use to remember important things."

Input. Students must acquire new information about the knowledge, process, or skill they are to achieve. To design the input phase of the lesson so that a successful outcome becomes predictable, the teacher must have analyzed the final objective to identify knowledge and skills that need to be acquired.

Modeling. "Seeing" what is meant is an important adjunct to learning. To avoid stifling creativity, showing several examples of the process or products that students are expected to acquire or produce is helpful.

Checking for understanding. Before students are expected to do something, the teacher should determine that they understand what they are supposed to do and that they have the minimum skills required.

Guided practice. Students practice their new knowledge or skill *under direct teacher supervision*. New learning is like wet cement; it is easily damaged. An error at the beginning of learning can easily "set," so that correcting it later is harder than correcting it immediately.

Independent practice. Independent practice is assigned only after the teacher is reasonably sure that students will not make serious errors. After an initial lesson, students frequently are not ready to practice independently, and the teacher has committed a pedagogical error if unsupervised practice is expected.

Source: Adapted from Hunter, 1984, pp. 175–176.

by introducing peer instruction and group rewards into the instructional equation. It capitalizes on the social aspects of the learning process and greatly expands the number and types of interactions students encounter.

Direct Instruction

Although not as well known as mastery learning, mastery teaching, or cooperative learning, the model designed by Carnine and his colleagues (Carnine, 1991; Carnine, Granzin & Becker, 1988; Carnine & Kameenui, 1992), roughly referred to as direct instruction (Carnine, Grossen, & Silbert, 1995), also has a strong research base. Direct instruction differs from the other instructional models discussed here: Using materials—specifically, well-scripted lessons—is central to the model.

Direct instruction is, however, based on a set of general principles about effective instruction. Perhaps the most salient is that instruction should explicitly focus on the critical feature of the information or skill that is the focus of a given lesson. To illustrate, Carnine, Grossen, and Silbert (1995) explain that if a lesson's focus is the cause of the Revolutionary War, then instruction should focus on the problem-solution-effect pattern that is the central feature in an analysis of that particular episode in history. Instruction would highlight a generalized pattern of causes and effects that relate to many, if not most, wars. This approach sharply contrasts with the traditional approach to the causes of the war, which presents students with a series of acts (e.g., the Wool Act, Hat Act, Iron Act, Navigation Act, Sugar Act, and Stamp Act) to which the colonial revolt was a reaction. In this approach, students are typically expected to infer their own conclusions about the pattern of causes and effects that resulted in the Revolutionary War. The core of direct instruction, then, is to identify the sine qua non of a lesson or unit and teach it explicitly.

HOW WILL THE 20TH CENTURY INFLUENCE THE 21ST CENTURY?

Twentieth century pedagogy has provided much that the 21st century can build on. Two areas of research and theory stand out as pillars: insights from cognitive psychology and insights from brain research.

INSIGHTS FROM COGNITIVE PSYCHOLOGY

Although advances in cognitive psychology began to influence theories on teaching and learning as early as the 1950s, psychology principles that could be directly applied to classroom practice did not emerge until the end of the century. Two of these principles are briefly reviewed below.

Principle 1: Learners construct their own meaning. In the 1990s, constructivism became popular among educators, although it is based on decades of psychologists' research, particularly in the field of schema theory (Abelson, 1975; Bransford, 1979; Schank & Abelson, 1977). Constructivism refers to the general principle that learners use their prior knowledge to construct a personally meaningful understanding of new content that is the focus of learning.

The instructional principles engendered by constructivism require that teachers actively engage students in designing their own unique understanding of new content, and that teachers legitimize and even celebrate the design differences from student to student. Brooks and Brooks (1993) describe the underlying principle of constructivism:

> Each of us makes sense of our world by synthesizing new experiences into what we have previously come to understand. Often, we encounter an object, an idea, a relationship, or a phenomenon that doesn't quite make sense to us. When confronted with such initially discrepant data or perceptions, we either interpret what we see to conform to our present set of rules for explaining and ordering our world, or we generate a new set of rules that better accounts for what we perceive to be occurring. Either way, our perceptions and rules are constantly engaged in a grand dance that shapes our understandings (p. 4).

Principles were developed to guide classroom pedagogy (see Brooks & Brooks, 1993). They specified actions that constructivist teachers should follow:

• Encourage and accept student ideas and initiatives.
• Use raw data and primary sources along with manipulative, interactive, and physical materials.
• Encourage students to engage in dialogue, both with the teacher

and with one another.

• Encourage student inquiry by asking thoughtful, open-minded questions and encouraging students to ask each other questions.

• Seek elaboration of students' initial responses.

• Allow wait time after posing questions.

• Provide time for students to construct relationships and create metaphors.

Principle 2: Learning and thinking involve interactive systems. Cognitive psychology provided one of the more powerful realizations about learning: The human mind can be thought of as having interacting "components." According to psychologist Robert Sternberg (1977, 1979), a component is a mental process that operates on information stored internally and performs a specific function or set of functions. Various psychologists identified different types and numbers of components (Baron, 1985; Carroll, 1993). Most recognized the existence of at least three major components: cognitive, metacognitive, and executive. Cognitive components generally address processes that deal with retrieving knowledge and analyzing information (e.g., comparison, induction, and deduction). Metacognitive components address identifying goals and constructing strategies to accomplish those goals. Executive components address the effective functioning of tasks and the integration of behavior with beliefs and attitudes.

The identification of these various components of human thought greatly expanded the view of instruction in the 20th century. Teachers now had more to address than knowledge per se. If the various components were the working parts of the mind, then they were viable targets for instruction. Instructional models began to reflect this realization. For example, the Dimensions of Learning model (see Marzano, 1992) addresses student acquisition of knowledge, but it also provides teacher guidance on classroom activities that would help students not only extend and refine their knowledge of the subject matter but also use their knowledge in meaningful ways. The model further specifies that while these activities occur, the teacher should interact with students to enhance students' use of higher-level mental dispositions. Examples of such interactions include monitoring progress, seeking accuracy, and pushing the limits of a student's ability. Models that emphasize similar components include those developed by Danielson

(1996), Winocur (1991), and Pogrow (1990). (For a comprehensive listing of programs, see Costa, 1991.)

INFLUENCE OF BRAIN RESEARCH

The 1990s saw an explosion of information about the brain's internal workings. Books such as *A Celebration of Neurons* (Sylwester, 1995) and *Nature's Mind* (Gazzaniga, 1992) sought to educate the public on the brain's mechanical features.

One awareness that has the potential to dramatically influence classroom pedagogy is the influence of affect on the learning process. Given the biology of emotions, many brain researchers assert that emotions affect almost every aspect of human behavior. A good case can be made for the contention that emotion exerts a controlling influence over human thought. This case is well articulated in LeDoux's (1996) *The Emotional Brain: The Mysterious Underpinnings of Emotional Life*. After analyzing the research on emotions, LeDoux concludes that human beings (1) have little direct control over their emotional reactions; and (2) once emotions occur, they become powerful motivators of future behavior. LeDoux describes this lack of control over emotions:

> Anyone who has tried to fake an emotion, or who has been the recipient of a faked one, knows all too well the futility of the attempt. While conscious control over emotions is weak, emotions can flood consciousness. This is so because the wiring of the brain at this point in our evolutionary history is such that connections from the emotional systems to the cognitive systems are stronger than connections from the cognitive systems to the emotional systems (p. 19).

LeDoux also explains the power of emotions once they occur:

> They chart the course of moment-to-moment action as well as set the sails toward long-term achievements. But our emotions can also get us into trouble. When fear becomes anxiety, desire gives way to greed, or annoyance turns to anger, anger to hatred, friendship to envy, love to obsession, or pleasure to addiction, our emotions start working against us. Mental health is maintained by emotional hygiene, and mental problems, to a large extent, reflect a breakdown of emotional order. Emotions can have both useful and pathological consequences (pp. 19–20).

For LeDoux, emotions are primary motivators that often outstrip an individual's system of values and beliefs relative to their influence on human behavior.

The influence of emotions on learning implies that they should be a major consideration in a pedagogical model. Such an emphasis began in the 1990s in the form of instructional practices that directly addressed enhancing students' awareness and control over emotions. Goleman (1995) popularized the term "emotional intelligence" and established student awareness and control over emotion as a viable focus of classroom instruction.

PREDICTIONS FOR THE 21ST CENTURY

It would have been impossible for someone at the beginning of the 20th century to predict the incredible advances in classroom pedagogy that occurred in the next 100 years. There is no reason to assume that such a task would be any less difficult at the beginning of the 21st century. Given the advances in the latter part of the 20th century, however, the following two predictions seem fairly safe.

Prediction 1: Instruction will become more of a science. Even if one considers only those studies that Fraser (1987) and his colleagues reviewed in their meta-analysis, thousands of studies specifically on instruction have been published in the last four decades. One of the most amazing findings is the overwhelmingly positive effect of the instructional techniques studied. For example, Fraser and others found that the average effect size for the studies included in their synthesis was around 0.40, indicating that the average percentile gain expected when using the instructional interventions they reviewed is 16 points. Similarly, Lipsey and Wilson (1993) found that the average effect size within the 302 studies they reviewed was 0.50, indicating a percentile gain of 19 points. Only a small fraction of the studies reported effect sizes that were negative or close to zero. These findings were powerful enough to lead Lipsey and Wilson to comment:

> There is little in conventional reviews and past discussions . . . that prepares a reviewer for the rather stunning discovery that meta-analysis shows nearly every treatment examined to have positive effects. . . .

Indeed, the effect size distribution is so overwhelmingly positive that it hardly seems that it presents a valid picture of the efficacy of treatment per se (p. 1192).

This pattern of findings supports the conclusion that instruction has been studied in enough breadth and depth to provide the basis for a science of instruction. In an article, researcher Larry Hedges (1987) stated that educational research does, in fact, provide as much concrete guidance for educators as does the research in physics for scientists. Historically, educators have failed to use the wealth of generalizations explicit in their research; scientists do. The 21st century will reverse this trend. Instruction will become a science.

Prediction 2: Instructional models will become more comprehensive. The 21st century will likely see new instructional models that attempt to integrate three areas of knowledge: experimental research on instruction; what is known from cognitive psychology about the nature of learning; and what can be gleaned from the research on brain functioning. Although instructional models were certainly a part of the 20th century, new ones will greatly expand the research and theory base from which they draw. To illustrate, I offer a model I have developed as a first step (see Marzano, 1998). That model posits the interaction of four elements of human thought operating in most, if not all, situations: (1) the self-system, (2) the metacognitive system, (3) the cognitive system, and (4) knowledge. These four elements are engaged any time an individual is presented with a new task (see Figure 4.5).

A new task is defined as an opportunity to change whatever we are doing or attending to. For example, a student in a history class might be daydreaming about an upcoming social activity after school and be asked by her teacher to pay attention to the new information that is being presented about history. The request to pay attention to the history is a new task that is externally generated. Similarly, the student might independently conclude that paying attention to the information presented in class would be a good idea. This conclusion, that it is perhaps more advisable to pay attention to history than to continue daydreaming, is an internally generated new task. In both cases, the student engages her self-system, metacognitive system, and cognitive system as well as her knowledge.

The self-system contains a network of interrelated beliefs and

FIGURE 4.5
A MODEL SHOWING INTERACTION AMONG KNOWLEDGE,
COGNITIVE SYSTEM, METACOGNITIVE SYSTEM, AND SELF-SYSTEM

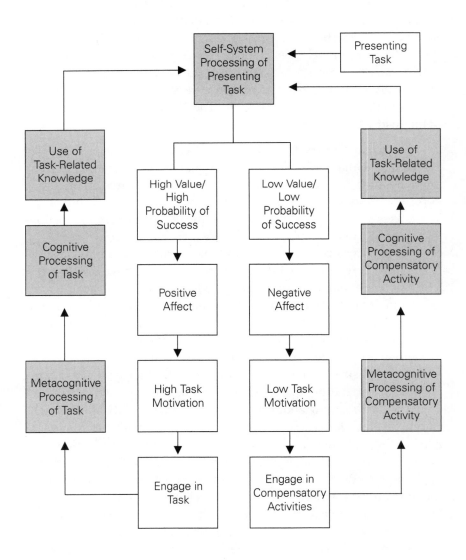

Source: Marzano, 1998, p. 88.

goals (Markus & Ruvulo, 1990; Harter, 1980) that helps us decide whether to begin a new task. It is also a prime determiner in how much motivation we have for a task (Garcia & Pintrich, 1991, 1993, 1995; Pintrich & Garcia, 1992). As shown in Figure 4.4, if a task is judged as important and the probability of success is high, positive affect is generated, and the individual is motivated to engage in the presenting task (Ajzen, 1985; Ajzen & Fishbein, 1977, 1980; Ajzen & Madden, 1986). If the new task is evaluated as low relevance or with low probability of success, negative affect is generated, and motivation is low. In this latter case, compensatory activities are selected, one of which might be to continue the status quo.

In addition to determining the level of motivation for a specific task, the self-system also determines the emotion associated with almost every element of knowledge or skill in long-term memory; that is, the beliefs and assumptions within the self-system tell us whether information—old or new—is to be associated with specific emotions.

The metacognitive system is engaged regardless of whether a new task or a compensatory activity is selected. This system processes information about the nature and importance of plans, time lines, resources, and their interactions (Schank & Abelson, 1977). It is also responsible for designing strategies to accomplish a given goal (Sternberg, 1977, 1984a, 1984b, 1986a, 1986b). The metacognitive system continually interacts with the cognitive system throughout a task.

The cognitive system processes information essential to completing a task. For example, if the task requires solving a problem, the cognitive system is responsible for executing the steps involved in problem solving. If the task requires generating a novel idea, the cognitive system constructs the new idea.

The amount of one's knowledge about a task dictates how successfully one can complete the task (Anderson, 1995; Lindsay & Norman, 1977). For example, if the task is to pay attention to new history information, then the cognitive system activates and acts upon the knowledge the student already possesses about history. If the task is to read an article about the planets, then the cognitive system activates the knowledge the student possesses about the planetary system.

These four elements are important to pedagogy because each (and their components) is necessary for effective learning. Stated negatively, a breakdown in any one of the components within any one of the three systems or knowledge can make a learning situation unproductive. For example, if a student has no personal goals within the self-system that would allow him to interpret the new task as important, the student might select a compensatory activity. If the student does not have effective goal-monitoring procedures in the metacognitive system, the chances of completing a task are severely compromised. If the student does not effectively process information necessary to the task through the cognitive system, the task will be executed inefficiently. Finally, if the student does not possess knowledge critical to the completion of the task, his efforts will probably falter.

Given their relevance, all four elements of this model are legitimate filters through which to interpret the research on instruction. I used meta-analysis to synthesize the findings across almost 5,000 studies related to the model. By using instructional strategies that employ the self-, metacognitive, and cognitive systems, respectively, I was able to determine the effects on students' knowledge gain. The results are shown in Figure 4.6.

The figure reports the average effect sizes for strategies within the various systems of thought. The average effect size for instructional techniques that employ the metacognitive system is 0.72, signaling an achievement gain of 26 percentile points. Strategies within this category include setting explicit instructional goals for students, providing feedback, and asking students to revise instructional goals.

FIGURE 4.6
OVERALL EFFECTS OF INSTRUCTIONAL STRATEGIES
FOR THREE SYSTEMS OF THOUGHT

System	Effect Size	Percentile Gain in Points
Self-System	0.74	27
Metacognitive System	0.72	26
Cognitive System	0.55	21

Source: Marzano, 1998, p. 88.

The average effect size for strategies that use the cognitive system is 0.55, indicating that these instructional techniques produce a gain of 21 percentile points in terms of students' understanding and use of knowledge. Strategies within this category include having students generate metaphors, create mental pictures for the knowledge they are learning, activate prior knowledge, and generate hypotheses about what they are learning.

The average effect size for instructional techniques that use the self-system is 0.74, indicating an achievement gain of 27 percentile points—the largest gain of the three. This finding is interesting because student attitudes and beliefs are commonly ignored as fruitful avenues for enhancing student achievement. Garcia and her colleagues (Garcia & Pintrich, 1991, 1993; Pintrich & Garcia, 1992) note that educators have almost excluded the self-system from the instructional equation, even though psychologists have recognized its importance in the learning process. Also, much of the popular literature critiquing current educational practice seems to downplay and even condemn teachers' attempts to bolster students' beliefs about sense of self (see Hirsch, 1987, 1996; Bennett, 1992). The average effect size for strategies that use the self-system (0.74) indicates that targeting this system should be a key aspect of instructional design. As Bandura (1997) notes: "A fundamental goal of education is to equip students with self-regulatory capabilities that enable them to educate themselves. Self-directedness not only contributes to success in formal instruction, but also promotes life-long learning" (p. 174). Instructional strategies that use the self-system include praising students and reinforcing the belief that effort will enhance performance.

Another interesting finding is that instructional strategies using student affect had an effect size of 0.86; that is, those instructional strategies that attempted to generate positive affect in students produced an average gain in achievement of 31 percentile points.

It is important to note that this model is presented as an example only of the more sophisticated and useful models that will be developed in the 21st century.

CONCLUSION

The last 100 years have produced amazing advances in our understanding of the workings of the mind and the nature of learning. Although the 20th century began with a fairly myopic view of teaching as the presentation of knowledge, it concluded with a panoramic perspective on instruction that addressed such diverse aspects of learning as the importance of affect, the role of attitudes and beliefs, the importance of metacognition and prior knowledge, and information analyses. Many of these advances came at the end of the 20th century. Certainly the 21st century will produce many new awarenesses and see the translation of those generated in the previous century into explicit and sound pedagogy.

References

Abelson, R. (1975). Concepts for representing mundane reality in plans. In D. Bobrow & A. Collins (Eds.), *Representation and understanding: Studies in cognitive science.* New York: Academic Press.

Aiken, W. (1942). *The Story of the Eight-Year Study.* New York: Harper and Row.

Ajzen, I. (1985). From intentions to actions: A theory of planned behavior. In J. Kuhl & J. Beckman (Eds.), *Action-control: From cognition to behavior.* Heidelberg: Springer.

Ajzen, I., & Fishbein, M. (1977). Attitude-behavior relations: A theoretical analysis and review of empirical research. *Psychological Bulletin, 84,* 888–918.

Ajzen, I., & Fishbein, M. (1980). *Understanding attitudes and predicting social behavior.* Englewood Cliffs, NJ: Prentice-Hall.

Ajzen, I., & Madden, T. J. (1986). Prediction of goal-directed behavior: Attitudes, intentions, and perceived behavioral control. *Journal of Experimental Social Psychology, 22,* 453–474.

Anderson, J. R. (1995). *Learning and memory: An integrated approach.* New York: John Wiley & Sons.

Athappilly, K., Smidchens, V., & Kofel, J. W. (1983). A computer-based meta-analysis of the effects of modern mathematics in comparison with traditional mathematics. *Educational Evaluation and Policy Analysis, 5,* 485–493.

Bandura, A. (1997). *Self-efficacy: The exercise of control.* New York: W. H. Freeman.

Baron, J. (1985). *Rationality and intelligence.* New York: Cambridge University Press.

Bennett, W. J. (1992). *The devaluing of America: The fight for our culture and our children.* New York: Summit Books.

Bloom, B. S. (1976). *Human characteristics and school learning.* New York: McGraw-Hill.

Bransford, J. D. (1979). *Human cognition: Learning, understanding, and remembering.* Belmont, CA: Wadsworth.

Bredderman, T. A. (1983). Effects of activity-based elementary science on student outcomes: A quantitative synthesis. *Review of Educational Research, 53,* 499–518.

Brooks, J. G., & Brooks, M. G. (1993). *In search of understanding: The case for constructivist classrooms.* Alexandria, VA: Association for Supervision and Curriculum Development.

Brophy, J. (1981, Spring). Teacher praise: A functional analysis. *Review of Educational Research, 51,* 5–32.

Brophy, J., & Good, T. L. (1986). Teacher behavior and student achievement. In M. C. Wittrock (Ed.), *Handbook of research on teaching* (3rd ed., pp. 328–375). New York: Macmillan.

Bruner, J. (1960). *The process of education.* Cambridge, MA: Harvard University Press.

Carnine, D. (1991). Curricular interventions for teaching higher-order thinking for all students. Introduction to the special series. *Journal of Learning Disabilities, 24*(5), 261–269.

Carnine, D., Granzin, A., & Becker, W. (1988). Direct instruction. In J. Graden, J. Zins, & M. Curtis (Eds.), *Alternative educational delivery systems: Enhancing instructional options for all students* (pp. 327–349). Washington, DC: National Association of School Psychologists.

Carnine, D., Grossen, B., & Silbert, J. (1995). Direct instruction to accelerate cognitive growth. In J. H. Block, S. T. Everson, & T. R. Guskey (Eds.), *School improvement programs* (pp. 129–152). New York: Scholastic.

Carnine, D., & Kameenui, E. (1992). *Teaching higher-order thinking to all students.* Austin, TX: Pro Ed.

Carroll, J. B. (1993). *Human cognitive abilities: A survey of factor-analytic studies.* New York: Cambridge University Press.

Costa, A. L. (Ed.). (1991). *Developing minds: Vol. 2. Programs for teaching thinking* (Rev. ed.). Alexandria, VA: Association for Supervision and Curriculum Development.

Crismore, A. (Ed.). (1985). *Landscapes: A state-of-the-art assessment of reading comprehension research: 1974–1984. Final report.* Washington, DC: U.S. Department of Education. (ERIC Document Reproduction Service No. ED 261 350)

Danielson, C. (1996). *Enhancing professional practice: A framework for teaching.*

Alexandria, VA: Association for Supervision and Curriculum Development.

Dewey, J. (1916). *Democracy and education.* New York: Macmillan. Available: http://www.ilt.columbia.edu/academic/texts/dewey/d_e/title.html

Dunkin, M., & Biddle, B. (1974). *The study of teaching.* New York: Holt, Rinehart, and Winston.

Flanders, N. (1970). *Analyzing teacher behavior.* Reading, MA: Addison-Wesley.

Fraser, B. J., Walberg, H. J., Welch, W. W., & Hattie, J. A. (1987). Synthesis of educational productivity research. *Journal of Educational Research, 11,* 145–252.

Garcia T., & Pintrich, P. R. (1991, August). *The effects of autonomy on motivation, use of learning strategies, and performance in the college classroom.* Paper presented at the annual meeting of the American Psychological Association, San Francisco.

Garcia, T., & Pintrich, P. R. (1993, August). *Self-schemas as goals and their role in self-regulated learning.* Paper presented at the annual meeting of the American Psychological Association, Toronto, ON.

Garcia, T., & Pintrich, P. R. (1995, April). *The role of selves in adolescents' perceived competence and self-regulation.* Paper presented at the annual meeting of the American Educational Research Association, San Francisco.

Gazzaniga, M. (1992). *Nature's mind: The biological roots of thinking, emotions, sexuality, language, and intelligence.* New York: BasicBooks.

Goleman, D. (1995). *Emotional Intelligence.* New York: Bantam Books.

Guskey, T. R. (1995). Mastery learning. In J. H. Block, S. T. Everson, & T. R. Guskey (Eds.), *School improvement programs* (pp. 91–108). New York: Scholastic.

Guskey, T. R., & Gates, S. L. (1986, May). Synthesis of research on the effects of mastery learning in elementary and secondary classrooms. *Educational Leadership, 43*(8), 73–80.

Haller, E. P., Child, D. A., & Walberg, H. J. (1988). Can comprehension be taught? A quantitative synthesis of "metacognitive studies." *Educational Researcher, 17*(9), 5–8.

Hansford, B. C., & Hattie, J. A. (1982). The relationship between self and achievement/ performance measures. *Review of Educational Research, 52,* 123–142.

Harter, S. (1980). The perceived competence scale for children. *Child Development, 51,* 218–235.

Hattie, J. A. (1992). Measuring the effects of schooling. *Journal of Education, 36,* 5–13.

Hattie, J., Biggs, J., & Purdie, N. (1996). Effects of learning skills interventions on student learning: A meta-analysis. *Review of Educational Research, 66,* 99–136.

Hedges, L. V. (1987). How hard is hard science; How soft is soft science? *American Psychologist, 42,* 443–455.

Hirsch, E. D., Jr. (1987). *Cultural literacy: What every American needs to know.* Boston: Houghton Mifflin.

Hirsch, E. D., Jr. (1996). *The schools we need: Why we don't have them.* New York: Doubleday.

Hunter, M. (1967). *Reinforcement.* El Segundo, CA: TIP.

Hunter, M. (1969). *Teach more faster!* El Segundo, CA: TIP.

Hunter, M. (1971). *Teach for transfer.* El Segundo, CA: TIP.

Hunter, M. (1976). *Rx: Improved instruction.* El Segundo, CA: TIP.

Hunter, M. (1984). Knowing, teaching, and supervising. In P. Hosford (Ed.), *Using what we know about teaching* (pp. 169–192). Alexandria, VA: Association for Supervision and Curriculum Development.

Hunter, M. (1995). Mastery teaching. In J. H. Block, S. T. Everson, & T. R. Guskey (Eds.), *School improvement programs* (pp. 181–204). New York: Scholastic.

Johnson, D. W., & Johnson, R. T. (1995). Cooperative learning. In J. H. Block, S. T. Everson, & T. R. Guskey (Eds.), *School improvement programs* (pp. 25–56). New York: Scholastic.

Johnson, D. W., Johnson, R. T., & Holubec, E. J. (1994). *Cooperative learning in the classroom.* Alexandria, VA: Association for Supervision and Curriculum Development.

Johnson, D., Maruyama, G., Johnson, R., Nelson, D., and Skon, L. (1981). Effects of cooperative, competitive, and individualistic goal structures on achievement: A meta-analysis. *Psychological Bulletin, 89,* 47–62.

Jones, B. F., Palincsar, A. S., Ogle, D. S., & Carr, E. G. (1987). *Strategic teaching and learning: Cognitive instruction in the content areas.* Alexandria, VA: Association for Supervision and Curriculum Development.

LeDoux, J. E. (1996). *The emotional brain: The mysterious underpinnings of emotional life.* New York: Simon and Schuster.

Lindsay, P. H., & Norman, D. A. (1977). *Human information processing.* New York: Academic Press.

Lipsey, M. W., & Wilson, D. B. (1993). The efficacy of psychological, educational, and behavioral treatment. *American Psychologist, 48,* 1181–1209.

Madaus, G. F., & Stufflebeam, D. (Eds.). (1989). *Educational evaluation: Classic works of Ralph W. Tyler.* Boston: Kluwer Academic Press.

Markus, H., & Ruvulo, A. (1990). Possible selves. Personalized representations of goals. In L. Pervin (Ed.), *Goal concepts in psychology* (pp. 211–241). Hillsdale, NJ: Lawrence Erlbaum.

Marzano, R. J. (1992). *A different kind of classroom: Teaching with Dimensions of Learning.* Alexandria, VA: Association for Supervision and Curriculum Development.

Marzano, R. J. (1998). *A theory-based meta-analysis of research on instruction* (Tech. Rep.). Aurora, CO: Mid-continent Regional Educational Laboratory.

Ogle, D. (1986). The K-W-L: A teaching model that develops active reading of expository text. *The Reading Teacher, 39,* 564–576.

Perkins, D. N. (1986). *Knowledge as design.* Hillsdale, NJ: Lawrence Erlbaum.

Perkins, D. N. (1992). *Smart schools: From training memories to educating minds.* New York: Free Press.

Pintrich, P. R., & Garcia, T. C. (1992, April). *An integrated model of motivation and self-regulated learning.* Paper presented at the annual meeting of the American Educational Research Association, San Francisco.

Pogrow, S. (1990). *HOTS: A validated thinking skills approach to using computers with at-risk students.* New York: Scholastic.

Popham, W. (1971). Performance tests of teaching proficiency: Rationale, development, and validation. *American Educational Research Journal, 8,* 105–117.

Pressley, M., & Levin, J. R. (Eds.). (1983a). *Cognitive strategy research: Educational applications.* New York: Springer-Verlag.

Pressley, M., & Levin, J. R. (Eds.). (1983b). *Cognitive strategy research: Psychological foundations.* New York: Springer-Verlag.

Redfield, D. L., & Rousseau, E. W. (1981). A meta-analysis of experimental research on teacher questioning behavior. *Review of Educational Research, 51,* 237–245.

Rickover, H. G. (1959). *Education and freedom.* New York: E. P. Dutton.

Rosenshine, B. (1970). Evaluation of instruction. *Review of Educational Research, 40,* 279–301.

Rosenshine, B., & Stevens, R. (1986). Teaching functions. In M. Wittrock (Ed.), *Handbook of research on teaching* (3rd ed., pp. 326–391). New York: Macmillan.

Ross, J. A. (1988). Controlling variables: A meta-analysis of training studies. *Review of Educational Research, 58,* 405–437.

Schaefer, R. J. (1971). Retrospect and prospect. In *The curriculum: Retrospect and prospect. Seventieth yearbook of the National Society for the Study of Education, Part I* (pp. 3–25). Chicago: University of Chicago Press.

Schank, R. C., & Abelson, R. (1977). *Scripts, plans, goals, and understanding.* Hillsdale, NJ: Lawrence Erlbaum.

Slavin, R. E. (1987). Mastery learning reconsidered. *Review of Educational Research, 57,* 175–213.

Stallings, J., & Kaskowitz, D. (1974). *Follow-Through classroom observation evaluation 1972–1973* (SRI Project URU-7370). Stanford, CA: Stanford Research Institute.

Sternberg, R. J. (1977). *Intelligence, information processing, and analogical reasoning: The componential analysis of human abilities.* Hillsdale, NJ: Lawrence Erlbaum.

Sternberg, R. J. (1979). The nature of mental abilities. *American Psychologist, 34,* 214–230.

Sternberg, R. J. (1984a). *Beyond IQ: A triarchic theory of human intelligence.* New York: Cambridge University Press.

Sternberg, R. J. (1984b). Mechanisms of cognitive development: A componential approach. In R. J. Sternberg (Ed.), *Mechanisms of cognitive development* (pp. 163–186). New York: W. H. Freeman.

Sternberg, R. J. (1986a). Inside Intelligence. *American Scientist, 74*(2), 137–143.

Sternberg, R. J. (1986b). *Intelligence applied.* New York: Harcourt Brace Jovanovich.

Sylwester, R. (1995). *A celebration of neurons: An educator's guide to the human brain.* Alexandria, VA: Association for Supervision and Curriculum Development.

Taba, H. (1962). *Curriculum development: Theory and practice.* New York: Harcourt, Brace, and World.

Tyack, T., & Tobin, W. (1994). The "grammar" of schooling: Why has it been so hard to change. *American Educational Research Journal, 31,* 453–479.

Unruh, G. G., & Unruh, A. (1984). *Curriculum development: Problems, processes, and progress.* Berkeley, CA: McCutchan.

Weinstein, C. E., & Mayer, R. E. (1986). The teaching of learning strategies. In M. Wittrock (Ed.), *Handbook of research on teaching* (3rd ed., pp. 315–327). New York: Macmillan.

Winocur, S. L. (1991). IMPACT. In A. L. Costa (Ed.), *Developing minds: Vol. 2. Programs for teaching thinking* (Rev. ed., pp. 33–35). Alexandria, VA: Association for Supervision and Curriculum Development.

Wright, C. J., & Nuthall, G. (1970). Relationships between teacher behaviors and pupil achievement in three experimental elementary science lessons. *American Educational Research Journal, 7,* 477–491.

5

Curriculum for the New Millennium

Allan A. Glatthorn and Jerry Jailall

"The more things change, the more they stay the same." That sentence seems to sum up the history of curriculum change over the past 50 years. Much apparent activity occurred, especially at the advocacy level, but also much continuity, especially at the classroom level. It also describes the future of curriculum change, implying a somewhat predictable pattern: New curriculum projects touch the surface of schooling, with comparatively little change at the heart of the educational system. To explain these general assertions, this chapter examines the lessons of the past and then suggests some goals for the future.

LESSONS FROM THE PAST

Rather than simply recounting the major changes that have taken place, delineating what has been learned from that past seems more useful.

CURRICULUM IS STREAMS OF VARYING STRENGTH

A metaphor of several streams works well to describe how the curriculum has been moving. It flows through the system, ebbing at times, then gathering strength and flowing together in a dynamic confluence. Such a metaphor seems more helpful than the cliché of a pendulum, which connotes a simple back-and-forth motion. The streams metaphor instead suggests that at any given time in our curricular history, several curriculum streams or orientations are operating. At a particular point in our past, one stream is weak in influence; later, it gathers strength and becomes powerful. At times, the streams are widely separated; at other times, they flow together. And the strength of a given stream is clearly influenced by many factors, especially complex societal and cultural forces.

Perhaps the best analysis of the streams is that presented by Elliot Eisner (1979), who used the term "curriculum orientations," rather than "streams." He identifies five such orientations:

• Cognitive processes. Exemplified in Gardner's (1995) multiple intelligences approach, this orientation is based on the belief that the curriculum should be primarily concerned with helping students solve problems, develop their thinking skills, and learn how to learn. As Eisner points out, this stream goes back at least to the 19th century, when phrenologists and faculty psychologists argued for the primacy of mental development.

• Academic rationalism. Found in the curriculum standards movement, which is strongly subject centered, this orientation is predicated on the assumption that the academic disciplines should constitute the basis for curriculum. Proponents believe that understanding a discipline's concepts and syntax of inquiry should be the central goal of all curriculums. Such a belief can be traced, of course, to the medieval concepts of the trivium and quadrivium. The proliferation of state curriculum standards—all of which are subject based— illustrates this stream's strength.

• Personal relevance. The continuing interest in whole language programs in elementary language arts indicates this stream's presence. Based on the assumption that the curriculum should begin with students' needs, its goal is to enable students to find personal meaning in what they study. (In an earlier work, Eisner and Vallance (1974) termed this orientation "self-actualization, or curriculum as consummatory experience.") The curriculum advocated by Neill (1960) is an excellent example of a student-centered curriculum.

• Social adaptation and social reconstruction. This orientation manifests itself in programs that emphasize preparation for adult living, such as the current school-to-work programs. It is grounded in the belief that the curriculum should find its foundations in society's needs. Those committed to social adaptation believe that schools should help students adapt to the existing social order. They argue that schools should prepare students to fill the work force needs of the nation and to accommodate themselves to societal values and norms. The argument of the ill-conceived *A Nation at Risk* (National Commission on Excellence in Education, 1983) was that the schools are failing the society by not producing the kinds of workers that the nation needs.

On the other hand, educators and other citizens who believe in social reconstruction want the curriculum to enable students to improve the society. Radicals want to transform the society; liberals wish to improve it. For example, Wood (1988) argues persuasively for a curriculum that would result in what he terms "democratic empowerment" (p. 176). Such empowerment, he notes, would enable students to know "that alternative social arrangements to the status quo exist and are worthwhile" (p. 176). Thus, although social adaptation and social reconstruction are considered one stream here, they are diametrically opposed in their goals.

• Technology. This stream views curriculum as a technical process, emphasizing a means-end orientation. A curriculum designed for mastery learning principles uses a technological approach, even though most mastery learning programs are strong on means, but weak on ends. The starting point is to identify goals; then all that matters is designing the means to accomplish those goals. This orientation goes back at least to an influential book by Franklin Bobbitt (1918) and can be found today in the work of many curriculum consultants, including Glatthorn (1994).

How have these streams flowed in the past? Any attempt to reduce a complex educational past to a single diagram is necessarily fraught with error; however, the streams shown in Figure 5.1 may be useful in illustrating major trends and suggesting future directions. (See the last section of the chapter for a discussion of the implications.)

The analysis reflected in the figure has two implications. The first is that the foundations of curriculum are multiple, resulting in what Kliebard (1988) terms an "absence of purpose" in a school curriculum (p. 31); this situation might also be described as a complexity of

FIGURE 5.1
THE FOUNDATIONS OF CURRICULUM
AS CURRICULAR STREAMS OR ORIENTATIONS

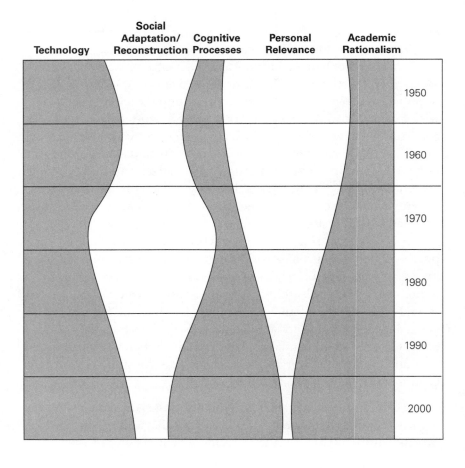

purposes. At any given time, the five foundations may be competing for attention. Such complexity is especially frustrating for a classroom teacher, who faces conflicting demands from school administrators and parents. A striking example of this conflict is given in a report (Marzano, Kendall, & Cochineal, 1999) on parent expectations for the curriculum. At a time when teachers are under extreme pressure to emphasize academic standards, researchers determined that parents rated health information and work-related skills higher than academic subjects.

The second implication is that one or two streams may seem to dominate both dialogue and action at the same time. For example, cognitive processes and academic rationalism seem most powerful now. Such dominance can be the result of several factors working together: the general world view and economic status of the society; recommendations of prestigious committees; influence of the stars of the consulting circuits; and emergence of new technology.

INERTIA PREVENTS MAJOR CHANGES

Curriculum change is difficult to achieve. As Anderson (1996) points out in his study of curriculum reform, significant barriers get in the way: beliefs and values of those involved; lack of teacher preparation to teach in the new ways an innovative curriculum requires; the need to reeducate students; the need for new assessment approaches; and the complexities of initiating the new curriculum while operating an old system. Those barriers result in what might be termed "curriculum inertia," a tendency among educators to leave the curriculum as it is.

Lack of teacher preparation should not be construed here as another example of blaming the victim. Most teachers do their best under difficult circumstances—and the problems they face go beyond their preparation. They are often expected to teach two or more subjects. Elementary teachers typically teach four or five subjects and often are required to implement two or more new curriculum guides in the same year. Also, teachers lack the time needed to plan the new curriculum. Anderson notes that the most important teacher learning takes place in collaborative work with other teachers—and time for such collaboration is scarce indeed. More experienced teachers have been indoctrinated into the practices of traditional instruction and find using new instructional approaches, such as constructivism, difficult.

MAJOR CURRICULUM CHANGES TEND TO HAVE A SHORT LIFE SPAN

Looking back over the past 50 years of curriculum change, one can become cynical about educational faddism, especially in curriculum. Or one can simply note that continual change is a manifestation of a basic cultural value: New is good. To substantiate this claim, consider the short life of these innovative conceptions of curriculums. The approximate dates they were introduced and then abandoned are in parentheses.

Life Adjustment Curriculums (1945–1952)

During the complacent post-World War II period, many educational leaders advocated a special brand of social adaptation that was appropriately termed "life adjustment." Behind this movement was the theory that the curriculum should help students adjust to adulthood demands, especially those related to pursuing careers. The key publication that caused much discussion was *Life Adjustment Education for Every Youth* (U.S. Office of Education, 1951), which expressed a special concern for students in the general curriculum track (at that time, 60 per cent of high school age students). Life adjustment ended when both critics and the general public perceived it as too soft; the attack was part of a more general reaction against progressive education (Tanner & Tanner, 1980).

Structure of the Discipline Curriculums (1960–1970)

In responding to the shock of the Soviet's launching of Sputnik, scholars used federal funds to develop demanding curriculums that emphasized the concepts and syntax of inquiry of the academic disciplines. Thus, such curriculums were clearly in the academic rationalism camp. The argument was simple: The best way to compete with the Soviet Union was to reform U.S. schools' curriculum so that it would provide students with in-depth knowledge of the disciplines.

The basic tenets of this curriculum theory were explained in *The Process of Education* (Bruner, 1960): The structure of the disciplines should constitute the heart of curriculums; each discipline has its own concepts, theories, and ways of knowing; and children can learn such abstract concepts as the distributive property of numbers if taught by trained teachers. Despite such claims, classroom teachers and their students had great difficulty in understanding the concepts.

Free Curriculums (1960–1975)

The term "free curriculums" is used here to describe the curriculums that advocates claimed would bring freedom to children and youth, especially the oppressed. These personal relevance curriculums were a response to the Civil Rights movement of the '60s and early '70s.

This child-centered approach took three forms. Some curriculums were avowedly radical, designed to reconstruct society, as Freire (1970) argued. Most radicals believed that this reconstruction should enable people to live a liberated existence. Thus, it is classified here as an example of free curriculums, although, obviously, it might also be seen as social reconstruction. A milder form was the electives movement, which high school teachers developed and advocated, perhaps in reaction to scholars' efforts to take over schools' curriculums. Rather than enrolling in Sophomore English, a student would be offered a choice of perhaps 20 minicourses, such as Black Voices, Youth Speak Out, and Power to the People. Glatthorn remembers attending principal conferences where participants played a variety of curriculum one-upmanship: "Our school offers 150 courses—how many do you have?" Elementary teachers developed a third type of free curriculum for the open classroom. The teacher determined which learning experiences and materials students could use to achieve developmentally appropriate outcomes, and then equipped several learning centers that children could use as they wished.

Computerized Curriculums (1980–present)

The starting date represents the approximate time when technology became widely used in schools. "Computerized curriculums" is used to describe several ways of using a computer with the curriculum. When the computer is used for drill and practice in a nonbranching manner, the orientation is obviously technological. The computer and allied technology are instructional tools for delivering the curriculum

(Bozeman & Baumbach, 1995). The computer also has several other functions that affect the curriculum:

• Stores the curriculum, making it readily accessible. For example, several packaged curriculums are available in communication skills, math, science, and other subjects.

• Monitors the curriculum. Using an instructional management system, a teacher can input data on instructional plans, instructional objectives and activities, and student achievement.

• Aligns the curriculum by simplifying the task of aligning the taught, the tested, the written, the learned, and the supported.

• Enriches the curriculum by expanding the sources of knowledge and supplementing text with multimedia (see Dede, 1998, for further details).

As these examples show, the computer can be used with several orientations; it need not be only a technological instrument. Interactions between technology and the curriculum result in several subtle curricular changes. A technologically based curriculum tends to have the following features: more specific and less general; more complex and less linear; more visual and less verbal; more administrative driven and less teacher centered; more interactive and less uni-directional; and more global and less parochial.

Total Quality Education Curriculums (1985–present)
Based on the management concepts of W. E. Deming, total quality education (TQE) curriculums could be classified as technological because they advocate a means-end orientation and emphasize using technology to achieve quality. Although TQE is strong on both the ends (quality learning) and the processes (frequent monitoring for quality), it seems to give scant attention to curriculum. For example, Bonstingl's (1992) widely read book mentions curriculum only in passing.

Several signs suggest that TQE's influence is declining: Fewer publications focus on it; educational conference programs include only one or two sessions about it; and professional "buzz" about it in gatherings of school administrators is minimal. The reasons might be that many TQE publications did not clearly describe school reform, and the reform model lacked strong empirical support.

Outcome-Based Education Curriculums (1985–1995)

Outcome-based education (OBE) was clearly a technological model of curriculum change: It delineated a linear process that moved from general educational goals to specific classroom behaviors (see Spady, 1988, 1994). As explained earlier, any curriculum that has a tight means-end orientation can be seen as technological. It seemed to present a useful model that promised to tighten up the connections among the several levels of curriculum. Initially, OBE was widely adopted. The Pennsylvania Department of Education, for example, strongly recommended that it be used as a model throughout the state. But it was attacked from two directions. Scholars criticized it for overemphasizing outcomes over processes, and conservative parents and other citizens attacked it because it seemed to take over parental functions. One other cause of its demise was that too many educators misunderstood OBE's basic principles.

Constructivist Curriculums (1990–present)

Constructivism as a curriculum foundation can be classified as having a cognitive processes orientation. Based on the findings of cognitive psychology and building on earlier work on thinking skills, constructivism emphasizes the learner as a meaning maker—a constructor of meaning. It emphasizes depth, not coverage; poses a contextualized and complex problem for students; ensures that students have a sound knowledge base for solving the problem; and sees the teacher's role as a problem structurer and a scaffolder. (For additional details about its application in schools, see Brooks & Brooks, 1993.)

Standards-Based Curriculums (1992–present)

The present concern for content standards clearly represents the views of those who advocate academic rationalism, even though they probably do not use the term. State standards and their related benchmarks are all subject divided. And those developed by several professional organizations even more strongly represent an academic orientation. (For an excellent compilation of the professional standards and benchmarks, see Kendall & Marzano, 1997.) Most educators and citizens seem to welcome the standards, although two criticisms are frequently heard. Several reviewers have criticized the quality of the standards, chiefly on the grounds that they are too vague about content (see, for example, Gandal, 1995). And many classroom teachers complain that the standards are too numerous and demanding (Glatthorn & Fontana, in press).

As Figure 5.2 shows, one stream seems to systematically progress to another, in a pattern of action-reaction. Note that three of the most recent five innovations have had a technological orientation.

THE GENERAL PUBLIC HAS A ZONE OF ACCEPTANCE OF NEW CURRICULUMS

The term "zone of acceptance," borrowed from management theory, is used to suggest that the general public seems to set broad limits for schools' curriculum. People are inclined to accept major curriculum changes unless they perceive those changes as too radical. If the limits are breached, controversy results—and in many cases, public pressure causes the innovation to be abandoned. Two examples come to mind. In the 1970s, Bruner and his colleagues developed a course entitled Man: A Course of Study (MACOS), which scholars and educators widely heralded as an exemplary curriculum. Developed with funds from the National Science Foundation, MACOS was billed as an elementary school introduction to the concepts of anthropology. As Shaver (1987) analyzed the ensuing controversy, MACOS presented a social science view of reality, one that highlighted a basic conflict between scientific and traditional values. The public uproar reached the halls of Congress, where politicians reacted by withdrawing federal funds from several curriculum projects.

The second project that suffered the same fate is outcome-based education (OBE). As developed by Spady (1988), OBE is a comprehensive reform strategy involving all the significant components of schooling. Spady argued for a tightly coordinated curriculum that moved systematically from publicly announced exit outcomes to specific classroom objectives. Again, acceptance seemed to be widespread. Then conservative parents began to question the movement, arguing that its transformational outcomes infringed upon family responsibilities. Those parents were joined by leaders of the political right, who saw OBE as a convenient way of attacking liberal educators. When conservative talk-show hosts joined the attack, the movement was clearly doomed.

FIGURE 5.2
RELATIONSHIP BETWEEN CURRICULAR STREAMS AND INNOVATIONS

Curriculum Innovation	CURRICULAR STREAMS OR ORIENTATIONS				
	Academic Rationalism	Technology	Personal Relevance	Social Adaptation/ Reconstruction	Cognitive Processes
Life Adjustment (1945–1952)				X	
Structure of the Disciplines (1960–1970)	X				
Free (1960–1975)			X		
Computerized (1980–present)		X			
Total Quality Education (1985–present)		X			
Outcome-Based Education (1985–1995)		X			
Constructivism (1990–present)					X
Standards-Based (1992–present)	X				

ENVISIONING THE FUTURE

Making predictions is tempting but risky. Consider, for example, Glatthorn's prediction in a 1980 publication that the then-current conservative trend would last only a few years. Describing the general features of the desired future seems more useful—a vision that we hope can provide direction for reform efforts.

STRUCTURE OF THE NEW CURRICULUM

For the 21st century, a new curriculum is needed—one that has the power to make a difference in the lives of the young and in the society where they live. The following discussion examines both the structure and the content of the new curriculum. "Structure" is used here to denote the organizational features of the curriculum, and they apply to all curriculums. Figure 5.3 contrasts the structural features of the new curriculum to those of traditional curriculums.

In describing the desired structure of the millennial curriculum, educators can turn to the research for common characteristics:

• Has greater depth and less superficial coverage. For example, in studying the Civil War, students would learn in depth about two battles that were turning points, rather than skipping through every battle. Depth of knowledge leads to power. Several studies conclude that focusing in depth on a smaller number of skills and concepts will lead to greater understanding and retention and will also support efforts to teach problem solving and critical thinking. (See, for example, Knapp et al., 1991; McDonnell, 1989; Brophy, 1990; Cotton & Northwest Regional Educational Laboratory, 1999.)

• Focuses on problem solving that requires using learning strategies. Solving complex and situated problems lies at the heart of the new curriculum. And embedded in the problem solving are learning strategies. Although the initial interest in critical thinking led many innovators to teach isolated thinking skills, research in cognitive psychology clearly indicates that such skills or learning strategies are better learned and retained when they are embedded in problem-solving units dealing with complex meaningful problems, situated in a context. Thus, students studying the features of early European explorations would be taught the learning strategy of using a matrix to organize information.

• Emphasizes both skills and knowledge of the subjects. For many years, educators foolishly argued about the primacy of content or process. Recent advances in cognitive psychology show that such a dichotomy is dysfunctional. Students can solve complex problems in science, for example, only when they are given access to the knowledge required to solve the problem. Cognitive psychologists distinguish between inert knowledge—knowledge that is not used—and generative knowledge—knowledge that is used in solving meaningful problems. Psychologists agree that generative knowledge should be the goal of the curriculum (Brooks & Brooks, 1993).

• Provides for students' individual differences. Three types of adaptations are recommended. First, the curriculum should use varied modes of representation—different ways to display or transfer knowledge. Most curriculum developers emphasize verbal modes; more effective teachers add visual means, such as flow charts and web diagrams (Hyerle, 1996). Second, the curriculum should allow teachers to provide high structure at the beginning of the year through cues, suggestions, and explanations, and then let students solve problems on their own as the year progresses. This systematic variation is called "scaffolding." Finally, the curriculum should recognize students' multiple intelligences, rather than stressing only the verbal and mathematical. Such adjustments are designed to accommodate significant learner differences.

• Offers a common core to all students. In responding to individual differences, curriculum leaders should be sure that the curriculum does not lead to a fragmentation of the student body. Such fragmentation occurs when curriculum tracking separates students on the basis of ability or career goals. One study concludes that high schools had more "character" when they offered a "centripetal" curriculum—a common curriculum for all students. The centripetal curriculum draws students together; the "centrifugal" curriculum throws them in different directions (Hill, Foster, & Gendler, 1990).

• Coordinates closely. Three types of coordination are recommended. First, the curriculum should coordinate related subjects, such as science and mathematics: The mathematics curriculum supports and closely relates to the science curriculum.

Second, the various levels of the curriculum in a given subject should be coordinated; thus, 4th grade science builds upon 3rd grade content and leads to the 5th grade curriculum. Such a curriculum is more effective than stand-alone courses that have no relationship to the rest of the curriculum. Although offering stand-alone courses for enrichment at all levels may have some value, McDonnell's (1989) research stresses that multiyear sequential curriculums will have greater payoff.

Finally, the sequence of units in a given grade level in one subject should make developmental sense; Unit 3 should build upon Unit 2 and lead to Unit 4. In too many curriculums, the units seem entirely unrelated when seen over the span of a year.

FIGURE 5.3
A COMPARISON BETWEEN NEW AND TRADITIONAL CURRICULUMS

| Area | EMPHASIS | |
	New Curriculum	Traditional Curriculums
Depth or Coverage	Depth	Coverage
Problems	Authentic, contextualized; learning strategies in context	Contrived; thinking skills isolated
Skills and Knowledge	Both emphasized in solving problems	Overemphasis on knowledge
Individual Differences	Provided for	Ignored
Common Core or Curriculum Tracks	Common core	Curriculum tracks
Coordination	Closely coordinated	Fragmented
Integration	Selectively integrated	All subjects separated
Focus	Focus on results	Focus on activities
Streams	Emphasis on personal relevance, with other streams used	Emphasis on academic rationalism

• Integrates selectively. Numerous studies have concluded that integrated curriculums have resulted in better achievement and improved attitudes toward schooling (Vars, 1991). Leaders, however, should proceed with caution, because experts are concerned about excessive integration. In their view, excessive integration slights the subject knowledge (see Gardner & Boix-Mansilla, 1994; Roth, 1994). How much integration should be used can best be resolved at the school level. The principal and teachers together can decide the type and extent of curriculum integration for their school, using guidelines the district provides. (For further analysis of this approach to integration, see Glatthorn, 1998.)

• Emphasizes the learned curriculum. Curriculum leaders should be primarily concerned with results—improved learning for all students. The written curriculum—whether integrated or subject focused—is only a means to an end: high-quality learning for all students. Such quality learning can be best achieved if the written curriculum is teacher-friendly in its format and organization, if objectives are clearly delineated, and if less attention is given to mindless activities.

• Pays greater attention to personal relevance, while drawing upon other streams as well. The new curriculum restores some balance in the content. It emphasizes personal relevance but uses the other perspectives: The structure of the disciplines receives adequate attention; students use cognitive processes to solve problems; a technological approach helps in designing curriculums; and the curriculum gives students the tools they need to make the society an even better one.

CONTENT OF THE NEW CURRICULUM

In contrast to figuring out the new curriculum's structure, which can be determined by turning to research, decisions about content depend upon the values of the developers. Thus, debates about whether the curriculum should stress the basics or respond to student concerns are simply matters of values. Two major factors influenced how we envision the new curriculum's content: society and its future, and the needs of youth.

111

Society and Its Future

The first factor is an analysis of the society and its predictable future. One does not have to be a futurist to see a nation and a world characterized by the following challenges:

• Globalism/Nationalism. The interrelatedness of all nations, accompanied by continuing pressure for statehood and separatism.

• Technology. The overwhelming influence of new technologies that will enrich the entire learning process.

• Conflict. Battles between nations, within nations, and between generations and ethnic groups.

• Equity. The struggle for fairness and justice in accessing and allocating resources.

• Aging. The graying of the world—all developed nations will resemble Florida in its demographics.

• Alienation. A loss of commitment to political parties, the electoral process, moral codes, and religious institutions.

• Continuing change. An unstable world, where major changes are experienced in all aspects of our lives—technology, work, family, and leisure.

Schools can help students live productively in such a world with the new curriculum that gives them the tools to confront and overcome those challenges.

Needs of Youth

The other influential factor is the needs of youth. Although critics vehemently assert that the major problem in schools is low student academic achievement, the real problem is student alienation. We believe that low achievement and high dropout rates are consequences of much deeper problems. Consider the evidence from a comprehensive study of schools in California (Institute for Education in Transformation, 1992). Both students and teachers identified their most troubling problems:

• Human relationships between teachers and students seem to be in a sorry state. Students report that their teachers, support staff, and other students do not like or understand them.

• The schools seem biased about race, culture, and class. Some

112

students doubt the substance of what is being taught. They feel their teachers do not understand or value their life experiences.

• Students feel the schools are amoral institutions, where discussions of values are forbidden. Although students believe that their values are different from those of their teachers, the researchers conclude that there is a consensus around the core values of honesty, courage, caring, and justice. This misperception probably stems from the fact that such matters are not discussed during a regular school day.

• Both students and teachers feel that what is taught is meaningless. Students are bored and see little relevance in the curriculum presented to them; teachers feel pressured to teach what is mandated and also doubt the curriculum's appropriateness.

• Neither students nor teachers feel safe in the schools. In the middle and high schools especially, they worry about deadly violence that might erupt at any time. An alarming number of elementary students report that they do not believe that they will live to be adults.

• The physical environment is often depressing. Students feel that the poorly maintained facilities and the unappetizing food are symbols of the society's lack of priority for education.

In summary, the real problem is that too many schools are without heart. If the preceding list describes the real problem, then the solution is not to be found in many of the current reform efforts. If this picture is accurate for many schools, then who would want a longer school day or a longer school year?

A school with heart is one that is a learning community, where everyone feels known, is considered important, and works for the common good. To understand the essential qualities of a school as a learning community, imagine that a student is speaking about what the school means to her:

> I feel that I belong here. There is a place for me.
> I make a difference here. I have the power and the skills to change what needs to be changed.
> I am known as an individual, and I am prized for what I am.
> I know that people here care about me. They know when I am absent, they sense when I am hurt.
> I feel needed; I am part of a learning family, who need each other.
> I feel safe here. And most of all, I feel fully myself.

Such learning communities would not only address the problem of heartlessness but also have a positive effect on achievement. A growing body of research indicates that schools that structure themselves as caring communities have better holding power for at-risk children and youth. Such schools seem to develop in students a greater sense of belongingness, greater involvement in academic work, and improved achievement (see Wehlage, Rutter, Smith, Lesko, & Fernandez, 1989).

Developing a school with heart involves many factors, such as school size, teacher-student relationships, and school and classroom climate. The next section focuses only on curriculum, the subject of this chapter. One caution should be noted: Both we and many other educators perhaps place too much confidence in curriculum's power to change attitudes and behavior. A review of "contemporary issues" curriculums found that these ambitious curriculums achieved 66.6 percent of their knowledge outcomes, 32.6 percent of their attitudinal objectives, and 27.5 percent of their behavioral goals (Leming, 1992). Even though the data are discouraging, they do not necessarily lead to despair. Educators can set realistic goals, bargaining for incremental improvement. And they can choose programs more carefully, adopting only those that solid research supports.

CONTENT OF THE NEW CURRICULUM IN A SCHOOL WITH HEART

What would the new curriculum look like in the year 2010? We present two answers. The first answer describes general principles; the second, transformed content.

GENERAL PRINCIPLES

General principles are guidelines that can be applied in any school. They are especially useful to leaders wishing to make incremental curricular changes, such as revising courses. Here are the guidelines:

• The curriculum should be meaningful. The curriculum helps students make sense of their lives, find purpose in what they are doing, and live with a sense of intentionality. In English language arts, the meaningful curriculum emphasizes writing for real problems, real solutions, and real audiences. The 500-word theme is jettisoned; instead, students write memos, letters, reports, résumés, and responses to literature—all addressed to real audiences.

• The curriculum should have both unity and diversity. Such a curriculum emphasizes the unity of this nation by honoring the traditions and values that bind citizens together. At the same time, it celebrates the diversity that is our strength. The need for this balance is shown clearly in a report by Farkas and Johnson (1998). Among other significant findings, the report determines that parental support for emphasizing national unity is strong. When asked whether schools should give higher priority to teaching students to be proud of the United States or to focusing on each student's ethnic identity, 79 percent of all parents thought schools should give higher priority to national pride. The ethnic breakdown of those favoring national identity is especially interesting: African American parents, 66 percent; Hispanic parents, 80 percent; and foreign-born parents, 73 percent. A need to value the strengths of diversity remains—the means should not be divisive.

• The curriculum should make connections. The connecting curriculum begins with ephemeral student interests, such as cars, and then connects them with deeper student concerns, such as the need for power and control. It lifts students out of the confines of the present and connects them with their past. It connects them with this country's history through an informed patriotism that acknowledges the mistakes and celebrates the triumphs of the past. It connects them with the rest of the world, destroying their parochialism by helping them understand that they are part of a global community. It reduces their self-centeredness by making them sensitive to the plight of the poor and the war-weary around the world. It strips away their cultural blinders by helping them see the world through the eyes of other people. And it reminds the students that on this planet Earth all people are recent immigrants.

• The curriculum should reflect human values. The curriculum is anchored in the bedrock of universal values that transcend ethnic preferences, party politics, and sectarian differences. To amoral youth who believe that their fleeting wishes justify any action, the curriculum places a renewed emphasis on ethical decision making. Too many educators have avoided the awesome task of developing character because they fear the attacks of extremists. Educators can take comfort in the results of polls conducted in 1993 and 1994 by the Gallup organization. More than 90 percent of the people polled supported teaching the following values: honesty, democracy, acceptance of people from different races, patriotism, caring for friends and family, moral courage, the Golden Rule, respect for others, the value of hard work and persistence, fairness, compassion, civility, and self-esteem (Elam, Rose, & Gallup, 1994).

• The curriculum should emphasize responsibility. A continuing need to respect the rights of students, parents, and teachers is balanced with a countervailing need to emphasize responsibility. For we have become an irresponsible people. We mindlessly respond to the whims and caprices of our individual needs, without considering the impact of our actions on those whom we touch. We deny responsibility for what we have become—blaming our parents, teachers, or the larger society in an endless whine of "It's not my fault." We need instead to speak of the obligations of being human. To the teacher who wastes a class session on mindless seatwork, we say, "You wasted 30 learning hours; you are responsible." To the student who comes unprepared, we say, "You are not able to contribute to our work today and thus you hurt us all; you are responsible." And to the parent who sees the school only as a baby-sitting service, we say, "You are not carrying your fair share of the burden; you are responsible." And we need to reaffirm our responsibility for the persons we are, acknowledging our human frailty and shouldering the burden of our own errors.

The importance of character development is underscored by a Michigan state survey of employers reported by Carson, Huelskamp, and Woodall (1993). When asked about skills needed for employment, employers listed these five as the most important: no substance abuse, honesty, ability to follow directions, respect for others, and punctuality. The five least important skills were mathematics, science, social sciences, computer programming, and foreign language. Schools in Japan seem to put a higher priority on character development than do U.S. schools: Japanese middle school teachers spend twice as much time as their American counterparts in providing moral education and counseling individual students (Yang, 1994).

116

TRANSFORMED CONTENT

As noted earlier, leaders can make incremental changes. Or they can transform the program of studies—that is, make radical changes in the entire set of learning experiences offered at a particular grade level.

Little program transformation is taking place in these conservative times. Many educators believed that the charter school movement would prove to be an excellent opportunity to make radical changes in the program of studies, because most were freed from curriculum regulations. The evidence, however, suggests that charter school founders have not seized this opportunity. In an otherwise excellent introduction to charter schools, Nathan (1996) gives scant attention to charter schools' programs of study. Anecdotal reports from charter school leaders indicate that their programs of study differ little from those of existing public schools.

If educators could wipe the curriculum slate clean and develop a new curriculum that truly responded to student needs in a changing world, what specific content would be included and how would that content be organized? Consider the following learning experiences, which exemplify what a middle school transformed program might include (note that the set of learning experiences includes all of the curriculum streams):

• Creative studies. This new course or learning experience includes the following topics: the nature of creativity; creative problem solving; creating with wood, fabric, food, and sound; paint; metal; and words. This set of learning experiences fuses personal relevance and cognitive processes.

• Wellness. This course synthesizes health, physical education, and social and emotional learning, helping adolescents make informed choices about their well-being. It is a manifestation of the personal relevance stream.

• The natural world. This course focuses chiefly on the sciences, integrating appropriate content from applied mathematics and social studies. It develops scientific knowledge in depth, challenging students to find feasible solutions to contextualized problems. The course fuses the academic rationalism and social adaptation streams.

• Communication. Drawing much of its content from English

language arts, the course provides students with useful knowledge of reading; technological communication; interpersonal communication and verbal and nonverbal communication; language history, language change, and dialect studies; languages around the world; and second language acquisition. Much of the course would use a technological orientation, along with personal relevance.

• Humanness. This course emphasizes the social sciences, giving greater attention to psychology, anthropology, geography, sociology, and economics, and reducing attention to history by eliminating tiresome repetition. The stream of academic rationalism is chiefly represented here.

• Decision making and problem solving. This course is designed to help students solve problems and make decisions. These topics are included: decision models, consumerism and decision making, ethical decision making, and problem-solving strategies. The course emphasizes the cognitive processes orientation.

• Mathematical reasoning. Although many opportunities are available to integrate applied mathematics into other offerings, the concepts, principles, and strategies of pure mathematics need special attention. This course primarily represents the academic rationalism stream, with a mixture of personal relevance and social adaptation in the mathematical applications.

• Aesthetic appreciation. This course builds upon a foundation of personal relevance and academic rationalism, helping students find enjoyment in the act of appreciating—literature, music, the visual arts, architecture, and everyday objects.

A CONCLUDING NOTE

The curriculum will change in the years ahead. The hope expressed here is that it will become more effective in responding to the significant challenges that education will face.

References

Anderson, R. D. (1996). *Study of curriculum reform* (ORAD-96-1309). Washington, DC: U.S. Department of Education.

Bobbitt, F. (1918). *The curriculum.* New York: Alfred A. Knopf.

Bonstingl, J. J. (1992). *Schools of quality: An introduction to total quality management in education.* Alexandria, VA: Association for Supervision and Curriculum Development.

Bozeman, W. C., & Baumbach, D. J. (1995). *Educational technology: Best practices from America's schools.* Princeton Junction, NJ: Eye on Education.

Brooks, J. G., & Brooks, M. G. (1993). *In search of understanding: The case for constructivist classrooms.* Alexandria, VA: Association for Supervision and Curriculum Development.

Brophy, J. (1990). Teaching social studies for understanding and higher-order applications. *Elementary School Journal, 90,* 351–417.

Bruner, J. S. (1960). *The process of education.* Cambridge, MA: Harvard University Press.

Carson, C. C., Huelskamp, R. M., & Woodall, T. D. (1993). Perspectives on education in America. *Journal of Educational Research, 86,* 259–311.

Cotton, K., & Northwest Regional Educational Laboratory. (1999). *Research You Can Use to Improve Results.* Portland, OR: Northwest Regional Educational Laboratory.

Dede, C. (Ed.). (1998). *Learning with technology: 1998 ASCD yearbook.* Alexandria, VA: Association for Supervision and Curriculum Development.

Eisner, E. W. (1979). *The educational imagination.* New York: Macmillan.

Eisner, E. W., & Vallance, E. (1974). *Conflicting conceptions of curriculum.* Berkeley, CA: McCutchan.

Elam, S. M., Rose, L. C., & Gallup, A. (1994). The 26th annual Phi Delta Kappa Gallup Poll of the public's attitudes toward the public schools. *Phi Delta Kappan, 76,* 42–56.

Farkas, S., & Johnson, J. (1998). *A lot to be thankful for: What parents want children to learn about America.* New York: Public Agenda.

Freire, P. (1970). *Pedagogy of the oppressed.* New York: Continuum.

Gandal, M. (1995, March). Not all standards are created equal. *Educational Leadership, 52*(6), 16–21.

Gardner, H. (1995). Reflections on multiple intelligences. *Phi Delta Kappan, 76,* 200–209.

Gardner, H., & Boix-Mansilla, V. (1994). Teaching for understanding in the disciplines—And beyond. *Teachers College Record, 96,* 198–218.

Glatthorn, A. A. (1994). *Developing a quality curriculum.* Alexandria, VA: Association for Supervision and Curriculum Development.

Glatthorn, A. A. (1998). *Performance assessment and standards-based curriculums.* Larchmont, NY: Eye on Education.

Glatthorn, A. A., & Fontana, J. (in press). *Standards and accountability: How teachers see them.* Washington, DC: National Education Association.

Hill, P. T., Foster, D. E., & Gendler, T. (1990). *High schools with character.* Santa Monica, CA: Rand.

Hyerle, D. (1996). *Visual tools for constructing knowledge.* Alexandria, VA: Association for Supervision and Curriculum Development.

Institute for Education in Transformation. (1992). *Voices from the inside.* Claremont, CA: Author.

Kendall, J. S., & Marzano, R. J. (1997). *Content knowledge: A compendium of standards and benchmarks for K–12 education.* Aurora, CO: Mid-continent Regional Educational Laboratory; and Alexandria, VA: Association for Supervision and Curriculum Development.

Knapp, M. S., Adelman, N. E., Needels, M. C., Zucker, A. A., McCollum, H., Turnbull, B. J., Marder, C., and Shields, P. M. (1991). *What is taught and how to the children of poverty* (LC 88054001). Washington, DC: U.S. Department of Education.

Kliebard, H. M. (1988). Fads, fashions, and rituals: The instability of curriculum change. In L. N. Tanner (Ed.), *Critical issues in curriculum* (pp. 16–34). Chicago: University of Chicago Press.

Leming, J. S. (1992). The influence of contemporary issues curriculums on school-aged youth. In G. Grant (Ed.), *Review of research in education* (Vol. 18, pp. 111–162). Washington, DC: American Educational Research Association.

Marzano, R. J., Kendall, J. S., & Cochineal, C. (1999). *What Americans believe students should know.* Aurora, CO: Mid-continent Regional Educational Laboratory.

McDonnell, L. M. (1989). *Restructuring American schools: The promise and the pitfalls* (Conference Paper No. 10). New York: Institute on Education and the Economy, Teachers College, Columbia University.

Nathan, J. (1996). *Charter schools: Creating hope and opportunity for American education.* San Francisco: Jossey-Bass.

National Commission on Excellence in Education. (1983). *A nation at risk: The imperative of educational reform.* Washington, DC: U.S. Government Printing Office.

Neill, A. S. (1960). *Summerhill.* New York: Hart.

Roth, K. J. (1994). Second thoughts about interdisciplinary studies. *American Educator, 19*(1), 44–48.

Shaver, J. P. (1987). Implications from research: What should be taught in social studies. In V. Richardson-Koehler (Ed.), *Educators' handbook: A research perspective* (pp. 112–138). New York: Longman.

120

Spady, W. G. (1988, October). Organizing for results: The basis of authentic restructuring and reform. *Educational Leadership, 46*(2), 4–8.

Spady, W. G. (1994). *Outcome-Based education: Critical issues and answers.* Arlington, VA: American Association of School Administrators.

Tanner, D., & Tanner, L. S. (1980). *Curriculum development: Theory into practice* (2nd ed.). New York: Macmillan.

U.S. Office of Education. (1951). *Life adjustment education for every youth* (Bulletin No. 22). Washington, DC: U.S. Government Printing Office.

Vars, G. (1991, October). Integrated curriculum in historical perspective. *Educational Leadership, 49*(2), 14–15.

Wehlage, G. G., Rutter, R. A., Smith, G. A., Lesko, N., & Fernandez, R. R. (1989). *Reducing the risks: Schools as communities of support.* New York: Falmer.

Wood, G. H. (1988). Democracy and the curriculum. In L. E. Beyer & M. W. Apple (Eds.), *The curriculum: Problems, politics, and possibilities* (pp. 166–190). Albany, NY: State University of New York Press.

Yang, H. (1994). Roles of the middle school teacher in Japan and the United States. *Journal of Curriculum and Supervision, 10,* 77–93.

6

Assessment in Education: Where Have We Been? Where Are We Headed?

Elliott Asp

recently read an account of how a state superintendent of instruction, concerned about the shortcomings of the schools in his state, convinced the state school board to initiate an assessment[1] program. The assessment methodology was short answer with some essay, in place of the oral assessments used by teachers earlier. The program's purpose was to evaluate schools' performance and to classify students according to what they knew and were able to do within a framework of efficiency and equity of instruction. That assessment effort produced a number of reactions:

• When the test results were released, a panel charged with evaluating the effectiveness of the state's largest school system issued a scathing report on the quality of local schools.

• After viewing the test results, the public decried the students' poor performance on the number of items they answered incorrectly and the large number of punctuation errors they made, even though punctuation had not been assessed.

• Ideology went searching for data. Educational "theorists," whether advocating a traditional-basics philosophy or favoring a more progressive approach, used the test results to support their position. Policymakers, who before the assessment had believed that the schools were not performing at the level they should, sought to use the results to objectively confirm what they already knew to be true.

• Teacher-developed classroom assessments took a back seat to the state assessment because the public and policymakers wanted to have an objective measure to assess the quality of instruction.

• Teachers expressed concern about the mismatch between the test's format and the way they taught, and about how the test would affect instruction.

• School administrators complained that the test results were being used to compare schools having varying parameters. Not all students at each school took the test, and the rules for exempting students were not equally applied.

• Some critics questioned the mismatch between the test items and the schools' curriculum. They wanted to know if the test measured what was being taught.

• Educators and parents alike worried that the assessment classified students inequitably.

Does any of this sound familiar? These are reoccurring themes in the popular and professional literature of our day. This list could easily have come from recent issues of the *New York Times* or *Education Week*. The events, however, occurred over 150 years ago, when the first large-scale (given to more than one class of students), standardized testing program in the United States was initiated during Horace Mann's tenure as the Secretary of the State Board of Education in Massachusetts (U.S. Office of Technology Assessment, 1992).

Mann's assessment program had a variety of goals, and they parallel the primary purposes for today's assessment efforts as well. Here are the main features:

• Accountability. Evaluating the effectiveness of educational systems and programs.

• Feedback. Providing specific feedback to individual teachers to inform instruction and to students to improve achievement.
• Classification and certification. Putting students into categories in the name of efficiency and equity in instruction and certifying that students have achieved particular knowledge and skills.
• Reform. Improving instruction on a broad scale and increasing student learning.

As policymakers, educators, and assessment experts have tried to determine the priority for these assessment aims, many issues have loomed large: test fairness for individual students and educational systems, impact of testing on instruction and student learning, appropriate interpretation and use of test results, and the relationship between large-scale and classroom assessment. These concerns arose with the onset of large-scale assessment in the mid-19th century, and we are still wrestling with them today. These concerns, along with other factors, such as advances in technology, changes in national demographics, and political disputes about what students should be learning and who should be tested, will influence the future of educational assessment in the United States.

This chapter examines the issues and trends in assessment and predicts where the field is headed as we enter the new millennium. To provide a context, I briefly review the major historical developments in educational assessment in America, and then discuss the current state of affairs.

WHERE HAVE WE BEEN?

To understand where we are headed we need to know where we have been. The past 150 years have seen notable developments in educational assessment that will continue to influence the field in the next century:

• Emergence of external accountability.
• Advances in the technology and science of assessment.
• Advent of large-scale testing in schools.
• Impact of large-scale assessment on instruction and the call for reform.

EMERGENCE OF EXTERNAL ACCOUNTABILITY

Initially, American schools served only the children of the elite. The main purpose of assessment, which was classroom based, was to provide feedback to students, parents, and teachers about student progress in meeting the teacher's goals so that the teacher could modify instruction and students (and parents) would know where they needed to improve. Existing external assessments determined which students would be admitted to the few centers of higher education then in operation (U.S. Office of Technology Assessment, 1992). As education became more accessible to all Americans and citizens began paying for education with their tax dollars, the desire to know how well schools were doing and what students were learning quickly grew. This interest required some form of external audit—that is, beyond the classroom—that would assess all students using the same instrument. Large-scale, standardized testing in the United States was born.

The first attempt at an external accountability was the Massachusetts effort described earlier. Under the direction of the Secretary of the State Board of Education, Horace Mann, Massachusetts became the first educational jurisdiction to use standardized[2] written examinations. Mann wanted to have a more uniform way of classifying students and to provide a means to externally monitor the effectiveness of the state school system (U.S. Office of Technology Assessment, 1992). He hoped that these written exams would create a more efficient and rational (objective) classification of students than what existed at the time, which was mainly based on age.[3] Such efforts would allow teachers to better meet students' needs and help schools use their resources more effectively.

The program sponsors also hoped to use large-scale assessment to promote reform. Mann and his associates thought that standardized written examinations would show that the Boston grammar schools were doing a poor job of educating students because they emphasized rote learning. Mann favored a more applied approach of linking what students learn in school to what they experience outside school. He hired two colleagues to develop a testing program and report the results. Teachers did not see the written exams. As one might expect, his colleagues' report had little good to say about the state of education in the Boston schools (Katz, 1968).

The emergence of systematic testing outside the classroom changed the nature of educational assessment. No longer was assessment a tool for only the teacher. It now became an instrument of public policy, a means to bring about change. And, the test influenced instruction. Teachers took note of the test's form and content and felt pressure to prepare their students. A new set of assessment questions surfaced. Did the test actually measure what the schools were teaching? Did it classify individual students accurately? Was the test designed to meet those purposes? These issues have been magnified as large-scale testing has become more pervasive.

ADVANCES IN THE TECHNOLOGY AND SCIENCE OF ASSESSMENT

Other major developments occurred in educational assessment: Technological changes improved assessment, and assessment as a science emerged. The first technological milestone was the invention of the multiple-choice format, although some may not agree that it was an improvement (see Sheppard, 1989; Wiggins, 1989). Even though Mann's written exams were more consistently and efficiently scored than their oral predecessors, they covered only a small part of the curriculum and ignored many important aspects of schooling, in part, because they were still relatively time-consuming to administer and score, at least by today's standards (U.S. Office of Technology Assessment, 1992). Multiple-choice items are easier and faster to score, and many more items can be administered in a shorter time, allowing for greater coverage of the domain tested.

The first test to use a multiple-choice format was the Kansas Silent Reading Test, developed by Frederick Kelly in 1915 (U.S. Office of Technology Assessment, 1992). Arthur Otis, a psychologist at Stanford University, modified the Kansas model's format, for which he was deemed the "father" of multiple-choice testing. Multiple choice soon became the testing format of choice for most large-scale applications.

Following the invention of mechanical and then electronic scoring machines keyed to the multiple-choice format, low-cost and efficient testing of millions of students became possible. As a result, multiple choice, along with its selected-response relative, the true-false item, quickly became the predominant method of classroom assessment.

127

At the same time that assessment technology was advancing, assessment's scientific underpinning was growing as well. Thanks to the pioneering work of Binet, Hall, Guillford, Thorndike, Tyler, and others (Glaser, 1999), psychological and educational measurement was becoming a scientific enterprise. Policymakers discovered that this new science could be applied to real-world problems.

Advances in the technology and science of assessment led to the testing of millions of Americans during World War I, the first truly large-scale assessment effort. To sort recruits and assign them to various positions, a team of American psychologists created two intelligence tests. The validity (i.e., the accuracy and, hence, the fairness) of these tests for classifying soldiers in terms of their ability to perform various functions was questioned, and the practice was abandoned soon after the war ended. This testing effort, however, led to widespread use of intelligence testing in schools, a precursor to large-scale achievement testing that would soon become a common practice in American education.

Concurrent with increased large-scale group intelligence testing was the use of standardized multiple-choice tests to sort students for college admission. Early in this century, the College Board was formed to develop some consistency in the college admissions process. Examiners wrote a set of exams in various subject areas, and the board administered them around the country. These tests profoundly affected the curriculum of secondary schools, and teachers complained:

> These examinations now actually dominate, control, and color the entire policy and practice of the classroom. . . . Further, they have come, rightly or wrongly, to be at once the despot and headsman professionally of the teacher. Slight chance for continued professional service has that teacher who fails to "get results" in the "College Boards" (U.S. Office of Technology Assessment, 1992, p. 119).

In response to this kind of criticism—as well as to the belief of many in higher education that students were merely cramming for the exams, and therefore, their scores had little to do with their ability to do college work—the College Entrance Examination Board revised their tests to have them assess general intellectual ability. The Scholastic Aptitude Test (SAT), first administered in 1926, was then created, with the hope that it would provide institutions of higher learning a consistent tool to differentiate between students who were qualified for college and those who were not (U.S. Office of Technology Assessment, 1992).

Because of the high stakes attached to this process (i.e., college admission), the format and content of large-scale assessments soon found their way into classrooms, creating a need to make assessments like the SAT more secure and less sensitive to instruction. As we shall see, a tension between classroom assessment and large-scale assessment increased as external testing became more prevalent. Also, the concerns noted earlier, such as the appropriate use of assessment data, impact of assessment on instruction, and fairness, intensified.

ADVENT OF LARGE-SCALE TESTING IN SCHOOLS

As the technology and science of assessment grew rapidly from the 1920s through the 1950s, so did the use of standardized tests in schools. By the early '60s, students in K–12 took, on average, three standardized tests a year; from the 1960s to the early 1990s, revenue from commercial test sales doubled, compared to only a 15 percent increase in student enrollment (U.S. Office of Technology Assessment, 1992). New ideas in assessment theory and advances in technology made testing large numbers of students economically feasible,[4] but changes in educational policy at the federal level and the public's and policymakers' desire for accountability were the actual catalysts for the increase.

Elementary and Secondary Education Act

Passage of the Elementary and Secondary Education Act in 1965 accelerated large-scale testing. Title I, the principal component of the act, provides federal funding to support educational services in reading and math to children from low-income areas. Because of its evaluation and certification requirements, Title I affected educational assessment. The law requires school districts receiving these funds to use objective measures to identify children who will receive services and to periodically evaluate the outcome of their programs. Congress has changed the regulations governing Title I evaluation several times over the last 30 years, and the changes have affected assessment practices each time.

In the 1980s, Title I was renamed Chapter 1 and then changed back to Title I in the 1990s. Almost every school district in the United

States receives Title I dollars, as do over 75 percent of elementary schools.

National Assessment of Educational Progress

Another federal initiative that promoted large-scale testing was the National Assessment of Educational Progress (NAEP). NAEP was the by-product of years of study by many committees and commissions attempting to find a way to collect data about what children actually learned. Title I evaluations provided much information about the achievement of low-income youngsters, but there was no systematic, nationwide data on the achievement of all students. Congress and other policymakers were concerned about the state of education in the country, but they had no credible data for evaluating it. NAEP, first administered in 1969, was created to fill that void (U.S. Office of Technology Assessment, 1992). Sometimes referred to as a "barometer" of education or the "nation's report card," NAEP reports national and state data only. It was not intended to provide information about individual students, schools, or districts. In fact, a number of safeguards are designed into the program to prevent such comparisons from happening.

For the first 20 years of its existence, NAEP had little effect on educational policy at the district, state, or national levels, even though it supplied valuable data about educational achievement. The reason was probably due to the lack of consequences associated with test performance and the general nature of the data it produced (U.S. Office of Technology Assessment, 1992).

NAEP did play a significant role, however, as a model assessment program that incorporated a variety of new measurement techniques and methods. For instance, NAEP uses a matrix sampling design: Samples of students at the same grade level across the country take part of (a sample of) the assessment. No student takes the entire test in any subject area. Such sampling allows a broader coverage of content without making the assessment too time-consuming. NAEP also pioneered the use of open-ended items with multiple-choice questions. Further, NAEP provides a means of linking results from different versions of the assessment across time. This linkage allows the test to be updated to reflect new curriculum and subject matter concerns, while ensuring that trends in achievement can still be tracked.

As the call for accountability grew in the late 1980s, some policy-makers wanted to redesign NAEP so that it could be used to measure accountability in states, districts, schools—and even for individual students (U.S. Office of Technology Assessment, 1992). Educators concluded that this change would cause more problems than it would solve, so a compromise position evolved: NAEP was redesigned, but state participation was voluntary. Thirty-seven states (plus the District of Columbia, Guam, and the Virgin Islands) volunteered for the first state-level trial in 1990. Voluntary participation continues today. State-by-state comparisons have been and continue to be published, as some had feared, but they have also been a positive impetus for investigating factors that seem to influence student achievement (Grissmer & Flanagan, 1998).

When Congress reauthorized NAEP in 1988 and revised it, another interesting issue arose. NAEP is a criterion-referenced measure: Student performance is evaluated against a set standard or criterion rather than compared to other student performances, as in a norm-referenced approach. Before the 1988 revisions, NAEP described student performance in terms of what students *could* do; that is, points on the NAEP scoring scale corresponded to student behaviors in a particular subject area. For example, students who receive a particular score in reading would be able to "make inferences and summarize material from several texts." As part of the reauthorization, Congress called for NAEP standards to be recast in terms of what students *should* do (U.S. Office of Technology Assessment, 1992). Although that process and the results were controversial (Sheppard, Glaser, Linn, & Bohrnstedt, 1993), the new NAEP standards have been used as a comparison measure with state and local standards. Because the NAEP standards were set quite high, a large percentage of students did not score at the proficient level when the assessment was first used. Fortunately, we have seen some improvement in performance in more recent administrations (Grissmer & Flanagan, 1998). Many states have reported much higher percentages of their students scoring at the proficient level on the state assessments than on NAEP (Linn, 1999). Needless to say, this difference has raised political issues for educators and policymakers in those states.

Overall, NAEP has set the national standard for educational assessment and student performance and has prompted much research and discussion in applied measurement (e.g., the standard-setting process for criterion-referenced assessment). Its impact on educational policy, however, is still limited. It is often cited as a precursor to a national test for individual students, and some have advocated for an "individual student NAEP" (U.S. Office of Technology Assessment, 1992).

Minimum Competency Movement

Another impetus for large-scale achievement testing was the minimum competency (MC) movement. In the 1970s, concerned that students were graduating from high school without basic competency in literacy and numeracy, many states established a set of minimal skills and knowledge that all students would be required to master. State exams assessed students against these competencies, awarding a high school diploma for a passing score. Minimum competency testing (MCT) became increasingly widespread throughout the 1970s and 1980s, with some interesting results.

The MC movement pushed assessment to the forefront. Test-based accountability as a tool for school reform, first forwarded by Horace Mann and his colleagues, was clearly not the solution that many policymakers had thought. Although MCT initially seemed to lead to increased student achievement, many gains attributed to it were later shown to be artificial; teachers, under pressure to raise test scores, taught directly to the test (Koretz, Linn, Dunbar, & Sheppard, 1991).[5] Because the goals of the minimum competency movement were minimal, the measures used to assess them were aimed mostly at the basic skill level. Teachers tended to focus their instruction at that level and ignored higher-order thinking skills (Sheppard & Dougherty, 1991). In fact, because many teachers narrowed their focus to what MCT measured, student achievement in some areas of literacy and numeracy appeared to remain stagnant or actually decline during the heyday of the MC movement (Linn & Dunbar, 1990).

MCT raised the familiar issue of fairness to a new height. Many states required students to pass minimum competency tests to receive a high school diploma. That requirement triggered court challenges based on the match of the test with the curriculum, the amount of notice given to students about graduation requirements, and the opportunities for students to learn the content tested (among others). Until this point, fairness in assessment had been mostly a political issue that was argued in legislatures, editorial pages, professional journals, and school board meetings. It now became a legal matter, with consequences attached to court outcomes. From this point forward, it was clear that the tests themselves, the decision-making process directing their use, and the associated curricular and instructional programs would be under close scrutiny by the courts. These concerns are still with us today and will be prominent in the new millennium.

IMPACT OF LARGE-SCALE ASSESSMENT ON INSTRUCTION AND THE CALL FOR REFORM

Following on the heels of the massive increase in large-scale testing in the 1970s and 1980s came a call for assessment reform. This call arose primarily from the impact of MCT and standardized, norm-referenced tests. Both employed multiple choice as the primary assessment methodology, resulting in the almost exclusive use of multiple-choice tests in classrooms, particularly in those states and districts where high stakes were attached to scores on these measures.

A related area needing reform was teachers' lack of knowledge about high-quality assessment practices (Stiggins, 1991). Teacher preparation programs provided little or no training in assessment. Because they did not know much about assessment design and use, teachers were likely to turn to the format of large-scale assessment regardless of its usefulness.

Spearheaded by teachers and experts in curriculum and instruction (see Wiggins, 1989), this reform movement could be characterized as a search for alternatives, or the performance assessment revolution. Its rhetoric has often been emotionally charged, with performance assessment proponents using terms such as "authentic" or "alternative" to distinguish the performance assessment format from the multiple-choice format of most large-scale, standardized tests. Some in the performance assessment camp see no place for multiple-choice and other selected-response formats in the classroom and view large-scale test developers and publishers as the enemy. Many others, including both instructional and assessment experts, view performance assessment as another tool to help construct a comprehensive picture of student learning, and they have explored ways to systematically combine selected-response and performance assessment to measure student achievement (Asp, 1998).

The performance assessment revolution—even though performance assessment has been a part of classroom instruction since its inception—has strongly influenced both classroom practice and large-scale assessment. The content of professional journals and educational conferences and workshops over the past decade indicates that the topic of developing and using performance assessment to enhance instruction and improve student achievement has been and continues to be popular. The use of performance assessment in classrooms has greatly increased as a result. The use of performance assessment on a large scale has also received much attention during the 1990s. Many states have incorporated various forms of performance assessments into their testing programs, with varying degrees of success. Kentucky, Maryland, and Vermont are examples. Efforts to integrate selected response with performance assessment are continuing as states seek to use assessment as an instrument of reform.

As performance assessment in large-scale settings became more widespread, some familiar concerns began to surface. For example, because they are highly context bound, performance assessments may actually exacerbate ethnic or gender score differences, causing the scores to be less fair than their selected-response counterparts (Herman, 1997). Further, their narrow scope means that many performances are needed to get a consistent score in a particular subject area (Shavelson, Gao, & Baxter, 1993). Their use in high-stakes situations then becomes problematic because administering many assessments greatly increases the cost in money and instructional time. As we approach the millennium, many large-scale testing programs are turning away from performance assessments because of their high cost; problems with technical quality (Herman, 1997, 1999a); difficulty in linking classroom and large-scale applications (Borko & Elliott, 1999); and their political volatility (Herman, 1997). What impact that direction may have on classroom assessment remains to be seen.

After all the rhetoric of the 1990s, perhaps we can put performance assessment in its proper place; that is, performance assessment is a valuable assessment and instructional tool when used for the appropriate purposes, but it is not the answer to all our assessment woes.

WHERE ARE WE NOW?

Many factors that affected assessment in the past are still with us today. This section focuses on two current influences likely to have the greatest impact in the next century. The first is the central role of assessment in current reform efforts, and the second is the emergence of new assessment methods that federal and state educational policy initiatives demand. Both involve new variations on what are now familiar themes.

ASSESSMENT AS THE FUNDAMENTAL TOOL FOR EDUCATIONAL REFORM

Education is in an era where accountability is not an option (Popham, 1998). People are generally dissatisfied with public schools and the level of student achievement (Herman, 1997). The public and policymakers alike view assessment as the engine of reform, which can improve education rapidly and for relatively low cost (Linn, 1998).

Encouraged by the Goals 2000 legislation passed by Congress in 1994 and the National Governors' Association Conference in 1996, every state has established standards for student achievement in a variety of subject areas, or has mandated that local districts do so. Most states (48) have developed a state testing program of some kind based on those standards (Herman, 1997; Editorial Projects in Education, 1999). A majority of these state tests include both multiple-choice and performance items, particularly in writing. Yet those states that integrated performance assessment into their assessment systems in the most progressive and fundamental manner (e.g., Kentucky and California) are going the other direction, moving away from performance assessments and reinstating a norm-referenced component (Borko & Elliott, 1999; D. Carlson, personal communication, 1999).

Along with the push for high standards and powerful accountability systems based on test scores at the state and district levels, the Clinton administration continues to advocate for a voluntary national test that would provide data on the achievement of individual students as well as schools and districts (U.S. Department of Education, 1997). The feasibility of such a system is still under study,[6] and the lack of bipartisan political support makes the project's future somewhat uncertain—but it is not dead (Brandt, 1998). Perhaps the new century will be marked by the advent of a national test whose fundamental purpose is to bring about educational reform by giving feedback to parents about the progress of their children, with the expectation that they would put pressure on the schools to raise student achievement.

The logic of standards-based reform is appealing, and assessment plays a pivotal role in the process (Herman, 1997):

• Standards provide a basis for instruction and student learning.

• Assessments of the standards provide targets for districts, schools, teachers, and students—they make the standards real.

• Assessment results indicate where the various levels of the system need to improve (i.e., district, school, teacher, and students).

• Professionals and students use the results to improve their performance.

• Sanctions and rewards based on assessment results encourage schools, teachers, and students to improve.

As discussed earlier, using assessment to promote educational reform is not new, but it has greatly intensified in this era of standards, when people believe that assessment alone will bring about fundamental change in our educational system. For example, a recent yearbook for a national education publication evaluated state reform efforts on the basis of whether they ranked schools according to assessment results tied to their standards and the degree to which they rewarded high-performing schools and punished low-performing ones (Editorial Projects in Education, 1999). The publication's editors assumed, as did many policymakers at the state and national levels, that rewards, sanctions, and highly visible comparisons of schools on the basis of test scores alone are prudent public policies and will result in increased student achievement and improved instruction. Our review of the history of assessment would suggest otherwise. Without a serious commitment to improving teachers' skills through professional development, it is likely that "pressure to improve test scores may well corrupt both the teaching and learning process and the meaning of the test scores" (Herman, 1997, p. 6).

For better or worse, pressure for district, school, and teacher accountability based on large-scale assessment will probably intensify. This pressure will, in turn, keep issues such as the impact of assessment on instructional practice and fairness (i.e., Who gets tested? How? How are data reported?) at the forefront as we enter the new millennium.

DEVELOPMENTS IN ASSESSMENT METHODOLOGY

Currently, two federal education policy initiatives are spurring the development of new methodologies of assessment.[7] These are the reauthorization of Title I and the Individuals with Disabilities Education Act (IDEA).

Title I Changes

Title I regulations greatly affected educational assessment earlier in this century, and the proposed changes appear to be having a similar impact today. The major change calls for using multiple measures to evaluate the performance of Title I programs. An example would be combining results from a norm-referenced test, a district criterion-referenced measure, and teacher judgment to get an index of student achievement in reading. Districts and states are examining ways of combining multiple measures of student achievement. Such research focuses on whether using multiple measures improves both the overall accuracy of the assessment process and the specific classification of students (Ryan & Hess, 1999). Educators also hope that multiple measures can offset the narrow focus of curriculum and instructional practice that occurs when accountability is based on a single measure (Asp, 1998). This work may help districts and states better integrate large-scale and classroom assessment to improve accountability and instruction.

IDEA Changes

The reauthorization of IDEA—regulations about federal funds for educating students with identified special needs—requires that *all* students, including severely handicapped youngsters, participate in state and district testing programs. States and districts must meet the requirement of "full participation" by 2001. They are already developing new assessment methods and adapting their content standards in an effort to include these students in the assessment process in a mean-ingful way. This work has led to exploring accommodations that enable these students to show what they know and can do on local and state assessments, and to exploring modifications of existing assessment instruments, so that special needs youngsters can participate with their regular education peers (Tindal, Kopriva, & Winter, 1999).[8]

Many states are developing alternative assessments. Within the context of special education, "alternative assessments" refers to ways of measuring student progress in the same content area as the regular state assessment. They are based on modified content standards. For example, an alternative assessment might measure whether a student could recognize environmental print, such as a stop sign or a logo on a billboard, rather than assessing the student's ability to read text in a book. Although these efforts are bearing fruit, the process raises a variety of issues:

- Who is eligible for accommodations? Who should be given modifications?
- How much can a student's individual needs be accommodated before the assessment no longer measures what it was designed to measure?
- When modifications are made to an assessment, what is it now measuring and how is that related to the domain of the original assessment?
- How can the results from modified and alternative assessments, developed for severely handicapped children, be meaningfully aggre-gated with the data from regular education assessments?

Value-Added Approaches

Besides these specific policy initiatives, the general push from state legislatures and school boards to make districts, schools, and teachers accountable has led to the development of value-added approaches to track student achievement. Value-added methodology measures the growth in individual student achievement from one point in time to another (e.g., from the beginning to the end of the school year). It takes into account student background factors that affect learn-ing but that the school has no control over (e.g., parents' income and education level and academic support within the home). These data are

138

aggregated across a classroom or grade level to provide an overall index of growth for the classroom or school.

Ideally, such an index would allow teachers, schools, and districts to determine how much value they have added in terms of student achievement, creating a more accurate measure of performance than examining the average scores of cohorts of students (e.g., How did this year's 3rd graders score compare to last year's?). The idea is to eliminate the inherent unfairness in comparing the absolute achievement levels of students from districts and schools with widely varying socioeconomic levels, as well as to provide a legitimate comparison of student achievement across classrooms where the entry achievement level varies greatly from year to year (Sanders, Saxton, & Horn, 1997).

The prime example of value-added methodology is the Tennessee Value-Added Assessment System (TVAAS), developed by William Sanders and his colleagues at the University of Tennessee (Ceperley & Reel, 1997). The Dallas public schools have used a value-added system for a number of years as well (Webster & Mendro, 1997). Both efforts have been criticized for technical[9] and educational[10] reasons. Given the accountability climate that is likely to persist into the next century, we will probably see continuing interest in value-added approaches. Conceptually, they seem to more fairly judge the true impact of schools and teachers on student achievement (Evans, 1999). Interestingly enough, even though the statistical models underlying value-added approaches are quite sophisticated, this methodology is haunted by the same issues that faced Horace Mann 150 years ago. Is the system fair? Does it measure what we want students to learn? Does it have a positive impact on instruction? Does it promote real reform, or is it just "teaching to the test"?

After reviewing the history of assessment and examining the current state, one could argue that we have greatly improved our understanding of, and methods for, assessing student learning over the past two centuries. On the other hand, we are still dealing with the same issues educators faced in the early days of public schooling in America. How will assessment play out in the future? Will new developments in assessment methodology or technology make dealing with these problems easier? A discussion of these concerns is our next topic.

WHERE ARE WE HEADED?

As the old joke goes, making predictions is not easy, especially when you are talking about the future. In line with that dictum, my intent here is not to predict events per se, but rather to identify the factors that I believe will affect assessment in the coming century, and to explore what that impact might be.

What are the factors that will determine the future of educational assessment? They are much the same as those that have influenced its development to this point, with several new twists. Here is what the list includes:

- Improvements in assessment technology and methodology.
- Differing views on the nature of learning.
- Testing as big business.
- Inclusion of *all* students in testing programs.
- Competing purposes for assessment.

IMPROVEMENTS IN ASSESSMENT TECHNOLOGY AND METHODOLOGY

How will technology affect educational assessment in the new millennium? Technology is likely to make assessment more flexible and tailored to the individual needs of students and teachers.

Computer Adaptive Testing

Already, computer adaptive testing (CAT) has changed assessment in some school districts. CAT customizes the assessment process and improves the accuracy of results by allowing the computer to determine which questions to pose to the student (U.S. Office of Technology Assessment, 1992). Here is how it works: Every student starts the assessment by taking an item of medium difficulty; if the student answers the item correctly, then she would receive a more difficult item; if she does not answer correctly, then she would move to a less difficult item. This process continues until the student has answered enough items to give her a score on the test scale or determine if she has met a certain standard. CAT allows schools and districts to administer on-demand assessments to students and track their progress across a particular school year and throughout their academic careers. The data can easily be aggregated at the school and district levels to check accountability.

This kind of assessment technology is expensive to develop for several reasons. First, before the assessments can be developed, districts and schools have to be very clear about what they want students to know and be able to do at various levels. Second, the data processing capability of a computer has to be merged with a sophisticated measurement model. And third, all schools in a district must be networked together electronically. Because of the technological and instructional costs—customized to specific local standards—CAT will probably not be a common practice in many school districts for some time. Many CAT off-the-shelf products, however, currently exist and are used in schools on an increasingly routine basis (e.g., STAR reading assessment).

Large-Scale Testing

The impact of technology on some forms of large-scale testing may be more immediate. For example, the days of sitting in an auditorium with 500 other students taking the American College Testing (ACT) Assessment Test or SAT (an experience some baby-boomer parents "wistfully" describe to their children) will soon be a thing of the past. Students can already take the Graduate Record Exam (GRE) online at a testing center (essentially a computer lab) and receive their score instantaneously. Students will soon probably be able to take college entrance exams online either at a computerized testing center in a school's counseling office or in one of their school's computer labs. The ability to take them at home may not be far behind—although issues such as verifying the identity of the test-taker and preventing cheating must still be resolved.

Classroom Assessment

Changing technology will likely influence how classroom assessment is done. Students in some schools can already download assessments at home, complete them, and send them to the teacher or computer for scoring. This capability will increase as the required technology becomes available to more students.

Expanded Formats

Technology will allow a variety of test-and-response formats that are not widely available today. For instance, test items could be contextualized in authentic ways using computers' video and audio capabilities. Questions could be posed orally so that students' reading ability would not be an issue when testing math skills or other "nonreading" content areas. In turn, students could respond orally or by constructing answers on the screen, enabling them to show what they know without having to write when writing is not being assessed (e.g., describing their thinking process in solving a math problem). Emerging technology will also help assess non-English-speaking students: Computer software could translate items into a variety of languages. Of course, the issues associated with translation and comparability of items across languages would still need to be addressed.

Technological Tools

Students currently use such technological tools as HyperCard stacks, digital cameras, and video production software to display the results of research and other complex tasks without having to write a research paper. In some schools, technology allows students to interact with authorities in the fields they are studying, providing students with information and feedback on their work that is not available locally.[11] Researchers at the National Center for Research on Evaluation, Standards, and Student Testing (CRESST) at the University of California, Los Angeles, are experimenting with using networked computers to assess students' ability to synthesize new information about a topic. For example, they have students create mind maps on particular concepts (Herman, 1999b). They are using the same technology to assess how well students can locate information, collaborate with others, and communicate their findings.[12] These advances will no doubt continue, allowing teachers to assess aspects of student learning that are difficult to assess using more print-bound methods.

What Educators Assess

New assessment technology will change what educators assess as well as how assessment is done. When students are not limited by what they can remember or locate in a classroom or school, then their ability to identify, evaluate, and apply information for a particular purpose becomes critically important. More and more, students will take tests that require them to look up and use relevant facts rather than spout them back. As educators become better able to measure the ability to apply or use information in meaningful contexts, those skills will take on a much higher priority in K–12 education than they do today (see Wiggins & McTighe, 1998; Resnick & Resnick, 1992; Resnick & Klopfer, 1989). Moreover, technology may be the impetus for changing the public's (and some educators') ideas about learning and what schools should be emphasizing. These advances will make the desirable feasible and maybe more palatable.

Even though technology will open up a new world of assessment possibilities, it also raises some old issues. Most important is that technology cannot be used as a tool if one does not have access to it. Concerns about equity and fairness for individuals and school systems will continue to arise. For example, assessments that use computer technology may be inherently biased against those students who have little or no experience with the technology. And, if individual scores on a large-scale assessment are aggregated to rank schools and districts—which often occurs with college entrance exams such as the ACT—those systems without the resources to purchase the technology and train teachers and students to use it may be unfairly judged.

Multiple Measures

As technology opens up new ways of assessing complex cognitive activities, we must find ways to solve the technical problems of integrating performance tasks into large-scale assessment programs. The use of multiple measures may be one way. Researchers are exploring methods of incorporating performance tasks, norm-referenced tests, and teacher judgment into an indicator of student achievement (Gribbons, 1999; Ryan, 1999). Combining multiple measures from a single domain may help solve the sampling problems that performance assessment generates and allow us to make use of emerging technological assessment tools on a large scale. Incorporating these kinds of assessments into high-stakes assessment programs would improve the programs' quality and have a positive impact on classroom instruction.

Another use of multiple-measures technology is to combine a multitude of school and district level data into a single performance index (Gribbons, 1999). Many states currently use school "grade cards," and the push for a simple or direct way for ranking schools will probably intensify, as evidenced by the Clinton administration's recent call for "report cards" on schools. A multiple-measures approach may be one avenue to increase the accuracy, fairness, and utility of such indexes because it provides for the inclusion of a variety of assessments in proportion to their relative importance.

Value-Added Methodology

Value-added methodology will receive additional attention in response to the increasing pressure to make schools and teachers accountable for student learning. As mentioned earlier, a value-added approach may be the fairest way to compare the effects of schools and teachers on student achievement. Unfortunately, most current value-added models use norm-referenced, multiple-choice measures. Performance tasks measuring higher-order application of knowledge need to be included if true reform is to be realized.

DIFFERING VIEWS ON THE NATURE OF LEARNING

The public's and policymakers' views on the nature of learning will greatly influence assessment in the 21st century. Cognitive psychologists and other researchers have abandoned the behavioral view of learning for a more constructivist approach in which learning is more than the reception of information. Rather, learning involves integrating new knowledge with what one has already learned and applying that new learning to construct additional knowledge (Glaser & Silver, 1994; Wittrock, 1991). To assess student learning, educators need to determine if students can organize information and use it to solve complex problems within a real-life context. Such work will require some form of performance assessment (Herman, 1997).

Although many scientists and educators have endorsed this new understanding of the nature of learning and how it takes place (i.e., what instruction needs to look like), the public at large has not (McDonnell, 1997).[13] Citizens and policymakers are concerned that schools are not emphasizing the basics enough (Johnson & Immerwahr, 1994).

144

Public opposition to this new view of learning and assessments has been so intense that it has led to revising or completely dismantling state assessment systems. This disagreement between what the public (and many politicians and policymakers) wants and how educators and the research community view learning shows no signs of abating.

The business community also has strong views about what students should be learning. Business leaders have been outspoken in their call for students to bring more than a knowledge of basic skills to the workplace (e.g., Secretary's Commission on Achieving Necessary Skills, 1991). They also have stressed the need for schools to train students to work effectively in groups, solve problems, make decisions, and meet deadlines. The assessments needed to measure these kinds of skills and knowledge are performance oriented, and several publishers have developed testing programs that tap this kind of learning. Business and community leaders have played a major role in improving student achievement in several states (Grissmer & Flanagan, 1998), and their influence may balance the impact of citizen groups and policymakers who advocate a more traditional view of school learning.

Who will win the learning wars is hard to predict. Whichever view predominates will undoubtedly be reflected in large-scale assessment, which, in turn, will affect what happens in the classroom.

TESTING AS BIG BUSINESS

Testing has grown into a major industry over the past 30 years. For example, revenues from testing increased from $40 million in 1960 to almost $100 million in 1989 (U.S. Office of Technology Assessment, 1992). Put simply, large-scale testing can make big money. This statement is particularly true in the current era of accountability, when almost every state and a large number of school districts need a variety of measures to provide the information on student achievement that their citizens and professional staff are demanding.

Most revenue in commercial assessment originally came from norm-referenced testing. But as the standards movement emerged in the last part of this century, state and district demands for criterion-referenced assessments, based on their specific content standards, have increased dramatically. Because many states and school districts do not have the technical expertise or resources to develop their own assessments, the commercial assessment market will only continue to grow.

Competition between test companies for market share is likely to increase the pressure for test publishers to adapt existing products, especially given the cost of developing new assessments quickly. For example, test companies have tried to adapt their norm-referenced products to provide criterion-referenced data, with varying degrees of success (see, for example, Glaser, 1999; Linn, 1998). As competition grows, we can expect marketing departments to play a larger role in test development, with decisions driven by profit margin as much as by psychometric quality. The effect that testing as big business will ultimately have on educational assessment is hard to predict, but we can expect that the testing market will probably be a conservative force in the coming century, tending to keep things as they are rather than being a force for change.

INCLUSION OF *ALL* STUDENTS IN TESTING PROGRAMS

Recent federal regulations require that district and state assessment programs include all students. Those regulations have fiscal and legal ramifications for every state and school district in the country. We will see a flurry of activity to develop alternative assessments and alternative testing formats for existing assessments (Kopriva, 1999), so that students with special needs, who traditionally have been excluded from large-scale testing, can be included. Whether such full inclusion can be achieved is open to question (Popham, 1999).

Changing demographics will also influence the nature of assessment. As we become a more diverse culture, assessment will also have to become more diverse. Educators will need to create formats that allow non-English-speaking youngsters to show what they know and can do, and that provide for aggregating that information with data from the mainstream population. There will be demands to accommodate students with a wider variety of needs than in the past in both large-scale and classroom assessment (Kopriva, 1999). New developments in technology may be our best hope of making this type of assessment a reality.

146

COMPETING PURPOSES FOR ASSESSMENT

> An assessment that attempts to perform too many functions—student diagnosis, curriculum planning, program evaluation, instructional improvement, accountability, certification, public communication—will inevitably do nothing well.
>
> —Linn & Herman, 1997, p. vi

The most important issue for us in the future may be one that has been with us since Horace Mann's day: how to balance the competing purposes for assessment to improve instruction and increase student achievement. We can expect that it will become even more pressing in an era where public demand for accountability has reached an all-time high.

The beginning of this chapter listed a variety of purposes for assessment: accountability, feedback to inform instruction and improve student achievement, student classification and certification, and educational reform. All are important. The history of educational assessment in this country is, in some sense, the story of our attempts to meet all these goals without slighting any. That story will continue into the future.

Large-Scale Assessment Versus Classroom Assessment

Why is balancing these competing demands so difficult? It is difficult (if not impossible) because different purposes for assessment require assessment methods with different characteristics. Assessments that work best for accountability (and other large-scale applications such as program evaluation) lend themselves to standardized administration in a relatively short amount of time; they can be scored quickly and reliably for relatively low cost. The most efficient large-scale assessment methodology is multiple choice. But as we have seen, multiple-choice tests for large-scale assessments, particularly when high stakes are involved, has had a negative effect on instruction. On the other hand, trying to incorporate more instructional-friendly assessments (e.g., performance tasks or portfolios) into large-scale efforts has proven quite difficult because of the costs in time and money and the technical issues involved (e.g., administering enough tasks to get a valid representation of the domain being assessed or achieving a level of consistency in scoring great enough to allow meaningful aggregation of the data).

Even when large-scale efforts incorporate assessments that model high-quality instruction and communicate high expectations, they typically do not provide teachers, students, and parents with much useful information. This deficiency is due to the lack of detailed results and the length of time it takes to get the data back after the assessment is administered.

The most meaningful information for informing instruction and providing explicit feedback to students is collected daily by teachers working with students. And yet, although a teacher's view is most valued when parents want feedback on their own children's progress, large-scale assessment is most valued when examining the performance of states, districts, schools, or teachers (Asp, 1998) or in certifying student achievement for high-stakes purposes (Baker, 1999).

If we are to have any hope of accomplishing our assessment goals, large-scale and classroom assessment must be meaningfully linked. Unfortunately, the inherent characteristics of classroom and large-scale assessment make that relationship difficult.

Layers of Assessments

Another issue complicates matters even more: overlapping and competing demands from layers of assessments facing teachers, schools, and districts (as well as students). Most school systems use a variety of large-scale assessments, including district assessments focused on local content standards, state tests reflecting state content standards, norm-referenced tests, and college admission exams. Their interaction greatly compounds attempts to link classroom and large-scale assessment.

How does that interaction work? Here is a real-life example that may look painfully familiar to some readers. A district I am familiar with has been in the process of implementing standards-based education for several years because of a mandate from the local board of education (and later required by state legislation). Classroom teachers (K–12) are required to assess students' progress in meeting the district's content standards. Teachers have some discretion in choosing the assessments they can use, but they must all use some common assessments the district provides. Results are reported to parents and the board of education.

Like many across the country, the district has a long tradition of administering norm-referenced tests at transition grade levels across the system. The district scores relatively well on these tests, and the community expects the scores to remain high. Those schools that score substantially below the district average are under pressure from both the central office and the community to improve their scores. Further, a large percentage of students in the district go on to higher education, so parents and the school board watch college admission scores closely. Schools reports these scores annually. ACT scores have increased gradually over the past five years, putting them well above state and national averages. Unfortunately, SAT scores were down last year, falling below the state average. This drop has alarmed both the superintendent and the school board.

A state testing program, based on state content standards, has been in existence for a year. Like most state programs, scores in the initial years were low, producing a public outcry. Although the district did relatively well on the state tests, there is certainly room for improvement, particularly in some content areas such as writing.

What do all these results mean for teachers and schools in our sample district? The expectation, although not always formally stated, is that all results show steady gains on all these measures, and in the case of a few, dramatic turnarounds in performance are expected. Teachers in the district are confused and frustrated. Where are they supposed to focus their efforts? Is it the district's standards or the SAT? What about norm-referenced scores? Whose standards are most important, the district's or the state's? For teachers, this situation is like trying to win a prize at a ball toss at a school carnival, but with restrictions on how they can play. They get a handful of balls to throw at many targets, and they must throw them all at the same time, rather than using a ball to hit one specific target. They are not told which target is the most important. In fact, the value of each target seems to change from minute to minute without notice. Teachers end up trying to spray all the targets, thus ending up with few points (i.e., their efforts have little impact). And, some targets may be impossible to hit—because the targets are impervious to instruction (Popham, 1999).

In an era of accountability, where assessment defines what is important, we must *align* the targets. This alignment can only happen by eliminating some of them, linking others together, and clarifying the appropriate uses of particular assessments.

All levels of the educational system are responsible for this work. State policymakers and legislators can assist by clarifying the aims of their policies. They should start with understanding the appropriate uses of various assessment methods and the kind of information the methods provide. Then, they can make informed choices about assessment strategies. Once they have agreed upon a particular course of action, they need to stay the course. In state after state, as well as in many districts, goals are set and then changed, and accordingly, so are assessment schedules, methodologies, and subjects tested—leaving those who are supposed to carry out these policies (i.e., teachers) confused and frustrated.

Test publishers can help by *directly* informing policymakers, practitioners, and the public about the appropriate uses and limitations of their products. State education agencies can help clarify and align assessment targets by carefully considering who should be included in state assessment programs and how data are reported. District leaders should clarify what targets they truly value and help teachers see the link between classroom instruction and student scores on large-scale assessments.

The key is to link large-scale and classroom assessment together so that daily classroom work naturally prepares students for large-scale assessment. This connection means embedding the content and skills assessed on large-scale assessments into daily classroom life. Then teachers would not have to stop and prepare for the "big test" (whatever it happens to be). Teachers would already know how their students will do on large-scale assessments because they have been gathering daily data about student progress and using the data to inform their instruction and provide feedback to individual students. Of course, large-scale assessments have to be carefully chosen. Achievement goals have to be clear, and large-scale assessments must closely match those goals.

Some states and districts have been successful in this process (Linn & Herman, 1997; Asp, 1998), but many struggle with moving beyond simply preparing students for the big test. Why? Many try to do reform "on the cheap," expecting assessment alone to improve learning (Linn, 1998). Policymakers often throw assessments at the problem in hopes of a quick solution. Somehow they think that measuring more frequently or with a wider array of tools will lead to increased achievement. But, in this case, more is not better. Large-scale assessment does affect curriculum and instruction, and involving teachers in the process (e.g., scoring) is a powerful staff development activity. But a number of other supports (e.g., training and other professional development opportunities) are clearly needed if we are to fundamentally improve instruction (Herman, 1999a). Districts and states do not always provide adequate classroom instructional resources that incorporate the content and skills of a large-scale assessment. Therefore, teachers turn to commercial or homemade test prep materials to prepare their students, especially when the pressure is on. These materials are often just clones of the big test and do little to improve authentic achievement.

Assessment at the classroom, school, district, and state levels needs to be linked together to support and reinforce a set of clearly articulated goals. The primary responsibility for this alignment lies with the district. Expecting districts to have a single goal is unrealistic. What may work better is an ecological approach to assessment: Each succeeding assessment layer in the system is linked to and supports teachers in their daily work with students (Garbarino & Asp, 1981). When what teachers do everyday in the classroom is linked to student performance outside it, then large-scale assessment becomes another vehicle for students to show what they know and can do.

THE LONG-RANGE FORECAST

We have examined where we have been, where we are now, and where we are headed. Here is a short list of best hopes for the future:

• Performance assessment will play a more prominent role in both classroom and large-scale assessment as students' ability to apply knowledge in real-world situations becomes more valued as a goal of education and we are better able to assess that ability.

• Norm-referenced testing will decrease as accountability focuses more on what students actually know and can do, rather than on how much they know compared to other students' general content knowledge.

    • More coherent assessment systems will emerge that better integrate large-scale and classroom assessment (including performance assessment) for both teachers and students. Different forms of assessment and new ways of standardization that allow all students to participate will be used.

    • Criteria for evaluating the quality of assessments and assessment systems will include the influence of assessment on learning, teaching, and the school as an organization, along with psychometric characteristics (Sykes, 1997). The degree to which an assessment is sensitive to instruction will become a major indicator of quality.

    • A new role for assessment—helping provide more and better education for the learner—will become prominent over other goals such as accountability or the classification of students.

If we develop and integrate large-scale and classroom assessments that require children to think and apply their knowledge in new and different ways, and we help teachers to integrate those things in everyday instruction so that students all know what they know, then assessment has a bright future in the new millennium.

Endnotes

1. In this chapter, the terms "assessment," "test," and "testing" are used interchangeably. In other contexts, they may be defined separately.
2. "Standardized" refers to assessments given under the same conditions and scored in an identical manner.
3. Many educational reformers of this time believed that populating classrooms with children of widely varying levels of achievement was not only inefficient but also inhumane (Tyack & Hansot, 1982).
4. The expenses were feasible in terms of the actual cost of test materials and scoring, but when the costs for staff and instructional time were figured in, some questioned the practicality of large-scale assessment (U.S. Office of Technology Assessment, 1992).
5. This phenomenon of artificial gains on achievement tests was made public by West Virginia physician, John Cannell, who described this problem as the "Lake Woebegon Effect." His research addressed the question of how all 50 states could report scores above the national average on tests that were

designed so that half the students would score above the average and half below (Cannell, 1987).

6. A national test poses a variety of educational and political issues. For example, some contend that a national test would lead to a national curriculum, ending local control of education. Others are concerned about how non-English speakers would be assessed. Additional issues include the purpose and design of the instrument and its impact on students, teachers, and schools (Brandt, 1998).

7. These methodologies are new in the sense that they are receiving renewed and increased attention. Measurement experts have been exploring them for some time.

8. Accommodations are changes that alter how a test is administered without changing what it measures. Modifications are changes that actually alter what the test measures. Accommodations and modifications can be the same, depending on what the assessment is measuring. For example, reading a test to a student could be an accommodation if reading is not being measured. Obviously, it is a modification if the student is taking a reading test.

9. For example, some question the exclusion of certain student variables from estimating growth in achievement (Darlington, 1997); others have raised concerns about the statistical methods that are used to calculate student growth (Thum & Bryk, 1997).

10. Some question the impact on instruction; others raise concerns about the educational validity of the assessments used to gather data about student achievement (Sykes, 1997).

11. At a recent meeting of the ASCD Assessment Consortium in Ankeny, Alaska, I observed students using technology to produce presentations displaying their responses to complex tasks. They received feedback on their work from authorities in the field via the Internet. Students communicated frequently with a professor at the Massachusetts Institute of Technology who provided them with direction and evaluated their work.

12. For more information, see the CRESST Web site at www.cse.ucla.edu.

13. Disagreements over what it means to learn are not confined to the public arena. Recent issues of professional journals reveal numerous references to the math wars. Similar battles between whole-language and phonics-based approaches to reading have been raging for decades.

References

Asp, E. (1998). The relationship of large-scale and classroom assessment. In R. Brandt (Ed.), *Assessing student learning: New rules, new realities.* Arlington, VA: Educational Research Service.

Baker, E. (1999, April). *The assessment of student achievement: The hundred years war.* Paper presented at the annual meeting of the American Educational Research Association, Montreal, QC.

Borko, H., & Elliott, R. (1999). Hands-on pedagogy versus hands-off accountability: Competing commitments for exemplary math teachers in Kentucky. *Phi Delta Kappan 80,* 394–400.

Brandt, R. (Ed.). (1998). *Assessing student learning: New rules, new realities.* Arlington, VA: Educational Research Service.

Cannell, J. (1987). *Nationally normed elementary achievement testing in America's public schools: How all 50 states are above the national average.* Daniels, WV: Friends of Education.

Ceperley, P., & Reel, K. (1997). The impetus for the Tennessee value-added accountability system. In J. Millman (Ed.), *Grading teachers, grading schools: Is student achievement a valid evaluation measure?* (pp. 133–136). Thousand Oaks, CA: Corwin Press.

Darlington, R. (1997). The Tennessee value-added assessment system: A challenge to familiar assessment methods. In J. Millman (Ed.), *Grading teachers, grading schools: Is student achievement a valid evaluation measure?* (pp. 163–168). Thousand Oaks, CA: Corwin Press.

Editorial Projects in Education. (1999). *Quality counts: Rewarding results, punishing failure.* Bethesda, MA: Author.

Evans, R. (1999, February 3). The great accountability wars. *Education Week,* p. 32.

Garbarino, J., & Asp, E. (1981). *Successful schools and competent students.* Lexington, MA: Lexington Books.

Glaser, R. (1999, April). *The assessment of student achievement: The hundred years war.* Paper presented at the annual meeting of the American Educational Research Association, Montreal, QC.

Glaser, R., & Silver, E. (1994). Assessment, testing, and instruction. *Annual Review of Psychology, 40,* 631–666.

Gribbons, B. (1999, April). *Developing a valid and credible indicator system.* Paper presented at the annual meeting of the American Educational Research Association, Montreal, QC.

Grissmer, D., & Flanagan, A. (1998). *Exploring rapid achievement gains in North Carolina and Texas.* Washington, DC: National Goals Panel.

Herman, J. (1997). *Large-scale assessment in support of school reform: Lessons in the search for alternative measures.* (CSE Technical Report 446). Los Angeles: University of California, National Center for Research on Evaluation, Standards, and Student Testing.

Herman, J. (1999a). The state of performance assessments. *The School Adminis-trator, 55*(110).

Herman, J. (1999b, February). *Why standards-based assessment systems ought to improve classroom practice.* Presentation at the annual meeting of the American Association of School Administrators, New Orleans, LA.

Johnson, J., & Immerwahr, J. (1994). *First things first: What Americans expect from the public schools.* New York: Public Agenda.

Katz, M. (1968). *The irony of early school reform.* Cambridge, MA: Harvard University Press.

Kopriva, R. (1999, April). *A conceptual framework for valid and comparable measure-ment.* Paper presented at the annual meeting of the American Educational Research Association, Montreal, QC.

Koretz, D., Linn, R., Dunbar, S., & Sheppard, L. (1991, April).*The effects of high-stakes testing on achievement: Preliminary findings about generalizations across tests.* Paper presented at the annual meeting of the American Educational Research Association, Chicago.

Linn, R. (1998). *Assessments and accountability.* (CSE Technical Report 490). Los Angeles: University of California, National Center for Research on Evalua-tion, Standards, and Student Testing.

Linn, R. (1999). *Standards-Based accountability: Ten suggestions.* Los Angeles: Uni-versity of California, National Center for Research on Evaluation, Stan-dards, and Student Testing.

Linn, R., & Dunbar, S. (1990). The nation's report card goes home: Good news and bad about trends in achievement. *Phi Delta Kappan, 72,* 127–133.

Linn, R., & Herman, J. (1997). *Standards-Led assessment: Technical and policy issues in measuring school and student progress.* (CSE Technical Report 426). Los Angeles: University of California, National Center for Research on Evalua-tion, Standards, and Student Testing.

McDonnell, L. (1997). *The politics of state testing: Implementing new student assess-ments.* (CSE Technical Report 424). Los Angeles: University of California, National Center for Research on Evaluation, Standards, and Student Test-ing.

Popham, J. (1998, April). *Standardized tests should not be used to evaluate educa-tional quality: A debate.* Paper presented at the annual meeting of the Ameri-can Educational Research Association, San Diego, CA.

Popham, J. (1999, April). *Using and combining multiple indicators and assessment formats for accountability and guiding instruction.* Symposium conducted at the annual meeting of the American Educational Research Association, Montreal, QC.

Resnick, L., & Klopfer, L. (1989). Toward the thinking curriculum: An overview. In L. Resnick & L. Klopfer (Eds.), *Toward the thinking curriculum: Current cognitive research* (pp. 1–18). Alexandria, VA: Association for Supervision and Curriculum Development.

Resnick, L., & Resnick, D. (1992). Assessing the thinking curriculum: New tools for educational reform. In B. Gifford & M. O'Conner (Eds.), *Changing assessments: Alternative views of aptitude, achievement, and instruction.* Boston: Kluwer Academic Press.

Ryan, J. (1999, April). *Using multiple indicators for high-stakes decisions.* Symposium conducted at the annual meeting of the American Educational Research Association, Montreal, QC.

Ryan, J., & Hess. R. (1999, April). *Issues, strategies, and procedures for combining data from multiple measures.* Paper presented at the annual meeting of the American Educational Research Association, Montreal, QC.

Sanders, W., Saxton, A., & Horn, S. (1997). The Tennessee value-added assessment system: A quantitative, outcomes-based approach to educational assessment. In J. Millman (Ed.), *Grading teachers, grading schools: Is student achievement a valid evaluation measure?* (pp. 137–162). Thousand Oaks, CA: Corwin Press.

Secretary's Commission on Achieving Necessary Skills. (1991). *What work requires of schools: A SCANS report for America 2000.* Washington, DC: U.S. Department of Labor.

Shavelson, R., Gao, X., & Baxter, G. (1993). *Sampling variability of performance assessments* (CSE Technical Report 361). Los Angeles: University of California, National Center for Research on Evaluation, Standards, and Student Testing.

Sheppard, L. (1989, April). Why we need better assessments. *Educational Leadership, 46*(7), 4–9.

Sheppard, L., & Dougherty, K. (1991, April). *Effects of high-stakes testing on instruction.* Paper presented at the annual meeting of the American Educational Research Association, Chicago.

Sheppard, L., Glaser, R., Linn, R., & Bohrnstedt, G. (1993). *Setting performance standards for student achievement.* A report of the National Academy of Education Panel on the evaluation of the NAEP trial state assessment. Stanford, CA: Stanford University, National Academy of Education.

Stiggins, R. (1991). Assessment literacy. *Phi Delta Kappan, 72,* 534–539.

Sykes, G. (1997). On trial: The Dallas value-added accountability system. In J. Millman (Ed.), *Grading teachers, grading schools: Is student achievement a valid evaluation measure?* (pp. 110–119). Thousand Oaks, CA: Corwin Press.

Thum, Y., & Bryk, A. (1997). Value-added productivity indicators: The Dallas system. In J. Millman (Ed.), *Grading teachers, grading schools: Is student achievement a valid evaluation measure?* (pp. 100–109). Thousand Oaks, CA: Corwin Press.

Tindal, G., Kopriva, R., & Winter, P. (1999, April). *A single assessment system for all students including those with special challenges—disability, limited English fluency, and poverty: What will it take?* Panel discussion at the annual meeting of the American Educational Research Association, Montreal, QC.

Tyack, D., & Hansot, E. (1982). *Managers of virtue: Public school leadership in America, 1820–1980.* New York: BasicBooks.

U.S. Department of Education. (1997). *Voluntary national tests, 4th grade reading, 8th grade mathematics* [On-line]. Available: www.ed.gov/nationaltests

U.S. Office of Technology Assessment. (1992). *Testing in American schools: Asking the right questions* (OTA-SET-519). Washington, DC: Author.

Webster, W., & Mendro, R. (1997). The Dallas value-added accountability system. In J. Millman (Ed.), *Grading teachers, grading schools: Is student achievement a valid evaluation measure?* (pp. 81–99). Thousand Oaks, CA: Corwin Press.

Wiggins, G. (1989, April). Teaching to the authentic test. *Educational Leadership, 46*(7), 41–47.

Wiggins, G., & McTighe, J. (1998). *Understanding by design.* Alexandria, VA: Association for Supervision and Curriculum Development.

Wittrock, M. (1991). Testing and recent research in cognition. In M. Wittrock & E. Baker (Eds.), *Testing and cognition* (pp. 5–16). Englewood Cliffs, NJ: Prentice-Hall.

7

The Evolving Science of Learning

Ronald S. Brandt and David N. Perkins

What is our most important science? Some might say physics, because it discloses the fundamental mechanisms of nature. Others might say genetics, because it seems on the verge of yielding enormous power to manipulate the biological world. But a case can also be made for what might be called "mind science"—the scientific study of human beings as thinking and learning organisms.

The lawyer for the defense would emphasize the logic of the matter. Most fundamentally, we human beings are thinkers and learners. Without thinking and learning, we would have little of what we now possess, including powerful questions that promise to extend our understanding and capabilities even further. To the degree that we fathom the nature of the mind and how to cultivate it, we have mastered the essence of the human condition. Imagine a world in which every school child, every business person, every politician, every parent, and indeed every teacher thought much better and learned much more than at present!

The lawyer for the prosecution might acknowledge the potential, but would certainly accentuate a cautionary fact: The scientific study of learning is today not as unified or powerful as physics or genetics. At the heart of a science of learning must lie an accurate conception of how the human mind actually works. Unfortunately, contemporary psychology is home to multiple views of the mind. Educators who are determined to put learning science to work face a sampler of perspectives, some complementary, some in conflict, and some better suited to particular agendas than others.

Views of the mind over the past century fall broadly into the behaviorist view that dominated the first half of the century and the cognitive view that has dominated much of the second. Although treating the history of learning science in terms of this shift is tempting, the story is much more complicated. For example, contemporary cognitive science, a sprawling conglomerate of theories and stances, is much broader than behaviorism was. And recent developments in neuroscience are broadening the field even further, shedding new light on earlier findings by disclosing a physiological basis for thinking and learning.

Our focus in this chapter is only indirectly on the scientific study of thinking and learning. We are concerned here primarily with how various conceptions of the mind have influenced the practice of education, and how they may affect it in the future. We begin with behaviorism, then turn to cognitive science, leading to major themes influencing schools in recent decades: constructivism and human development, intelligence and the skills of thinking, and brain research. We conclude by discussing a few themes most likely to affect education in the decades to come.

BEHAVIORISM

SCENARIO 1

Dr. Bea Havior, principal of Rewards Elementary School, greets nine students who have been sent to her office to be honored for their achievements.

"Congratulations to each of you," she says warmly. "Your teachers have told me that you have earned a high score on our local test of one of the state standards of learning, demonstrating that you are prepared to take the state test for your grade level in the spring. Here is a certificate honoring you for the hard work you have done. And as you know, if you earn a certificate like this for all the standards at your grade level, you will be invited to a pizza party we will be holding the week before the state tests. So keep working, and our school will be proud of you."

SCENARIO 2

At nearby Warnum High School, students listen to an announcement over the public address system about a new policy the board of education had adopted a few days earlier:

"Beginning immediately, students with more than three unexcused absences are to be suspended from school until they return with their parents for a meeting with the assistant principal. To be readmitted, they must compose and sign an agreement to attend school regularly and propose a plan for how they will avoid unauthorized absences."

As mentioned earlier, the study of psychology was dominated for the first half of the century by behaviorism, the idea that mental processes are invisible and therefore not subject to scientific investigation. What could be observed was outward behavior, so rather than speculating on internal causes, scientists focused on how organisms responded to various stimuli, with rats and pigeons as favored laboratory animals. Because learning was defined as changed behavior, research on learning was concerned with what produced measurable changes. Much of this research dealt with the effects of positive and negative reinforcement—rewards and punishments—on learning.

The influence of rewards and punishments can certainly explain a substantial portion of our actions, as it does those of other animals. For many centuries, rulers, employers, and parents recognized and exploited this trait before it became the object of scientific investigation. By studying the phenomenon systematically, behaviorist psychologists added to our understanding of human learning.

Behaviorists argue that organisms learn through classical and operant conditioning. Complex behaviors are built up through "shaping," starting with parts of or rough approximations of the target behavior and providing reinforcement in ways that gradually shape the pattern of behavior in the intended direction. Much learning in natural circumstances occurs because the environment shapes behavior in this way. Not only direct rewards like food but also indirect "tokens" of reward shape behavior through learned associations. Research has yielded a body of findings about when reinforcement is best administered (broadly, immediately is best) and what kinds of reinforcement are most effective (in the long run, positive is generally better than negative, which can cause the learning organism to withdraw or become unresponsive).

What B. F. Skinner (1974) called "behavioral science" has been harshly criticized and is currently disparaged by most educational leaders, but a significant virtue of behaviorism is its emphasis on human adaptability. Because behaviorists believe that people's actions and capabilities are largely the result of environmental influences, behaviorists' work is a powerful counter to those who believe, or act as though they believe, that learning ability is unalterable. Behaviorism is therefore a positive force for democratic schooling, which assumes that all students have potential.

We should perhaps clarify that a focus on behavior is not necessarily behaviorist. One can analyze behavior or set detailed goals for desired behavior without believing that the best or only way to attain them is through a regimen of reinforcement. Likewise, one can have a behaviorist view of learning without long lists of specific target behaviors. The two are allied historically, but are not the same thing.

Poor practices are sometimes mistakenly criticized as behaviorist even though they have nothing to do with behaviorist theory. Giving a lengthy lecture to a group of bored, uninvolved students is not good behaviorist practice. A well-designed behaviorist lesson requires thoughtful attention to introduction of tasks, timing and character of reinforcements, and many other factors.

Some innovations that attracted educators' attention at various times throughout the century were explicitly or at least partially behaviorist. In the 1930s, evaluator Ralph Tyler, who later became an influential curriculum theorist, urged teachers participating in the famous Eight-Year Study (Aiken, 1943) to specify objectives for what their students should be able to do. A quarter century later, school systems required teachers to use "action verbs" as they wrote thousands of behavioral objectives. An influential theme in elementary, secondary, and higher education has been mastery learning (Bloom, 1968), which is at least partially behaviorist in its emphasis on creating the conditions under which students will learn successfully.

Some teacher education has a behaviorist flavor. To ensure that beginning teachers could demonstrate a defined set of professional skills, schools of education have sometimes developed elaborate programs of competency-based teacher education. The effective teaching research of the 1980s (Rosenshine, 1986) dealt with particular teacher behaviors—such as providing systematic feedback and corrections—found to be associated with high student test scores.

As illustrated by the scenarios at the beginning of this section, some practices considered fundamental to learning are partly behaviorist in their assumptions. Teachers of younger children use praise and symbolic rewards, such as stickers and stars, to positively reinforce behaviors they want to encourage. Schools also rely on various punishments to shape student conduct and maintain order. Grades given to assignments and overall coursework function as positive or negative reinforcements. From a behaviorist standpoint, such reinforcements are most effective when students understand not only *that* they did right or wrong but also *what* they did right or wrong, and what they should do to improve. Instructional settings often fail to provide this information.

Behaviorism may be somewhat unfashionable, but it continues to influence educational practice. Although some applications are undoubtedly simplistic, distorted, or even harmful (Kohn, 1993), educators cannot avoid behaviorism entirely. They must to some degree view behaviors as indicators of students' intentions and wishes, and they will always find reinforcement an important tool for directing attention and effort in some directions rather than others. Results from behaviorist research can guide their work.

ENTER COGNITIVE SCIENCE

SCENARIO 1

Mr. Explicit is teaching his middle school science students about torque and balances. He shows them a balance scale with pegs on each side and different numbers of rings on the pegs.

Rather than saying just, "What do you think will happen?" he says, "Three weights on the third peg versus two weights on the fourth peg; what do you think will happen?" He also gives each student an external memory aid: a printed diagram of the problem. When students develop a hypothesis about a possible relationship between the weights and distances, he asks them to check the hypothesis using data from previous problems they have compiled on previous diagrams (Bruer, 1993, p. 48).

Scenario 2

Students in a reading class sit in groups of three to five. In an activity known as "reciprocal teaching" (Palincsar, Ransom, & Derber, 1988), one student at a time acts as teacher. As others in the group follow along, Anita reads aloud a paragraph from a story set in a Native American village in 1820. When she finishes reading, she briefly summarizes what the paragraph said and asks the other students a question about it. Satisfied with the answers, she tells one thing she isn't completely clear about and makes a prediction about what might happen next. Then another student reads the next paragraph and does the same.

In the years following World War II, psychologists began turning away from behaviorism to embrace a broader view eventually characterized as "cognitive science." Behaviorism had captured the field of psychology because it replaced unproductive introspection with quantifiable scientific procedures. Unfortunately, behaviorists tended to overstate their ability to fully explain all aspects of human thought and behavior. So when cognitivists made referring to internal mental processes academically respectable again, mind scientists regarded the renewed interest as a fresh opportunity.

A development often cited as particularly damaging to behaviorism was Chomsky's (1980) insight that rule-governed language—children's ability to construct linguistic structures they had never heard before—could only be explained by the existence of inherent mental and neurological structures. Behaviorists had assumed that language mastery was entirely the product of stimulus-response learning mechanisms. Plotkin (1998) explains that behaviorism did not permit

> Causal explanations if they did not lie within the limits of ordinary everyday experience. Scientifically this was an extraordinarily bankrupting stance. Cognitivism rescued psychology from this crippling narrow vision. It liberated psychologists conceptually and allowed causal powers to be relocated in the mind and brain, only a very small part of whose workings are visible (p. 33).

Many educators welcomed the shift to a cognitive orientation because it meant that consideration of mental activity was no longer ruled out as unscientific. Teachers are, after all, concerned with students' thinking. They want students to understand and appreciate, and the effort to translate these aims into desired behaviors can be cumbersome at best. Yet cognitive science is still science, so its investigation of the mind goes beyond naive terms and concepts used in everyday conversation, like "idea" or "hunch."

Cognitive science has many branches and variations, and no simple description applies to them all. Obviously, the central theme is cognition, the process of knowing. Early research focused primarily on information processing, especially pattern recognition, memory, and problem solving. The mind was considered a rule-governed computational device. A scientist's task was to identify the specific rules by which the mind manipulates symbols to arrive at results. Over time, cognitive scientists gradually expanded their attention to include a remarkable array of human activities: the formation of judgments, decision making, creativity, critical thinking, and even the emotions.

For much of this work, the computer and information processing remained central metaphors. That the evolution of cognitive science paralleled the development of electronic computers is no coincidence, because cognitivists often emphasized similarities between the two. Concerned with information-processing functions, leading cognitive scientists described themselves as "functionalists." Francis Crick, the Nobel prize-winning scientist who collaborated in discovering the molecular structure of DNA, has observed that

> Just as it is not necessary to know about the actual wiring of a computer when writing programs for it, so a functionalist investigates the information processed by the brain, and the computational processes the brain performs on this information, without considering the neurological implementation of these processes (Crick, 1994, p. 18).

Crick's charge that functionalists have ignored the physiological basis for the processes they studied may be unfair, because until recently scientists had few ways to investigate the brain directly. As we show later, however, neuroscientists like Crick now insist that mental activity cannot be fully understood without reference to structure and operation of the brain itself.

Even so, cognitive scientists have profoundly influenced how informed professionals view learning (Bransford, Brown, & Cocking, 1999). They have produced an extensive literature on cognition and a wide range of potentially useful programs and practices, although as happens in almost all initiatives of educational change, most of these efforts have seen only occasional use, generally in more progressive settings.

We discuss cognitive science from two points of view. First, we show how the cognitive orientation has affected educators' understanding of the learning process and therefore influenced how teachers teach. Then we consider how new views of learners' capabilities have contributed to attempts to improve students' intelligence and thinking skills.

CONSTRUCTIVISM AND HUMAN DEVELOPMENT

SCENARIO 1

Mr. N. Ductive asks his chemistry students to work in small groups with a list of 95 book titles, each with a classification name and a number. They are to arrange the books on a seven-shelf bookcase with space for 32 books per shelf, according to a set of rules. When all groups have finished, with several different results, he reintroduces the task as a metaphor for the periodic table of elements (Brooks & Brooks, 1993, pp. 50–53).

SCENARIO 2

Students are working in groups to prepare presentations about the American Revolution, but when asked whether he's beginning to shape a plan for his part, Jeremy says, "Not really." Mr. Meta has him read a passage aloud and asks him what is most important. Jeremy chooses the words "ammunition" and "military stores" because, he explains, "I like guns and stuff."

"You're thinking about how the text reminds you of your own life," says Mr. Meta. "That's one way to decide what's important. Let's break this passage down a little to make it easier to decide what's important. Great readers are thinking all the time as they read, 'What's most important?' I'm going to read that sentence you just pointed to. You listen, and I want you to tell me what you think is most important in that one sentence, Okay?" (Keene & Zimmermann, 1997, pp. 83–86).

The Mind's Role in Constructivism

Part and parcel of the cognitive revolution is a theme called constructivism (see, for example, Duffy & Jonassen, 1992). Both a philosophical and psychological stance, constructivism argues that the human mind does not simply take in the world but makes it up in an active way. The creative role of the mind is obvious in contexts such as scientific inquiry and artistic endeavor, but constructivists believe that the constructive process also figures prominently even in such seemingly routine mental operations as perception and memory.

Much evidence demonstrates that both operations are highly constructive. When we form a perception of the room around us, a new acquaintance's personality, or an event we have witnessed, we do not simply register it like a camera. We engage in a complex act of information processing, combining the information our senses give us with a host of expectations to fill in the gaps, devising something much more like an interpretation than a snapshot. Likewise, remembering, far from replaying some mental tape recorder, works more like problem solving. It involves reconstructing a version of what happened from memory traces and a range of expectations.

The mind's pervasively constructive character is both bad news and good news for the effectiveness of cognition. On the down side, perception and memory, as well as more obviously interpretive activities, such as writing fiction, turn out to be highly susceptible to a range of mistaken presumptions and biases. On the up side, the mind's constructive character means that we can make sense of things with much less information than if we had to draw conclusions mostly from the data at hand.

Philips (1995) distinguishes three strands in constructivism: the active role of the thinker and learner, the creative role of the thinker and learner in making up knowledge, and the social construction of knowledge. Different theorists foreground various combinations and offer different pedagogical prescriptions. In the same spirit, Perkins (1992b) distinguishes between without-the-information-given (WIG) constructivism and beyond-the-information-given (BIG) constructivism. Ardent WIG constructivists argue that for real learning, students must virtually reconstruct knowledge for themselves, with appropriate support. BIG constructivists believe that giving learners information directly is fine and often preferable; but to learn it, they must then apply it actively and creatively. Infighting among moderate and extreme schools of thought about what teaching in a constructivist way means inevitably weakens the momentum.

HOW CHILDREN'S THINKING DEVELOPS

Another theme closely allied with constructivism is that of human development. The premise for a developmental view of mental maturation came from observations that youngsters often had difficulties in thinking and understanding that went beyond simple lack of knowledge. Certain kinds of reasoning, ways of using numbers, or manners of appreciating another person's perspective seemed beyond youngsters of certain ages, no matter how much explanation or practice they received. Perhaps such things depended on broad waves of development, which brought into place necessary cognitive equipment.

The most renowned advocate of this view was undoubtedly the Swiss psychologist Jean Piaget (Inhelder & Piaget, 1958; Piaget, 1954). With his colleague Inhelder, Piaget proposed that development proceeded through several stages of cognitive capability, culminating in what he termed "formal operations." Before children attained the highly general cognitive schemata underlying formal operations, they could not be expected to handle deductive reasoning or, among other things, manage scientific inquiry well. Early applications of Piaget's model led to curriculums that did not even attempt to engage young children in scientific reasoning, on the grounds that they were not up to it.

A number of studies conducted since Piaget's research program argue that Piaget's proposed stages are too broad. Development proceeds in a more modular way within different domains or kinds of thinking. Neo-Piagetians adopting this view have outlined more focused developmental tracks. For instance, Case (1992) argues that development travels along the tracks of several central conceptual structures, including understanding of quantity and of social matters such as intentionality.

Both the more modular view of development and a number of teaching experiments have shown that youngsters can manage various kinds of reasoning considerably earlier than had been thought. An early champion of this sort of flexibility was the seminal cognitive and developmental psychologist Jerome Bruner, who wrote in 1960 the well-known statement, "We begin with the hypothesis that any subject can be taught effectively in some intellectually honest form to any child at any state of development" (Bruner, 1973, p. 413).

At the most general level, constructivism and developmental science offer two guidelines for education: Cast the learner in an active, creative role rather than that of a passive receptacle; and take into account what the learner is ready for developmentally. Thus, in the opening scenarios, Mr. N. Ductive and Mr. Meta both insist that their students think things out rather than just give them the answers or even routine procedures with which to find the answers. From a developmental standpoint, activities like Mr. N. Ductive's rule-following classification task should work well for high school students but would need dramatic simplification for 3rd graders. Mr. Meta's rather generalized "think about what's important" focus, however, would work more or less as is across a wide range of grades and developmental levels, with Mr. Meta making on-the-fly adjustments in the sophistication of the discourse.

Although both constructivism and a developmental perspective have generated bold calls for pedagogical reform, the calls have generally been louder than the response. A good deal has happened to revise teaching practices and developmentally appropriate curriculums (see, for example, Bruer, 1993; Perkins, 1992a), but not nearly as much as champions would like to see. On the practical side, these agendas generate a variety of problems with classroom management, materials support, time required for covering the curriculum, teachers' stock of developmental knowledge, and the like. Moreover, different stances on both constructivism and human development have often confused teachers.

INTELLIGENCE AND THE SKILLS OF THINKING

SCENARIO 1

Ms. Ima Thinker has asked her elementary school students to meet in groups of three or four. She gives each group a collection of small tools often found in

169

kitchens, such as can openers, vegetable peelers, and potato mashers. She asks them to group the items in a way that makes sense to them and think of an appropriate name for each group. Then, after returning everything to a common pile, they are to sort the items again in a different way, and again name the groups. Later Ms. Thinker explains that this is an exercise in classifying, and that next they will be classifying words rather than things. She gives each group a list of words and asks them to write the words on slips of paper and sort them. When the students report out various ways of classifying the words, she introduces the idea of "parts of speech."

SCENARIO 2

At Socrates Elementary School, students are involved in an animated discussion. After the class has read a story about two young friends who get angry with one another, Ms. Logic asks questions about friendship. "If a friend does something you don't like, is she still a friend?" Students express their ideas, with the teacher leading but not dominating the discussion. Her purpose is to encourage students to define terms precisely and to support their positions logically, but not to get them to arrive at any particular conclusion.

The prospects of improving human thinking and learning have long been recognized. The disciplined inquiries of Socrates and Plato, built on the discoveries of Greek rhetoric, pointed toward using the mind more rigorously. Aristotle extended the available tools with the logical forms of the syllogism. Church scholars such as Saint Augustine picked up on the power of systematic reasoning, and Francis Bacon in the early 1600s articulated basic principles of the scientific method.

The last half century has seen a groundswell of attention on directly cultivating thinking and learning. Cognitive science was partly responsible. Early studies of problem solving and memory disclosed that effectiveness was partly a matter of strategy. Some people managed their minds better than others. Why not, then, teach people good practices of problem solving, memorizing, and other sorts of thinking? The other wellspring was philosophy, a discipline that had long stood back to examine the process of thinking itself. Some philosophers concentrated on pre-university education, exploring what could be done to bring into the classroom some of the concepts and practices that had invigorated philosophical inquiry since the Greeks.

The most visible result of all these efforts is a variety of curriculum materials that have as their primary purpose improving students' cognitive abilities. Such materials have strikingly diverse approaches. Some focus on basic operations of classification and discrimination, emphasizing tasks like those that appear on IQ tests. The first scenario in this section and the first part of the Odyssey program (Adams, 1986; Herrnstein, Nickerson, Sanchez, & Swets, 1986) are examples of this focus. Other programs, such as Instrumental Enrichment, encourage students to develop more precise, systematic, and attentive processes of information intake, manipulation, and output (Feuerstein, 1980). Still others focus on familiar kinds of thinking, such as problem solving, decision making, and creativity, as in other parts of Odyssey or Edward de Bono's (1973–1975) CoRT program. Some are based on developmental psychology, for instance, the work of Piaget (Adey & Shayer, 1994). A few, notably Philosophy for Children, deal with classical matters, such as using syllogisms and clarifying the meaning of words, as in Scenario 2 (Lipman, Sharp, & Oscanyan, 1980). Recommended teaching methods range from assigning problem sets of open-ended thinking activities to leading Socratic conversations.

Although many educators are intrigued by the possibility of augmenting students' mental abilities, relatively few elementary and secondary schools have taken steps to incorporate published thinking skills programs into their official courses of study. Schools often find that making time for a substantial addition to already packed schedules is difficult. Recent years have probably seen even fewer applications than in the mid-1980s, in part because the adoption of state content standards has narrowed the scope of curriculums.

Another factor impeding advancement of the thinking skills movement has been the existence of theoretical controversies, such as disputes over the nature of human intelligence. A view common since the turn of the century is that intelligence is largely determined by genetic factors and not subject to much educational influence. As recently as 1994, Herrnstein and Murray advocated this position in the well-known book *The Bell Curve*. This discouraging stance certainly has not won the day. A number of serious challenges have been posed from the perspectives of multiple intelligences (e.g., Gardner, 1983; Sternberg, 1985) and various ways of cultivating intelligence (e.g., Baron, 1988; Perkins, 1995). Indeed, considerable evidence exists that intelligence can be enhanced to a useful, albeit limited, extent (Perkins, 1995;

Perkins & Grotzer, 1997). The very existence of the controversy, however, has made many educators wary of investing in efforts to enhance learners' thinking and learning.

Another such controversy arose from a different quarter. Some theorists challenged the idea that general cross-domain strategies of thinking and learning had much leverage. Instead, they believed that knowledge and understanding were profoundly "situated"—specific to various disciplines and areas of practice. Thinking could be taught, they contended, but it should be taught through the various disciplines in ways fine-tuned to their particular styles of problem solving and inquiry (Brown, Collins, & Duguid, 1989; Lave & Wenger, 1991). Undoubtedly, this view has a measure of truth, but strong counterarguments have been offered against extreme situated stances (e.g., Anderson, Reder, & Simon, 1996). The truth likely lies somewhere in between, with room for some strategies of thinking and learning, but suitably adapted to particular contexts (compare to Perkins & Salomon, 1989). Again, controversy has discouraged some educators.

Partly as a consequence of the situated view and partly to dodge scheduling issues, perhaps the most common approach to the teaching of thinking and learning is "infusion," as it is sometimes called. Infusion means systematically incorporating thinking and instruction into subject matter classes. Besides stand-alone courses, some systematic approaches to infusion exist (e.g., Swartz & Parks, 1994; Tishman, Perkins, & Jay, 1995; Marzano, Pickering, et al., 1997). Teachers' efforts are sometimes made easier by subject matter textbooks that call for students to classify information, compare concepts, or use other such skills, a practice that has become more common as the importance of thinking skills has become more widely accepted.

Integrating content and thinking is certainly desirable, but this approach brings problems of its own. Under pressure to cover content, teachers may find the thinking side of a curriculum giving way to the content side. Moreover, individual student efforts are difficult to monitor or coordinate. Some published intensive programs show considerable evidence of effectiveness, but we simply don't know the extent to which teachers of regular classes provide explicit teaching of thinking or, if provided, what such integrated instruction accomplishes.

As understanding of the human mind continues to grow, and as knowledge about reliable means of developing students' cognitive capabilities continues to expand, educators will need to resolve the responsibility issue. Schools must determine how they propose to use this knowledge systematically to help all students sharpen their thinking and learning abilities.

Brain Research

Scenario 1

Students in Metro Middle School are practicing self-control in their social and emotional learning class. Two volunteers agree to role-play a typical situation. Pretending to be walking in the school hallway, one bumps against the other. The bumped student, who would ordinarily feel he must defend his honor by hitting back, uses the "red light, yellow light, green light" strategy (Elias et al. 1997, p. 29).

Speaking aloud in this case, he says, "Red light: Don't do anything yet. Yellow light: Think of things you might do and what might happen if you did them. Green light: Decide what is best and do it." He decides the bump probably wasn't intentional, or maybe it was just in fun, so he will ignore it for now.

Scenario 2

A high school biology class has begun to study DNA. At the beginning of class, Ms. Rhea Member asks students to jot down notes about what happened yesterday and then meet with a partner to discuss what they remembered. As she provides more information about DNA, she pauses occasionally to have partners explain to one another what they've just heard. A few minutes before the class is to end, she asks students to represent some aspect of what they've learned by making a diagram or sketch in their notebooks. She tells them that tomorrow she will give them some time to meet in learning teams to begin planning for a presentation they are to give next week, complete with visual aids. They are to portray knowledge of DNA in relation to a television program, well-known book, or song.

In the last decade, educators have begun to tap a comparatively new source of knowledge about the mind: neuroscience. Curious investigators have studied the physical brain for many years, of course, but only in the last few years have new noninvasive technologies, such as functional magnetic resonance imaging (fMRI), revealed exciting new information about workings of a normal, undamaged brain. Opinions about the immediate usefulness of these new findings vary greatly.

Some interpreters believe brain research provides support for particular approaches, such as real versus symbolic input (Hart, 1998), active processing of experience (Caine & Caine, 1997), enrichment in early childhood (Diamond & Hopson, 1998), and use of color and movement (Jensen, 1998).

Scientists themselves are generally more cautious. For example, at an invitational meeting of educators and brain researchers held under the auspices of the Education Commission of the States (1996), "the scientists urged the educators not to attempt to apply new research findings" (p. vi). John Bruer, a cognitive psychologist and president of the McDonnell Foundation, states flatly that "right now, brain science has little to offer educational practice or policy" (p. 14). Stephen Pinker (1997), director of the Center for Cognitive Neuroscience at the Massachusetts Institute of Technology, apparently agrees. In *How the Mind Works*, he writes,

> This book is about the brain, but I will not say much about neurons, hormones, and neurotransmitters. That is because the mind is not the brain but what the brain does. . . . My point is not that prodding brain tissue is irrelevant to understanding the mind, only that it is not enough. Psychology, the analysis of mental software, will have to burrow a considerable way into the mountain before meeting the neurobiologists tunneling through from the other side (pp. 24–26).

To make sense of the differing stances, educators perhaps need to understand the professional orientations of these authors. As explained earlier, cognitive science was born a quarter century before the recent proliferation of brain research. Just as behaviorism made headway by ignoring vague and unmeasurable concepts about the mind, cognitive science progressed by excluding some aspects of mentality that brain researchers are now able to study. At least, that's how it seems to neuroscientists. Francis Crick, quoted earlier as saying cognitivists were interested only in the software and not the hardware of the brain, commented,

> This attitude does not help when one wants to *discover* the workings of an immensely complicated apparatus like the brain. Why not look inside the black box and observe how its components behave? It is not sensible to tackle a very difficult problem with one hand tied behind one's back (p. 18)(emphasis in original).

Educators' purposes are different, of course. Their intent is not to discover the workings of the brain; they just want to help students learn by making use of what *has been discovered*. They must be cautious, because much about the brain remains unknown, and much current knowledge is highly tentative. Nevertheless, Crick is right about the folly of trying to understand the mind "with one hand tied behind one's back." If no other knowledge existed about teaching and learning, we could not derive pedagogy from brain research. But we do have insights from several sources—including cognitive science, educational research, and thoughtful professional experience. Combined with this existing knowledge, brain research has the potential to enrich educational practice.

A good example of how neuroscience can help solve learning problems is *Fast ForWord,* created by researchers Paula Tallal and Michael Merzenich (1997). They developed the program in response to Tallal's findings that some children have trouble learning to read because they do not process speech sounds fast enough to hear phonemic differences. Based on Merzenich's research exploring the brain's plasticity, the program uses computer games incorporating artificially extended speech. Playing the games, children first learn to recognize sounds and then gradually increase their processing speed until they can hear the sounds in normal speech.

Knowledge about the human brain's functioning is far too extensive to be summarized in a paragraph or two. But here are a few generalizations that, in combination with other knowledge, suggest numerous implications about teaching and learning:

• The product of hundreds of millions of years of evolution, the brain is not a general-purpose, problem-solving device but rather a collection of systems (e.g., the ability to sing and the ability to count), each designed to serve a specific purpose (Restak, 1994). All human brains are alike in some ways, but each is also different. The general capabilities that make us human, such as language, have a neuronal substrate, so they are not developed solely through experience (Plotkin, 1998). The organization of each individual brain, however, changes in direct response to experience (Diamond & Hopson, 1998).

• The brain is incredibly complex, processing many inputs simultaneously and in multiple ways (Edelman, 1992). Emotions—which are probably related to chemical neurotransmitters found throughout the body as well as in the brain (Pert, 1997)—play an important role in determining what we pay attention to, how we make personal decisions, and what we remember (Damasio, 1994). Memories that are recalled from time to time are retained because the connections among neurons are repeatedly strengthened. For the same reason, tasks done frequently (like driving a car or tying shoestrings) require less conscious attention and less brain energy (Calvin, 1996). Memories are not stored whole but are reconstructed by recombining aspects of an original experience, so experiences most likely to be remembered are those "that are targets of elaborative encoding processes" (Schacter, 1996, p. 56).

• Each brain attempts to make sense of the input it constantly receives by matching incoming sensations with related information stored from previous experiences. This process gives each individual the illusion of coherence and consistency, even though memories are highly unreliable, and individuals' interpretations of reality often differ dramatically (Gazzaniga, 1998).

Many educators will find in these statements confirmation of, and possibly new insights into, what they already know about human learning. In general, the findings help explain why students learn best from purposeful, meaningful experiences that engage their imaginations and arouse their emotions. In Scenario 1 at the beginning of this section, Ms. Rhea Member uses numerous techniques to encourage students to process information about DNA in the belief that the more extensively the information is encoded, the easier it will be to retrieve.

Teachers have also found that exercises like "red light, green light" described in the second scenario can help students learn to restrain emotional impulses that might otherwise "hijack" their brains. Researchers think the reason emotions have such power is that they were needed to survive in the past, as to a lesser degree they still are.

THE FUTURE OF A SCIENCE OF LEARNING

Full recognition of emotions—their role and relationship to other mental functions—is, in fact, one aspect of the more inclusive science of the mind that advocates now believe is evolving (LeDoux, 1996). This new, all-encompassing discipline, while drawing on knowledge from many sources, will be firmly anchored in the study of the physical brain and related neural systems. Although that focus may seem obvious to some, it is not yet obvious to many of today's academics and was certainly not assumed by scholars in the past. Most systematic investigation of the mind was and still is conducted without reference to the brain (and the rest of the body) for good reason: Advanced tools for studying the normal, living brain have only recently been invented.

But keeping the mind and brain apart is no longer necessary. Damasio (1994) refers to this mistaken dualism as "Descartes' Error," complaining that "the Cartesian idea of a disembodied mind" nevertheless remains influential (p. 250). By contrast, neuroscientists take a position more like that of Crick (1994), who declares in *The Astonishing Hypothesis* that each of us is "in fact no more than the behavior of a vast assembly of nerve cells and their associated molecules" (p. 3). Although Crick casts this proposition as a hypothesis to be tested rather than an established fact, he plainly believes it himself. And though, as Crick acknowledges, his doctrine is "alien to the ideas of most people alive today" (p. 3), some version of it will undoubtedly be more widely accepted eventually.

Given the directions that the study of the mind and brain is headed, we are probably safe in making this prediction: The field of study now known as cognitive science will become even more diverse, paying more attention to the study of topics such as emotions and consciousness that previously have been less central, and assimilating insights from behaviorism. This expanded field, which may be known as mind science, and which we are calling the science of learning, will specifically include all aspects of neuroscience, meaning investigation of the physical brain and related biology. The current competition between some cognitive psychologists and some proponents of brain research will gradually change to one of collaboration. Behaviorism, now in partial eclipse among educational theorists, will be reexamined for a range of insights about learning.

What else might we expect for education's future? As other authors in this yearbook have noted, predicting future developments is a highly unreliable undertaking. Nevertheless, by projecting from current trends, we can propose several generalizations that seem likely to become reality:

• *The quantity and quality of brain research, which has multiplied enormously in the past decade, will continue to increase.* With the steady improvement in technological means of conducting brain research, the number of neuroscientists and the topics they investigate is growing larger year by year. Eventually (perhaps 25 to 50 years), we will have a much more complete understanding of brain functioning. This information, along with knowledge from other branches of mind science, will have substantial implications for education. Specifically, research will reveal the origins of, and develop new responses to, variations in mental functioning, including some that are now considered disabilities. Research will add to our understanding of the abilities we call intelligences, including ways education can enhance them. It will also produce more detailed information about the workings of neurotransmitters and other communication mechanisms in the brain and body, thereby shedding light on such phenomena as emotions, memory, and imagination. Information of this sort quite likely will lead to expanded use of drugs capable of modifying natural processes, such as heightening memory.

• *Over time, research and evolving practice will untangle controversies that have blocked systematic application of learning science to education.* An example of this process is the controversy concerning phonics versus whole language, which has troubled the teaching of reading for decades. At this point, the debate appears largely resolved in a kind of synthesis that recognizes the important place of phonics but incorporates many whole language practices. Similarly, controversies such as whether intelligence can be enhanced or whether understanding is almost entirely discipline-specific are gradually working their way toward resolutions that seem likely to have the character of syntheses rather than stark victories.

• *Knowledge about learning will be a fundamental part of every educator's professional preparation, as well as every student's education.* As knowledge about the mind continues to grow, applications of this knowledge to education will become ever more apparent. Educators will be expected to be informed about, and to use, practices in accord with these findings.

Much of what is known about learning will also be taught directly to students in elementary and secondary schools. Few subjects could possibly be more important than understanding oneself and others and improving the ability to manage one's own thinking and learning.

• *Applications of information technology will continue to evolve, with digital devices proliferating, many of them small, specialized, and inexpensive—designed to extend human capabilities or compensate for limits of the natural mind.* With extensive networking of such devices, it will become more difficult to differentiate between mental abilities of an unaided individual and capabilities of people linked to other humans and to machines. In recent years, parents and educators have often disputed whether children should use calculators before they have learned computation "by hand" or whether they should be able to write compositions on word processing programs equipped with spell checkers. Future educators will wrestle with similar questions involving newly created electronic aids, including speech recognition word processors.

• *The need for instruction in thinking skills will continue to grow to help public school students from families with limited means perform well in school.* For complex economic, social, and political reasons, the proportion of children living in undesirable conditions has been increasing in developed countries, especially the United States. Some of these children are from indigenous families with a history of neglect and impoverishment; others are part of the steady flow of immigrants out of underdeveloped countries. With economic and political unrest throughout the world, and the availability of modern transportation, this trend will undoubtedly continue, bringing even more children with different languages and traditions to public schools. Many of these children will be from families with rural backgrounds that are not equipped to provide the middle-class surroundings that contribute to school success. Because these are the children most able to profit from programs specifically designed to develop intellectual skills, the need for such programs will continue to grow.

Some developments we foresee are outside educators' scope of influence. Mind science, including study of the brain, will surely proceed in the 21st century regardless of what happens in schools. But some of the things we foresee will not happen, at least not as readily, without initiative and support from educators themselves.

In today's political climate, educators are under great pressure to somehow bring all children to higher standards of performance. In the years ahead, the pressure is sure to grow even more intense. We can succeed in meeting this challenge only with improved understanding of the thinking and learning process itself. Accurate knowledge about the human mind is essential to an enlightened education profession.

References

Adams, M. J. (Ed.). (1986). *Odyssey: A curriculum for thinking.* Watertown, MA: Mastery Education.

Adey, P., & Shayer, M. (1994). *Really raising standards: Cognitive intervention and academic achievement.* London: Routledge and Kegan Paul.

Aiken, W. (1943). *Thirty schools tell their story.* New York: McGraw-Hill.

Anderson, J. R., Reder, L. M., & Simon, H. A. (1996). Situated learning and education. *Educational Researcher, 25*(4), 5–11.

Baron, J. (1988). *Thinking and deciding.* New York: Cambridge University Press.

Bloom, B. S. (1968). Learning for mastery. *UCLA Evaluation Comment 1*(2), 1–12.

Bransford, J. D., Brown, A. L., & Cocking, R. R. (1999). *How people learn: Brain, mind, experience, and school.* Washington, DC: National Academy Press.

Brooks, J. G., & Brooks, M. (1993). *In search of understanding: The case for constructivist classrooms.* Alexandria, VA: Association for Supervision and Curriculum Development.

Brown, J. S., Collins, A., & Duguid, P. (1989). Situated cognition and the culture of learning. *Educational Researcher, 18*(1), 32–42.

Bruer, J. T. (1993). *Schools for thought: A science of learning in the classroom.* Cambridge, MA: MIT Press.

Bruner, J. S. (1973). Readiness for learning. In J. Anglin (Ed.), *Beyond the information given* (pp. 413–425). New York: W. W. Norton.

Caine, R. N., & Caine, G. (1997). *Education on the edge of possibility.* Alexandria, VA: Association for Supervision and Curriculum Development.

Calvin, W. H. (1996). *How brains think: Evolving intelligence, then and now.* New York: BasicBooks.

Case, R. (1992). *The mind's staircase: Exploring the conceptual underpinnings of children's thought and knowledge.* Hillsdale, NJ: Lawrence Erlbaum.

Chomsky, N. (1980). *Rules and representations.* New York: Columbia University Press.

Crick, F. (1994). *The astonishing hypothesis: The scientific search for the soul.* New York: Scribner.

Damasio, A. R. (1994). *Descartes' error.* New York: Grosset/Putnam.

de Bono, E. (1973–1975). *CoRT thinking.* Blandford, Dorset, UK: Direct Education Services Limited.

Diamond, M., & Hopson, J. (1998). *Magic trees of the mind: How to nurture your child's intelligence, creativity, and healthy emotions from birth through adolescence.* New York: E. P. Dutton.

Duffy, T. M., & Jonassen, D. H. (Eds.). (1992). *Constructivism and the technology of instruction: A conversation.* Hillsdale, NJ: Lawrence Erlbaum.

Edelman, G. M. (1992). *Bright air, brilliant fire.* New York: BasicBooks.

Education Commission of the States. (1996). *Bridging the gap between neuroscience and education: Conference report.* Denver, CO: Author.

Elias, M. J., Zins, J. E., Weissberg, R. P., Frey, K. S., Greenberg, M. T., Haynes, N. M., Kessler, R., Schwab-Stone, M. E., & Shriver, T. P. (1997). *Promoting social and emotional learning.* Alexandria, VA: Association for Supervision and Curriculum Development.

Feuerstein, R. (1980). *Instrumental enrichment: An intervention program for cognitive modifiability.* Baltimore: University Park Press.

Gardner, H. (1983). *Frames of mind: The theory of multiple intelligences.* New York: BasicBooks.

Gazzaniga, M. S. (1998). *The mind's past.* Berkeley, CA: University of California Press.

Hart, L. A. (1998). *Human brain and human learning* (Updated ed.). Kent, WA: Books for Educators.

Herrnstein, R. J., & Murray, C. (1994). *The bell curve: Intelligence and class structure in American life.* New York: Free Press.

Herrnstein, R. J., Nickerson, R. S., Sanchez, M., & Swets, J. A. (1986). Teaching thinking skills. *American Psychologist, 41,* 1279–1289.

Inhelder, B., & Piaget, J. (1958). *The growth of logical thinking from childhood to adolescence.* New York: BasicBooks.

Jensen, E. (1998). *Teaching with the brain in mind.* Alexandria, VA: Association for Supervision and Curriculum Development.

Keene, E. O., & Zimmerman, S. (1997). *Mosaic of thought: Teaching comprehension in a reader's workshop.* Portsmouth, NH: Heinemann.

Kohn, A. (1993). *Punished by rewards: The trouble with gold stars, incentive plans, a's, praise, and other bribes.* Boston: Houghton Mifflin.

Lave, J., & Wenger, E. (1991). *Situated learning: Legitimate peripheral participation.* New York: Cambridge University Press.

LeDoux, J. (1996). *The emotional brain: The mysterious underpinnings of emotional life.* New York: Simon and Schuster.

Lipman, M., Sharp, A. M., & Oscanyan, F. (1980). *Philosophy in the classroom.* Philadelphia: Temple University Press.

Marzano, R. J., Pickering, D. J., et al. (1997). *Dimensions of Learning trainer's manual* (2nd ed.). Alexandria, VA: Association for Supervision and Curriculum Development.

Palincsar, A. S., Ransom, K., & Derber, S. (1988, December–1999, January). Collaborative research and the development of reciprocal teaching. *Educational Leadership, 46*(4), 37–40.

Perkins, D. N. (1992a). *Smart schools: From training memories to educating minds.* New York: Free Press.

Perkins, D. N. (1992b). Technology meets constructivism: Do they make a marriage? In T. M. Duffy & D. H. Jonassen (Eds.), *Constructivism and the technology of instruction: A conversation* (pp. 45–55). Hillsdale, NJ: Lawrence Erlbaum.

Perkins, D. N. (1995). *Outsmarting IQ: The emerging science of learnable intelligence.* New York: Free Press.

Perkins, D. N., & Grotzer, T. A. (1997). Teaching intelligence. *American Psychologist, 52,* 1125–1133.

Perkins, D. N., & Salomon, G. (1989). Are cognitive skills context bound? *Educational Researcher, 18*(1), 16–25.

Pert, C. (1997). *Molecules of emotion.* New York: Scribner.

Philips, D. C. (1995). The good, the bad, and the ugly: The many faces of constructivism. *Educational Researcher, 24*(7), 5–12.

Piaget, J. (1954). *The construction of reality in the child.* New York: BasicBooks.

Pinker, S. (1997). *How the mind works.* New York: W. W. Norton.

Plotkin, H. (1998). *Evolution in mind.* Cambridge, MA: Harvard University Press.

Restak, R. (1994). *The modular brain.* New York: Scribner.

Rosenshine, B. V. (1986, April). Synthesis of research on explicit teaching. *Educational Leadership 43*(7), 60–69.

Schacter, D. L. (1996). *Searching for memory.* New York: BasicBooks.

Skinner, B. F. (1974). *About behaviorism.* New York: Alfred A. Knopf.

Sternberg, R. J. (1985). *Beyond IQ: A triarchic theory of human intelligence.* New York: Cambridge University Press.

Swartz, R. J., & Parks, S. (1994). *Infusing the teaching of critical and creative thinking into elementary instruction: A lesson design handbook.* Pacific Grove, CA: Critical Thinking Press and Software.

Tallal, P., & Merzenich, M. (1997). *Fast ForWord* [CD-ROM]. Berkeley, CA: Scientific Learning Corporation.

Tishman, S., Perkins, D. N., & Jay, E. (1995). *The thinking classroom.* Boston: Allyn and Bacon.

8

Technology in America's Schools: Before and After Y2K

Barbara Means

Technology in the broad sense has always been a part of America's classrooms. Certainly pencil and paper, chalk and blackboard, and the printing press helped to shape—and continue to shape—the activity structures that dominate our schools. In this chapter, I concentrate on the much narrower domain of computer-based and telecommunications technologies. These technologies have a much briefer history in U.S. schools and, I argue, have not yet reached their full potential in dramatically altering the nature of the teaching and learning that goes on there.

Unleashing the educational potential of these technologies requires serious thinking, research, and experimentation on the

Note: The preparation of this chapter was supported in part by National Science Foundation grant CDA-9729384. The opinions expressed herein are those of the author and do not necessarily reflect the policy or opinions of the Foundation.

185

connections between the learning sciences and technological capabilities. To date, the public discourse surrounding educational technology has made little connection with such research. Instead, optimistic futurists (Braun, 1990) clash with skeptical contrarians (Oppenheimer, 1997; Stolls, 1995).

I argue that although we have made great strides in increasing the technological infrastructure in America's schools, we are still far short of providing a seamless, convenient, robust, and reliable technology support structure for all students and teachers. Today's desktop computers and common uses of the Internet are not the educational ideal (Roschelle, Pea, Hoadley, Gordin, & Means, in press). Although many lament the paucity of up-to-date computers and network connections in classrooms, a look into almost any classroom with a sizable number of computers reveals all kinds of problems related to their size, weight, shape, and requirements for multiple cords and wires. Similarly, today's World Wide Web is disorganized, of uneven quality, and overrun with advertising. In all too many cases, students and teachers are either not using the technology available to them or are using technology to accomplish things that could be done offline more quickly and with less effort extraneous to the learning content (Healy, 1998).

Nevertheless, our experience with the less-than-ideal technology infrastructure available in schools today, and the work of researchers attempting to embody advances in our understanding of human learning in technology-based systems, point to important directions for the 21st century. The insights gained from these experiences, coupled with technology improvements that can be expected in the decades to come, give rise to cautious optimism about technology's role in the schools of tomorrow.

Before speculating on the educational technology infrastructure and usage patterns of the next century, I first try to impart a "30,000-mile-high" perspective on where we have come from and where we are now. Time moves rapidly in the arena of information technology. My look at the past focuses principally on the 1980s. I contrast that era with our present—roughly the 1990s—which I use as a point of departure for identifying emerging trends that provide hints of what we can expect in the first part of the next century.

YESTERDAY: CHANGING GOALS

The earliest attempts at software development for the purpose of teaching were based on behavioral learning theory. Developers strove to analyze curriculum areas down into small discrete objectives and then to provide information or skills practice on each objective. Patrick Suppes designed computer systems of this sort for arithmetic at Stanford University in the 1960s. Suppes's system offered learner feedback, lesson branching, and a system for tracking individual student progress. During the 1970s, a similar approach was implemented on a much broader scale by the University of Illinois Programmed Logic for Automatic Teaching Operations (PLATO) system. PLATO included hundreds of tutorials and drill-and-practice programs available through timesharing on a mainframe computer (Coburn et al., 1982). Integrated learning systems (ILSs) are direct descendants of the PLATO and Suppes systems. Typically sold as packages of networked computers and software, these systems offer individualized instruction in core curriculum areas along with extensive capabilities for tracking student performance.

At the same time, the increasing importance of computers in managing information led to the creation of computer programming and "literacy" classes, first at the college and high school levels, and later in the lower grades. In contrast to the computer-assisted instruction of Suppes, PLATO, and ILSs, these classes were designed to teach *about* computers rather than to teach *with* them.

INFRASTRUCTURE AND ACCESS

From a low base in 1980, the number of computers in U.S. schools grew exponentially during the '80s. In 1981, only about 18 percent of U.S. public schools had even a single computer designated for instructional use. In 1983, the number of computers in U.S. schools was estimated at 50,000. By 1990, the estimate was 2.6 million (Becker, 1990).

As the number of computers in schools started rising during the 1980s, attention shifted from the total number of computers per school to the student-computer ratio. The average number of computers per 30 students nearly tripled between 1984 and 1990, rising from 0.60 to 1.53 (Mageau, 1991).

187

PATTERNS OF USE

Results from national surveys indicated that in the early '80s, computers were used mainly for three tasks: to teach students about computers (i.e., computer literacy classes), to teach programming, and for rote learning through ILSs or other drill-and-practice programs (Becker, 1985). Teachers reported using computers primarily to provide enrichment activities and variety, or to teach students about computers—rarely to provide students with instruction in core academic subjects (Becker, 1990). This reported pattern of use was certainly compatible with the argument that computer technology is used at the margins of education but not as an integral part of schooling (Cohen, 1988).

Starting in the mid-1980s, however, using computers as tools increased, and teaching about computers per se decreased. This shift took place in the broader context of moving away from mainframe computers, which small numbers of technologists controlled, to desktop microcomputers, which all kinds of workers used as productivity tools. Education experienced a comparable shift toward having students engage in more authentic tasks, using tools identical or analogous to those that professionals in the work world employ (Means et al., 1993). An influential proponent of this emphasis was the Apple Classrooms of Tomorrow (ACOT) program. Teacher leaders of the ACOT program at West High School in Columbus, Ohio, wanted to equip their classrooms with Apple's most powerful computer—the then-new Macintosh. This choice presented a problem because at the time there was little instructional Macintosh software appropriate for high school students. The Apple staff and West teachers began to explore the educational uses of general computer tools, such as word processing, database, and spreadsheet software. In retrospect, they felt that this decision, forced by necessity, was one of the best directions they could have taken. Instead of doing mathematics exercises or reading about science topics on a computer, West ACOT students used computer tools to support their work in complex projects involving math, science, and other subject areas. At the same time, many schools were turning to word processing software to support student writing. Under this emerging model of using general applications to support student activities, technology use was connected to teaching core academic subjects and mediated by the teacher's design and orchestration of classroom activities.

EQUITY

Neither the technology infrastructure nor the way that technology was used was equally distributed across schools during the 1980s. In 1983, computers were found in four times as many of the nation's wealthiest schools as in its poorest schools (President's Committee of Advisors on Science and Technology [PCAST], 1997). Such differences exacerbated large differences in home access to technology (Sutton, 1991).

Even when schools serving low-income students had computers, they tended to use them less frequently and in different ways than did schools serving students from more affluent homes. Research studies indicate that students in low-ability classes tended to use computers for drill and practice, while higher-ability students were given opportunities to use technology more broadly, including using computers as tools, as described earlier (Becker & Sterling, 1987; DeVillar & Faltis, 1991).

Federal compensatory education programs had mixed effects with respect to equity. Government funds helped increase low-income students' access to computers, but they also increased the likelihood that this access would be focused on drill in basic skills. Title I (then called Chapter 1) funding requires schools to test program participants. Computer labs with integrated learning systems (ILSs) became a popular strategy for addressing the basic skills needs of low-achieving students while simultaneously producing the data required for federal reporting. By 1990, approximately 10,000 ILSs were in use, funded primarily with federal compensatory education monies (Mageau, 1990).

ASSESSMENT

Standardized tests using multiple-choice formats dominated assessment practices during the 1980s. These assessments closely matched the kind of assessment embedded in many ILS and other basic skills software programs. Research studies comparing students learning reading and mathematics skills on computers to those receiving conventional teacher-directed instruction began appearing in the literature. Meta-analyses of studies at elementary school (Niemiec & Walberg, 1985) and secondary school (Samson, Niemiec, Weinstein, & Walberg, 1986) levels generally showed a significant advantage for computer-assisted instruction. Kulik, Kulik, and Bangert-Drowns (1985) found, for example, that on average, elementary school students who received instruction through computers outperformed their counterparts without computer-assisted instruction (CAI). This empirical evidence for positive effects of computer-supported instruction applied to didactic, skills-based CAI; it did not provide evidence about the effectiveness of the then-emerging practice of using technology tools to support more student-centered instructional approaches.

TODAY: HALF EMPTY *AND* HALF FULL

The goal of incorporating general-purpose technology tools into instructional activities that emerged in the latter 1980s continues as a major objective for technology today. Such practices have spread, as have teacher professional development programs to promote them. The focus on adopting general tools for education received a major boost from the rise of the World Wide Web and search engines for locating Web sites on almost any topic. Slogans such as "connecting the classroom to the world" and "the world at your fingertips" reflect today's interest on accessing a much broader information base through the Web.

Although taking advantage of access to vast knowledge resources is the most salient change in school uses of technology in the '90s, earlier goals persist, and new ones are emerging. On the one hand, drill-and-practice environments continue to have broad appeal, especially in schools serving low-income students; on the other, emerging collaborative, cognitive technologies reflect research on the social nature of human learning and advances in the interactive capabilities of computer networks.

INFRASTRUCTURE AND ACCESS

Classrooms continue to lag behind the business and entertainment sectors of society in capitalizing on new technologies. But during the final decade of the 20th century, the increase in information technology access within U.S. schools has been phenomenal. As various computer-based and telecommunications technologies have evolved, we have witnessed not only dramatic increases in their presence within schools but also a change in how educators measure technology access: They expect high-quality equipment and easy access to that equipment for both teachers and students.

Computers

From an estimated one computer for every 20 students in 1990, the presence of computers in U.S. schools grew to one computer for every 6 students by 1998, according to a national survey commissioned by *Education Week* ("Technology Counts," 1998).

But even with this increase, student access to computers remains limited in most schools. When only computers in regular classrooms were counted, there were 17 students per computer in 1998, according to Market Data Retrieval's Public School Technology Survey ("Technology Counts," 1998). The most common arrangement, particularly at the high school level, is one or more computer labs of 20 to 30 machines each, into which whole classes are scheduled for small amounts of time. A majority of schools still do not have enough computers for most students to use frequently. Moreover, when the obsolescence of the equipment base in schools is considered, the number of students per computer is much higher: In 1998, for example, there were 13 students for each computer with CD-ROM capability.

Internet Access

The rise of the Internet and the World Wide Web as tools for communication and education has been so dramatic that we may not realize just how recent this change has been. At the start of the 1990s, the World Wide Web did not exist. Some schools were exchanging messages and text files, but educational (and business) applications of the Internet didn't take off until the commercial descendants of Mosaic made graphical user interfaces commonplace.[1]

In 1990, few U.S. schools had Internet connections, and many of these were low-speed dial-up modem connections from a single computer. By 1994, the percentage of schools with Internet access was significant—at 35 percent—and by 1997, the percentage had risen sharply to 75 percent. As happened earlier with computers, we stopped counting *school* connections and started looking at the availability of Internet access within regular classrooms.

In 1994, the percentage of U.S. *classrooms* with Internet access was just 3 percent. In 1996, President Clinton announced a set of national educational technology goals, which included connecting every class-room in the United States to the Internet. By 1997, the proportion of connected classrooms had grown to 27 percent (National Center for Education Statistics [NCES], 1999). In 1999, the U.S. Department of Education announced that over half of U.S. classrooms now have Inter-net access; by fall of 1999, the department expects 80 percent of U.S. classrooms to have Internet connections (L. Roberts, personal commu-nication, June, 1999). This achievement is attributed to the impact of the "E-rate," or telecommunications discount to schools and libraries (passed by Congress in 1996).

PATTERNS OF USE

Education reformers have stressed the importance of (1) involving students in challenging, authentic tasks performed with tools compara-ble to those of professional practitioners and (2) leveraging the intellec-tual and social resources available through collaboration (Collins, Brown, & Newman, 1989). Learning technology researchers argue that today's technology offers support for this kind of learning (Roschelle et al., in press). A few examples can serve to illustrate this support.

Using the inquiry-oriented ThinkerTools software, middle school students manipulate simulations and visualizations of the concepts of velocity and acceleration. In carefully controlled studies, these middle schoolers have outperformed high school physics students in their abil-ity to apply principles of Newtonian mechanics to real-world situations (White & Frederiksen, 1998).

The Global Learning and Observations to Benefit the Environment (GLOBE) program seeks to promote elementary and secondary school students' learning of science by involving them in real scientific investi-gations, following detailed data collection protocols for measuring the characteristics of their local atmosphere, soil, and vegetation. Thou-sands of students are using GLOBE data entry forms on the World

Wide Web to submit data to a central archive, where they are combined with data from other schools to develop visualizations that can be viewed on the Web. Both students and scientists use the data in the GLOBE database for Earth science investigations. Students in GLOBE classes have performed better on science assessments than their peers in other science classes. The assessments measured ability to take the kinds of measurements used in GLOBE, knowledge of sampling and measurement principles, and ability to interpret data and apply science concepts (Means & Coleman, in press).

Other projects are connecting teachers and students with scientists involved in exciting data collection expeditions. The JASON Project, originated by explorer Robert Ballard, provides "telepresence" connections over the Internet that permit students to communicate with scientists while the scientists are exploring coral reefs, rain forests, or other interesting ecologies. In the KidSat project, students can direct a camera's movement on the NASA space shuttle. The resulting pictures are made available for study over the World Wide Web.

An important difference between these uses of technology and the computer-assisted instruction model dominant in the '80s is the nature of the instructional activity: The activity is much more than the technology and is initiated and orchestrated by a teacher, rather than by a software system. Cuban and Kirkpatrick (1998) call this use "computer-enhanced instruction" to distinguish it from the earlier, more didactic "computer-assisted instruction."

Increasingly, teachers themselves are designing technology-supported classroom activities. An example of teacher-designed Internet use is found in the Challenge 2000 Multimedia project in California's Silicon Valley (Means & Golan, 1998). Three project teachers teamed up to design and execute an extended collaboration between 4th grade classes at two elementary schools. In a unit they called "Monsters, Mondrian, and Me," pairs of students were directed to describe a picture in an e-mail message to partner students in a distant classroom. Their writing had to be clear and precise enough that students in the other class could recreate the picture (monsters in the first phase, followed by abstract expressionist paintings and then self-portraits) without ever having seen the original. The final step for each phase involved exchanging electronically the second-generation drawings, so that the students who had composed the descriptive paragraphs could reflect on their writing, seeing where ambiguity or incomplete specification led to a different interpretation from their readers.

Although such examples of technology-enhanced, constructivist-oriented learning activities are prominent in education literature, they do not represent mainstream educational practice in the United States today. A national survey of 4,100 teachers, conducted by Hank Becker and Ron Anderson (Becker & Anderson, 1998), found that in the 1997–98 school year, word processing software was still the technology application teachers were most likely to assign to students (nearly 50 percent of surveyed teachers had done so in the previous year). Second in frequency was the use of CD-ROM references (around 35 percent). On the other hand, the survey indicates that Internet research for information gathering was the third most common teacher-directed student use of computers. Nearly 30 percent of all teachers—and over 70 percent of teachers with high-speed Internet connections in their classrooms—had their students do Internet research (Becker, 1999). Internet assignments were thus slightly more common than game and software drills, which were assigned by 29 percent of teachers. Interactive uses of the Internet like the kind described earlier were relatively infrequent. Only 7 percent of teachers reported having their students use electronic mail three or more times during the school year, and even fewer had their students work with students at a distance in cross-classroom projects.

Although we now have millions of Web pages either designed for education or with potential educational applications, from an instructional standpoint, most educational uses of the Web in the 1990s have more in common with instructional television and reference libraries than with what we know about how people learn (Bransford, Brown, & Cocking, 1999). For the most part, Web page developers tell their stories or post their information, and students search for and view these messages. For every truly interactive, two-way collaborative use of Web technology for teaching and learning, dozens of examples of the more didactic model are available. Nevertheless, collaborative models are available for classroom use, and the explosive growth of Internet use in the '90s shows just how fast an educational practice can grow from a very small base.

EQUITY

By 1997, when *Report to the President on the Use of Technology to Strengthen K–12 Education in the United States* (PCAST, 1997) was released, differences among schools in poorer and more affluent areas in numbers of computers on site were much reduced. Largely thanks to federal programs such as Title I, which financed computer labs for needy schools, the student-computer ratio in schools serving communities with limited economic resources had shrunk significantly. By the 1994–95 school year, schools where 80 percent of students were eligible for Tile I funds had one computer for every 11 students; the wealthiest schools, where less than 20 percent of students were eligible for Title I funds, had 1 computer for every 9.5 students.

The gap between poorer and wealthier schools (sometimes called the "digital divide") is much larger when measured in terms of classroom Internet access. Only 39 percent of classrooms in the poorest schools had an Internet connection in 1998, compared to 62 percent of classrooms in the wealthiest schools (NCES, 1999). This gap is just as large as the 14 percent versus 36 percent difference in classroom access found in the NCES 1997 survey (NCES, 1999).

Differences in school and classroom technology infrastructures are only the tip of the iceberg. Research suggests that students in poorer and wealthier schools continue to use the technology resources they have differently. Survey data from the 1996 National Assessment of Educational Progress (NAEP) in mathematics, for example, indicate that simulations and applications programs (which were associated with higher mathematics scores) were the dominant technology use for 33 percent of 8th graders who were ineligible for school lunch. In contrast, these programs were the dominant technology use for only 22 percent of 8th graders who qualified for free lunches (Wenglinsky, 1998).

ASSESSMENT

Although use of technology within schools has been shifting toward tool uses and student-centered projects with a technology component, the nature of the high-stakes examinations for students and schools has undergone much less change. If anything, emphasis on student performance on district- or state-mandated assessments has increased since the 1980s. The mismatch between assessment content and technology-supported learning is a major barrier to using innovative technology-enhanced programs (Means, 1998). Time spent preparing students to do well on tests of numerical calculations, vocabulary, or English mechanics cannot be spent on learning about Newtonian mechanics, data visualizations, or rainforest ecology. Moreover, demonstrating how technologies have contributed to students' deep understanding will be almost impossible without new kinds of assessments. Researchers at Carnegie Mellon University, for example, have found that urban high school students who have used their Practical Algebra Tutor system do much better than their peers who have learned algebra through conventional methods on complex performance assessments, but they show only a small advantage on standardized tests (Koedinger, Anderson, Hadley, & Mark, 1997; Koedinger & Sueker, 1996). Research on technology-enhanced innovations, which include measuring student learning, may provide strategies and tools for more meaningful assessments of student understanding and higher-order skills.

TODAY IN SUMMARY

Students and teachers today have access to massive amounts of information on the World Wide Web. They are also continuing to use general-purpose application packages for their school work; the most common is still word processing. Although the percentages are relatively small, students are becoming more involved in building Web pages and multimedia presentations to show how they solved a problem or what they learned in their research. Schools are also using network technology to support collaborations, both locally and at great distances, between students and students, between students and experts, and between teachers and other teachers.

Educational software in the form of CD-ROM-based references and enrichment materials is commonly used: 35 percent of teachers assign students to work with them. Game-like programs for practicing basic skills are also prevalent: 29 percent of teachers assign students to use them. Much less common in both usage patterns and shelf space are content-rich learning materials compatible with subject area curriculums at various grade levels. Designing for and selling into the splintered U.S. education market is notoriously difficult within the software industry (PCAST, 1997; Soloway, 1998). Smaller, innovative educational software firms have folded or been bought out by a few large conglomerates. Increasingly, the educational software business is producing and selling "edutainment" products marketed primarily to parents. School sales are regarded as frosting on the cake.

TOMORROW: NEW ARCHITECTURES FOR DISTRIBUTED COLLABORATION

Knowing that in the 1950s the head of IBM could not envision the United States ever needing more than five computers, I undertake the task of predicting 21st century educational uses of technology with great trepidation.

The insights that I offer should primarily be credited to the National Science Foundation-funded Center for Innovative Learning Technologies (CILT). Four core CILT partner institutions—SRI International, University of California at Berkeley, Vanderbilt University, and Concord Consortium—have brought together researchers, technology developers, and policymakers from industry, government, universities, and schools throughout North America. CILT meetings encourage rapid information exchange, followed by brainstorming about the most critical educational issues and opportunities, and conclude with forming new teams of individuals representing multiple organizations and sectors who wish to collaborate on a particular issue. The discussion here reflects ideas that several of these interdisciplinary teams developed.

In contrast to current and past emphases on didactic software on the one hand and the use of reference materials and general-purpose software tools on the other, CILT members foresee a future where network tools and digital appliances are designed specifically for education through an alliance of researchers, practitioners, and commercial partners. This technology will support active thinking and collaboration any time, any place. Learning will occur both online and offline, but technology tools will prove particularly important in supporting deeper and more timely assessments of student understanding.

INFRASTRUCTURE AND ACCESS: PERVASIVE CONNECTIVITY, LOWER COST, AND SPECIALIZED DEVICES

Today's desktop computers and the networks they run on offer a huge array of potential uses—from tracking student grades to manipulating digitized images. But they are bulky, expensive, and awkward to use in a classroom. Many technology trend watchers believe that the 21st century will see a move away from relying on such general-purpose computing devices toward lower-cost, portable devices (the digital equivalent to toasters and radios), often connected through global networks and tailored for specific applications (Norman, 1998). Nowhere is the potential impact of such a trend greater than in our nation's schools.

Light-weight, low-cost learning devices small enough to fit in students' backpacks and rugged enough to withstand student life could be used across settings as students move from class to class, school to home, or between school-based and community-based learning settings. When used in concert with higher-powered servers and teacher workstations, these devices would likely function more effectively but with a narrower scope than today's desktop computers and be much easier to use. Computing and networking will be taken for granted as a part of the school environment. Teacher workstations will exchange information with low-cost student devices and with school- or district-level servers. Complex, memory-hogging programs will reside on servers and be pulled down to local computers or appliances as needed.

PATTERNS OF USE: DISTRIBUTED, COLLABORATIVE SYSTEMS

In the fall of 1998, CILT brought together a group of learning researchers and technology designers to brainstorm about technologies that education could use in the computing environments described in the preceding section (CILT, 1998). The fictional scenario in Figure 8.1 is based on some ideas they generated.

Several points should be made about technology use in this scenario. First, the hypothetical MathPad is designed explicitly for educational use. Although some of its capabilities are similar to those of technologies developed for business and general markets, others—such as its ruggedness and the ability to communicate from a central source (i.e., a teacher workstation) to many devices—are explicitly tailored for classroom needs. Second, students move back and forth across a range of equipment, depending on their needs. A combination of small quantities of expensive equipment (say, one or several central workstations for each classroom and a top-notch display facility) and large numbers of inexpensive devices (such as the MathPads themselves) improves the performance per dollar of technology investment over today's record. Different pieces of equipment "talk" to each other—compatibility issues have been overcome—and students use technology to talk to each other and to other classrooms.

From a pedagogical standpoint, educational technologies increase classroom communication—with the teacher unobtrusively checking student comprehension and time requirements. Connections to a larger world are second nature. The students' data and analyses are part of much larger projects with real stakeholders. Students are expected to contribute to, as well as learn from, a community of investigators.

EQUITY: NARROWING THE DIGITAL DIVIDE

Low-cost educational devices and network computers increase the likelihood that technology access can be more equitable across different sectors of our society. If federal, state, and local governments keep pressuring for equitable access and competition and price decreases prevail, prospects for increasing equity in infrastructure look good. A necessary piece of this solution is a client-server architecture linking the low-cost devices to a powerful server.

A much harder problem will be providing equity in educational use. Research has repeatedly shown that technologies per se are of limited use if teachers do not know how to make them a worthwhile part of high-quality instruction (U.S. Office of Technology Assessment, 1995). I believe the capability of schools serving predominantly low-income students to attract and support the best teaching talent is less certain than the prospects for obtaining needed equipment and connections.

Rethinking what and how one teaches, and applying new approaches in everyday practice, are hard work. We are asking teachers

FIGURE 8.1

A SCENARIO FOR TOMORROW'S USE OF
LEARNING TECHNOLOGIES

Relatively little new technical capability would be needed beyond today's palm-top computing devices to develop specialized educational devices geared to different subject and skill areas. A "MathPad," for example, would be an educational appliance, smaller and lighter than today's handheld palm-tops, with capability for stylus input, display, and mathematical calculations and graphing. Such devices would also feature infrared transfer capabilities, permitting the beaming of data and applications between palm-tops or between a palm-top and another computing device, such as a teacher workstation, a "share board" display system, or sensors built into the environment. We can already connect palm-tops to "smart probes," which measure variables such as motion, light, heat, or pH.

Middle school students in a class on environmental science are monitoring local haze using sun photometers to measure attenuation of sunlight caused by haze, smoke, and smog. Seven small groups of students go out to their school's softball field at noon to take their photometer readings. Each group takes a reading, which is automatically sent to their MathPad. Their MathPads contain a template for displaying the readings of all seven groups, and they obtain these by beaming their readings to each other.

After returning to the classroom, one group beams the filled-in template for today's reading to the class's share board computer, and the teacher begins a class review and discussion of the data shown on the wall-size display. He uses the scatterplot of the student data as a point of departure for discussing the distinction between accuracy and precision.

One of the groups has a highly disparate reading, and the teacher asks the group members to check the calibration on their photometer. The teacher takes the opportunity to introduce the statistical concept of an "outlier" and has the students compute a class mean with and without the disparate reading. In the end, the class decides to throw out that group's data before averaging the other readings to obtain the class mean, which they will report to an online Haze project.

The teacher then introduces the next assignment: Students are to work in small groups on an investigation using haze data both from their own school and from other schools. Controlling the display from his workstation, the teacher accesses the online Haze project database and reminds students of the database contents and strategies for navigating the database Web site. To make sure they know how to read the data tables, he asks several comprehension ques-

FIGURE 8.1 *(continued)*
A SCENARIO FOR TOMORROW'S USE OF
LEARNING TECHNOLOGIES

tions, having students submit their answers over their individual MathPads and checking their responses on his workstation to make sure no one is lost. He directs students to go back to their small groups and suggests that each group spend some time exploring the data archive before deciding on a research question for a project that will take them several weeks. It will culminate in presentations for their class and submission of their work to the Haze project's online student journal.

One group decides to look at the haze readings for their school over the past two years. The online data archive makes possible the retrieval of not only data they have collected themselves but also information collected by students taking the same course in prior semesters. Piecing the data together, they decide to graph 24 months' worth of data on a MathPad. They notice that in May of the prior year, students at their school reported high readings. One student argues that these readings probably reflect seasonal patterns in the data, with higher readings over the summer. Several others think that the readings were unusually high even given that variation. This discussion leads them to comparing their school's data set to those of other sites who collected data over the same period. Students in the group each pick a different site and create a 24-month graph on their individual MathPads to compare to their school's data. The teacher is ready to move on to the next activity, but first asks the small groups to use the time slider on their MathPads to indicate how much more time they need to complete formulation of their research question. The time requests are transmitted to the teacher workstation, where he can see that five minutes would be adequate for almost everyone.

In subsequent weeks, the groups continue to work on their haze investigations. The group looking at the prior year's high readings for May contacts another school in their area that also had a high reading. After sending e-mail to the environmental science teacher at the other school, they arrange for an online discussion with her Earth science students. In real-time Internet conferences with these students, they are able to jointly look at and manipulate graphs of the two data sets. When a student at one school uses a stylus to circle an extreme reading on a graph, students at the other school can see the same data point circled on the graph on their own computer screen. Speech and gesture flow naturally as they debate the meaning of the readings.

to make massive changes and cannot expect a single day of staff development or a weeklong summer institute to bring about such transformations. Network technology has promise for supporting more continuous, collaborative forms of teacher professional development (Schlager & Schank, 1997); major changes, however, in how we attract, train, retain, and structure teachers' work for our most needy schools will also be needed if we are to surmount the digital divide.

ASSESSMENT: TECHNOLOGY SUPPORTS FOR MEASURING UNDERSTANDING

If one assumes that future uses of technology will be influenced by the desire to have students perform tasks in school that are similar to technology uses in workplace settings, one can logically predict that pressure for new kinds of assessments that better reflect these priorities will increase. At the same time, learning researchers are calling for assessments that measure students' deep understanding of content and their ability to appropriately transfer what they learn in one context to other situations (Bransford & Schwartz, in press). This kind of assessment is very demanding. Although psychological studies provide carefully sequenced performance tasks and clinical questioning techniques, such procedures are time-consuming and difficult to duplicate in a classroom of 30 students (let alone in five or six such classes a day). And ideally, such assessment should be done more than just at the end of a unit. To guide teachers, assessment should also occur at the beginning and at multiple points along the way.

The likelihood that teachers would have the capacity to perform the kind of individualized, deep assessment that learning theorists advocate without technological supports is small. One of the CILT research themes is the use of new technology capabilities to support better classroom assessments (see online at http://cilt.org).

Extensive capabilities for automatically recording the steps in product development and the progression of student thinking over time are already available for students who work online. These records have potential as a major resource for improved classroom assessments.

Several of today's systems give an idea of the capabilities likely to become more commonplace. Knowledge Forum (formerly Computer-Supported Intentional Learning Environments [CSILE]), for example, provides a communal database with both text and graphics capabilities.

Students create text and graphics "notes" about the subject under study, labeling their contributions in terms of the kind of thinking represented—for example, hypotheses ("my theory for now . . .") or questions ("what we need to learn about next . . ."). Other students can search and comment on these notes. With teacher support, students can use Knowledge Forum to share information and feedback with each other, accumulate knowledge over time, and practice collaboration skills. The communal hypermedia database provides a record of students' thoughts and electronic conversations (Scardamalia & Bereiter, 1996). Teachers can browse the database to review their students' emerging understanding of key concepts as well as their interaction skills (Means & Olson, 1999).

SpeakEasy, a component of the Knowledge Integration Environment (KIE) developed by Marcia Linn and her colleagues at the University of California, Berkeley, supports threaded conversations over the Internet as collaborators work together on science investigations (Linn, Bell, & Hsi, 1998). Students categorize their entries into classifications such as issues, evidence, and explanations.

Several research-based, online learning environments provide templates to record specific kinds of student work; some include rubrics and forms that teachers can use to evaluate these digital records. Inquiry Scorer, for example, is a piece of software developed by John Frederiksen and Barbara White (Frederiksen & White, 1998) to help teachers assess science inquiry skills demonstrated through student project activities. The system presents a teacher with key elements to rate, a rating scale, and a place to input a narrative rationale for the score. Similarly, the electronic Design Diary developed for the Learning by Design project at Georgia Tech University includes criteria that teachers (or students) can use in evaluating the quality of student designs.

These and other systems have promise for providing teachers with a window into their students' thought processes and into student growth in understanding and skill over time. Their chief deficiency from a practical standpoint is the amount of time required to review the digital record. As researchers hone in on important features of student work and developers provide software tools for automated aggregation of these features (e.g., over time for individual students or across all students in a group or in a class at one point in time), the potential for improving classroom assessment practice will be much higher.

Researchers are currently designing and developing tools to digest all the information we can capture about student online work and to boil that information down to a manageable number of indexes or summaries that teachers can use in making instructional decisions.

Ron Stevens at the UCLA School of Medicine has developed a technique and authoring shell (structured template for developing new computer-delivered problems) for presenting complex problems to students and then assessing their skills in attacking those problems. He was originally motivated by the conviction that multiple-choice items could not get at the diagnostic skills he was trying to foster in his microbiology and immunology students. Stevens presents online patient simulations: Students are given a case history, the option to run certain diagnostic tests and get feedback, and then the opportunity to give a diagnosis. Stevens's program, called Interactive Multi Media Exercises (IMMEX), tracks not just whether the student got the right diagnosis but also the process used to solve the problem.

The teacher can look at a student's performance or a summary of an entire group. "Search path maps" use color codes to represent different types of information and lines to represent the solution path the student took. A tangled line suggests that the student jumped back and forth across different types of information, with no clear direction; a single straight line shows a "shoot from the hip" guess. Analyzing IMMEX responses can help teachers diagnose where they need to concentrate further instruction. When a student fails to solve a problem, for example, the instructor can see if the student did not look at the relevant data, or in fact examined the data but did not realize their significance. Number values can be assigned to different solution patterns.

More than 270 teachers in southern California elementary, middle, and secondary schools have received training on how to author and use IMMEX problem sets. Stevens acknowledges that the current IMMEX analysis output is still somewhat difficult for teachers to read and interpret. His current efforts focus on experimenting with using neural networks to recognize patterns of more and less successful problem-solving behavior. Such automated pattern recognition could both ease the interpretation burden and provide students with "hints" as they are in the process of working on the problem.

In addition to making possible higher-quality assessments within classrooms, technology tools for capturing and scoring student work may also increase the likelihood that in-class assessments and large-scale assessments can be more meaningfully linked. In the past, using teacher-developed assessments for high-stakes decision making has been unattractive not only because of the differing content taught by different teachers but also because many teacher-developed tests lacked the measurement qualities needed for assessments to be used as a basis for decision making. On the other hand, more time will always be available for classroom-based assessments embedded in instruction than for stand-alone, externally imposed tests. In the future, technology may make it possible for teachers to pull down professionally developed, teacher-tested assessment modules from a network server and in turn to contribute their students' responses to large-scale databases of student work. On-going projects at SRI have demonstrated the feasibility of such an item bank and of online training for teachers on how to apply specific rubrics to student performance tasks (Quellmalz & Schank, 1998). Although complex issues of copyright, security, and psychometric quality will have to be resolved, the union of technology and assessment may indeed provide a powerful catalyst for improving education.

CONCLUSION

It has been argued that a time traveler from 1900 would be baffled by the operations in today's automobile assembly plant or video arcade but would feel quite at home in a typical American classroom. I acknowledge that our education system has been remarkably impervious to radical change. But I believe that the wave of new technology affecting every aspect of our society simply cannot be ignored. In one form or another, new technologies will find their way into U.S. schools.

The predictions I have made for the next century are quite conservative on the technology side. In part, this view reflects the limitations of my own vision, but it also reflects my knowledge that common practice today lags far behind what is technically feasible. Accordingly, I have projected a mere extension of technical capabilities available today. The more optimistic facets of my vision of tomorrow surround preparing teachers with the skills to make good use of the technological tools that will be available. I have also assumed that education will make a commitment to developing classroom assessment practices that better support student learning.

One could easily paint a different picture of the future. The increasing availability of Web-based alternative learning resources coincides with a decline in public confidence in the efficacy of schools, and increasing interest in alternatives, such as voucher programs, charter schools, and home schooling. Quite likely, over the next two decades, public schools are going to have to compete for resources and for students—not only with private schools and home-schooling options—but also with Internet-based alternatives. I personally doubt that brick-and-mortar schools will become obsolete (if only for their utility as places for children to spend their time), but they will become one among many kinds of organizations offering formally organized, distributed learning. The increased pressure of competition should stimulate schools to improve. Schools incorporating the technology of the future can offer the best combination of role models, socialization, and morale building from face-to-face instruction; increased participation in systems of distributed learning that engage broader communities; learning-enhancing representations of concepts and data; restructuring of teaching and learning roles; and more meaningful assessment practices.

My vision for educational technology use depends critically on improvements in teacher preparation and professional development and in assessment practices, topics for two other chapters in this yearbook. The vision I have laid out is technically feasible—the question is whether our education system—and society—will support and promote the policies and practices needed to make it a reality.

Endnote

1. Mosaic is an Internet information browser developed at the National Center for Supercomputing Applications at the University of Illinois in Urbana-Champaign. Mosaic was a major breakthrough because it permitted using the Internet—previously limited largely to the exchange of text—to exchange text, graphics, animation, and digitized video. These capabilities made it possible to create Web pages that someone using any kind of computer (with an adequate Internet connection) could explore and interact

with through a point-and-click interface rather than through arcane computer commands.

References

Becker, H. J. (1985). How schools use microcomputers: Results from a national survey. In M. Chen & W. Paisley (Eds.), *Children and microcomputers: Research on the newest medium* (pp. 87–107). Beverly Hills, CA: Sage.

Becker, H. J. (1990, April). *Computer use in United States schools: 1989. An initial report of U.S. participation in the I.E.A. computers in education survey.* Paper presented at the annual meeting of the American Educational Research Association, Boston.

Becker, H. J. (1999). *Internet use by teachers: Conditions of professional use and teacher-directed student use.* Irvine, CA: Center for Research on Information Technology and Organizations.

Becker, H. J., & Anderson, R. (1998). Teaching, Learning, and Computing: 1998 [Online]. Available: http://www.crito.uci.edu/tlc/html/tlc_home.html

Becker, H. J., & Sterling, C. W. (1987). Equity in school computer use: National data and neglected considerations. *Journal of Educational Computing Research, 3*(3), 289–311.

Bransford, J. D., Brown, A. L., & Cocking, R. R. (Eds.). (1999). *How people learn: Brain, mind, experience, and school.* Washington, DC: National Academy Press.

Bransford, J. D., & Schwartz, D. L. (in press). Rethinking transfer: A simple proposal with interesting implications. To appear in A. Iran-Nejad & P. D. Pearson (Eds.), *Review of Research in Education.* Washington, DC: American Educational Research Association.

Braun, L. (1990). *VISION: TEST (technologically enriched schools of tomorrow).* Eugene, OR: International Society for Technology in Education.

Center for Innovative Learning Technologies. (1998). *Datagotchi deep dive.* Menlo Park, CA: SRI International.

Coburn, P., Kelman, P., Roberts, N., Snyder, T. F. F., Watt, D. H., & Weiner, C. (1982). *Practical guide to computers in education.* Reading, MA: Addison-Wesley.

Cohen, D. K. (1988). Educational technology and school organization. In R. S. Nickerson & P. P. Zodhiates (Eds.), *Technology in education: Looking toward 2020* (pp. 231–264). Hillsdale, NJ: Lawrence Erlbaum.

Collins, A., Brown, J. S., & Newman, S. E. (1989). Cognitive apprenticeship: Teaching the craft of reading, writing, and mathematics. In L. B. Resnick (Ed.), *Knowing, learning, and instruction: Essays in honor of Robert Glaser* (pp. 453–494). Hillsdale, NJ: Lawrence Erlbaum.

Cuban, L., & Kirkpatrick, H. (1998). Computers make kids smarter—Right? *Technos, 7*(2), 26–31.

DeVillar, R. A., & Faltis, C. J. (1991). *Computers and cultural diversity: Restructuring for school success.* Albany, NY: State University of New York Press.

Frederiksen, J. R., & White, B. Y. (1998, April). *Assessing students' scientific inquiry: Enhancing validity by creating multiple warrants for performance standards.* Paper presented at the annual meeting of the American Educational Research Association, San Diego, CA.

Healy, J. (1998). *Failure to connect: How computers affect our children's minds—for better and worse.* New York: Simon and Schuster.

Koedinger, K. R., Anderson, J. R., Hadley, W. H., & Mark, M. A. (1997). Intelligent tutoring goes to school in the big city. *International Journal of Artificial Intelligence in Education, 8,* 30–43.

Koedinger, K. R., & Sueker, E. L. F. (1996). PAT goes to college: Evaluating a cognitive tutor for developmental mathematics. In *Proceedings of the Second International Conference on the Learning Sciences* (pp. 180–187). Charlottesville, VA: Association for the Advancement of Computing in Education.

Kulik, J., Kulik, C. L. C., & Bangert-Drowns, R. L. (1985). Effectiveness of computer-based education in elementary schools. *Computers in Human Behavior, 1,* 59–74.

Linn, M. C., Bell, P., & Hsi, S. (1998). Using the Internet to enhance student understanding of science: The knowledge integration environment. *Interactive Learning Environments, 6*(1–2), 4–38.

Mageau, T. (1990). ILS: Its new role in schools. *Electronic Learning, 10,* 22–32.

Mageau, T. (1991). Computer-Using teachers. *Agenda, 1,* 51.

Means, B. (1998, April). *Models and prospects for bringing technology-supported educational reform to scale.* Paper presented at the annual meeting of the American Educational Research Association, San Diego, CA.

Means, B., Blando, J., Olson, K., Middleton, T., Morocco, C. C., Remz, A. R., & Zorfass, J. (1993). *Using technology to support education reform.* Washington, DC: U.S. Government Printing Office.

Means, B., & Coleman, E. (in press). Technology supports for student participation in science investigations. To appear in M. J. Jacobson & R. B. Kozma (Eds.), *Learning the sciences of the 21st century: Theory, research, and the design of advanced technology learning environments.* Englewood Cliffs, NJ: Lawrence Erlbaum.

Means, B., & Golan, S. (1998). *Transforming teaching and learning with multimedia technology.* San Jose, CA: Joint Venture: Silicon Valley Network.

Means, B., & Olson, K. (1999). Technology's role in student-centered classrooms. In H. C. Waxman & H. J. Walberg (Eds.), *New directions for teaching practice and research* (pp. 297–317). Berkeley, CA: McCutchan.

National Center for Education Statistics. (1999, February). *Internet access in public schools and classrooms: 1994–98.* [Issue Brief, NCES 99-017]. Available: http://www.nces.ed.gov/pubs99/1999017.html

Niemiec, R. P., & Walberg, H. J. (1985). Computers and achievement in the elementary schools. *Journal of Educational Computing Research, 1,* 435–440.

Norman, D. A. (1998). *The invisible computer: Why good products can fail, the personal computer is so complex, and information appliances are the solution.* Cambridge, MA: MIT Press.

Oppenheimer, T. (1997, July). The computer delusion. *The Atlantic Monthly,* pp. 45–62.

President's Committee of Advisors on Science and Technology, Panel on Educational Technology. (1997, March). *Report to the President on the use of technology to strengthen K–12 education in the United States* [On-line]. Available: http://www.whitehouse.gov/WH/EOP/OSTP/NSTC/PCAST/ k-12ed.html

Quellmalz, E. S., & Schank, P. (1998, April). *Performance assessment links in science (PALS): Online, interactive resources.* Paper presented at the annual meeting of the American Educational Research Association, San Diego, CA.

Roschelle, J., Pea, R., Hoadley, C., Gordin, D., & Means, B. (in press). Changing how and what children learn in school with computer-based technologies. To appear in *The Future of Children,* special issue on Children and Computer Technology. Los Altos, CA: David and Lucile Packard Foundation.

Samson, G. E., Niemiec, R., Weinstein, T., & Walberg, H. J. (1986). Effects of computer-based instruction on secondary school achievement: A quantitative synthesis. *AEDS Journal,* pp. 312–326.

Scardamalia, M., & Bereiter, C. (1996, November). Engaging students in a knowledge society. *Educational Leadership, 54*(3), 6–10.

Schlager, M. S., & Schank, P. (1997). Tapped in: A new online teacher community concept for the next generation of Internet technology. In R. Hall, N. Miyake, & N. Enyedy (Eds.), *Proceedings of the Second International Conference on Computer Support for Collaborative Learning* (pp. 231–240). Hillsdale, NJ: Lawrence Erlbaum.

Soloway, E. (1998). No one is making money in educational software. *Communications of the ACM, 41*(2), 11–15.

Stolls, C. (1995). *Silicon snake oil: Second thoughts on the information highway.* New York: Doubleday.

Sutton, R. E. (1991). Equity and computers in the schools: A decade of research. *Review of Educational Research, 61*, 475–503.

Technology Counts. (1998, November). [Special issue]. *Education Week,* pp. 1–114.

U.S. Office of Technology Assessment. (1995). *Teachers and technology: Making the connection* (OTA-EHR-616). Washington, DC: U.S. Government Printing Office.

Wenglinsky, H. (1998). *Does it compute? The relationship between educational technology and student achievement in mathematics.* Princeton, NJ: Educational Testing Service.

White, B. Y., & Frederiksen, J. R. (1998). Inquiry, modeling, and metacognition: Making science accessible to all students. *Cognition and Science, 16,* 90–91.

9

Progressive Education in the 21st Century: A Work in Progress

Deborah Meier

What is the future of progressive school reform? Will more schools in the 21st century be like the small, pioneering alternative schools of our own time? Or will the few such schools we have be decimated by politically driven standardized reforms? As one who for 30 years has been involved in progressive education, I have been asked to look back on my experiences and think about future prospects.

I took for granted, when I began working in schools in the mid-60s, that I was in the "progressive" (democratic and egalitarian) camp. The teachers I identified with were struggling with some of the same issues I was, and looking for answers in the writings of Sylvia Ashton-Warner, John Holt, Jonathan Kozol, and Herb Kohl. We looked to places like Lillian Weber's Workshop Center at City College and Bank Street College of Education, and to the works of John Dewey, Jean Piaget, and Lucy Sprague Mitchell.

Copyright © 2000 by Deborah Meier.

These were the traditions I inherited intellectually and morally when I had the good fortune in 1974 to start "my own" public school in East Harlem. Along with colleagues I had met over the years, we began our soon-to-be-famous venture, the Central Park East schools. We began with one, then two, and finally three small elementary schools and one secondary school, all located in East Harlem. Together they helped launch a wider concept of public school choice that spread throughout the city during the following two decades. Over the next 25 years, I was directly involved in founding more than a dozen public secondary schools, and advising hundreds of others in New York City and elsewhere. As a result of our work and that of our counterparts in other cities, more urban public schools than ever before have dared to address the ideas of John Dewey and Jean Piaget.

As we enter a new century, I am proud of what has been accomplished, yet deeply worried about the prospects facing these schools. As Charles Dickens said, it is the best of times but also the worst.

COMPETING VISIONS OF PROGRESS

When my friends and I began the Central Park East schools, we soon found that we had rather strong differences of opinion. We were less conscious, though, of a completely different set of views that other reformers held equally as ardently. These reformers also saw themselves rooted in progressive tradition—but in a different aspect of that tradition than we drew upon.

In public education, as in politics, the term "progress" has conveyed vastly different values and images of what the world could and should be like. So when I ponder the future of progressive education, I realize that it's endangered not merely by devotion to the status quo, the weight of bad traditions, or even greedy privatizers who see schools as a new market for profits, but also by a notion of progressivism different from mine.

It's a contest clearly spelled out at the time of our nation's founding, between those who dreamt of an orderly and expertly driven society in the hands of the propertied and qualified, and those who saw democracy as "boisterous, highly partisan" and full of ordinary unruly passion. One version of progress was even compatible with slavery—in fact, as Eric Foner (1998) notes in his recent book, *The Story of American Freedom*, dependent on it. Democracy, one assumed, required a ruling elite with the time, leisure, and mental capacities for reasoned and objective thought. That version left out women, non-Europeans, and in the beginning, anyone lacking a sufficiently propertied stake in society.

As the century wore on, the advocates of progress included those enamored of a whole array of ever more standardized, even robot-like practices, glamorized in various ant-colony visions of a scientifically designed utopia. Factory-like standards replaced craftsmanly standards. Efficiency—trains running on time—became the measuring rod. Communists and capitalists were often attracted by the same vision of social organization, accepting the pain and hardship it inflicted in the present as the necessary price for a golden future.

In contrast with this view was the peculiarly American concept of democracy exemplified by town meetings in New England and country life on the prairies, which embodied respect for the practical genius of ordinary people. From this tradition come our anti-aristocratic and even anti-intellectual attitudes, along with unequaled acceptance of nonconformity. We love efficiency, too, of course, but Americans have been willing to sacrifice efficiency in the name of individual rights and democratic norms. We've linked ourselves to the idea of small, contentious, and self-governing communities more than to anonymous, harmonious, and uniform ones. But we've always been of two minds.

I was startled to realize in my youth that Skinner's *Walden 2*—which pictured a society beyond concern for petty "freedom and dignity"—was considered by its author and his fans not as an Orwellian 1984 but as a positive utopia. A surprisingly large number of well-educated adults apparently saw a controlled, smoothly functioning society as preferable to democracy's confusion, waste, and contentiousness. No wonder that some advanced thinkers flirted with both fascism and communism.

HOW THE TWO VIEWS OF PROGRESS AFFECTED EDUCATION

What the 21st century may bring us is the triumph of one of these two notions of progress. Of course, in the real world, the two

213

perspectives are rarely as far apart as Orwell and Skinner were. They overlap more than we sometimes acknowledge, especially in the education of children. In schools, we borrow a little from both traditions.

John Dewey's ideas of progressive education, intended as means to a more egalitarian and democratic society, were not the only progressive ideas of his time. And even Dewey's ideas were primarily practiced in schools serving families of power and privilege: private schools, well-to-do suburban schools, and university laboratory schools. The rhetoric of Deweyan progressivism became increasingly commonplace, but its actual practice rarely extended to the rest of society.

Instead, the thrust of mass education went in another direction, also in the name of progress: toward more bureaucratic organization, the modernization of curriculum to cover more relevant topics, and expanded professional training of teachers. The increased concern for all children was interpreted to mean that there must be a place designed for every child in our public system—an obligation made possible by scientifically designed tests and carefully calibrated tracks.

The non-Deweyan reformers argued that the interests of children and society would be best (and most efficiently) served by schools where all children—regardless of ability and future destiny—could coexist under a common roof, although engaged in different studies. Such an approach meant larger schools and larger school districts, thus removing schooling from more direct family and community participation. Class, race, and other parochial biases would thus be overcome. This model of progress dominated most of the 20th century. The new modern plants with up-to-date biology labs and auto shops, organized by master schedulers into complex seven- and eight-period days, became the norm. Where once the average school had a few hundred pupils, now the norm was in the thousands. These changes, too, were called progressive.

Even in Deweyan progressive schools, once students moved to the secondary level, the emphasis shifted—the vast majority were deemed unfit for the advanced academic or intellectually demanding studies needed for the leaders of tomorrow. The greater informality between teachers and learners and the focus on experimental pedagogies, along with the empowered role of faculty, were seen as less appropriate in the upper grades, even among many of Dewey's more ardent followers. The general view was that a life of the mind, a focus on abstract ideas, and above all the respect accorded uncertainty and skepticism were not what most children needed nor what most families wanted.

This was how things were when I began teaching in the mid-60s. What changed over the next 30 years was a revolutionary commitment—at least rhetorically—to provide all children with an elite education. The avalanche of reforms that teachers, children, and parents experienced over the next 40 years came from both wings of progressivism and everything in-between, all promising that their methods could close the gap between the masses and the elite and provide a new kind of worker-citizen for the 21st century.

Dewey's egalitarian and messy vision seemed once again the possible answer to this extraordinary commitment. For the next 30 years, Dewey's ideas finally got a toehold in urban and rural schools for ordinary children. Never had there been so many public schools that Dewey would recognize as stemming from his ideas. But they had—and still have—only a toehold, and a precarious one. Mainstream reformers, like those who launched the comprehensive and consolidated school reforms of the past, had their up-to-date versions of progress, too, their well-intended efforts to close the achievement gap. Their vision lies in creating a foolproof, ever more standardized system of schooling, with each learner-worker plugged into an expertly designed program tailor-made to meet individual needs. They visualize a teacher-proof school, where centrally driven expertise coupled with strong incentives and disincentives can overcome all roadblocks—in time. The plan is becoming more feasible, its proponents argue, as technology progresses. But in the meantime, these reformers make do with less technologically sophisticated tools: a uniform curriculum; scripted teaching; massive curriculum-aligned testing; reams of printouts to shape each child's enrichment or remediation; and constant, consistent monitoring of teacher and student outcomes, all backed by strong incentives and disincentives. It's the factory-model school redesigned for 21st century workplaces—and considered the latest in progressive thinking.

And so the debate remains unsettled. Is the future envisioned by the mainstream reformers, taken to its increasingly impersonal extreme, an exciting idea or a chilling one? Is it utopia or dystopia? Does it seem enticing only because we can't imagine the possibility that Dewey's ideas could or would work for all those ordinary children our schools now encompass? Or does it appeal because democracy itself seems more illusive and elusive?

Trying to Put Dewey's Vision into Practice—
1970 to 2000

When we began the first of the Central Park East schools in 1974, New York City was retreating from a short-lived and small-scale romance with progressive innovations. Democratic progressivism was under siege because of both a post-60s backlash and a major financial crisis. It was in this context that we launched the Central Park East schools as an effort to at least keep promising innovative practices alive—such as open education and whole language. Surprisingly, to friends and foes alike, our version of progressivism continued to flourish in New York City. As I embarked in 1997 on creating a Central Park East-like school in Boston's Roxbury community, the early struggles and arguments in New York were relived once again in strikingly similar fashion. Though always cast in their idiosyncratic particulars, the big questions remained the same: How much freedom, how much choice? How much individuality and how much collectivity? Who rightly decides what in a democratic community? What evidence counts in making informed decisions? What does everyone need to know? And who should decide that?

Central Park East School was founded by a bunch of teachers who, like home schoolers in part, wanted their own one-room schoolhouse where they could "do their own thing." We were also leftovers from the '60s, kibbutzniks without a homeland searching for the ideal community. But we were also seeking a way to school all citizens to be rulers of a democratic society. We wanted to know what the rhetoric of "all men are created equal" might mean in terms of children's everyday experiences.

As we reread the works of Dewey and his followers, we found that defining progressive practice was hard—except by what it wasn't. It didn't lend itself to an idealized model. For us, such impreciseness

216

was a virtue, but also frustrating. We couldn't look up the answers. The progressive schools I knew about were the outgrowth of many histories. They could best be summed up in Jefferson's odd dictum that self-government is better than good government. In some form or other, they all rested on self-governance—but who was that self? The kids? Their families? The staff? The larger public? Because such schools involved different selves, their stories always idiosyncratic, it sometimes seemed as if nothing could be learned from them. Policymakers would complain that such ideas couldn't be put into systematic practice.

And it's true; they can't. The ideals of the progressive schools I'm talking about are not fixed. Each such school is unique, the outgrowth of a particular history, not a branch of a single divine inspiration or mental blueprint. Such schools are easier to describe than define. They are not embarrassed to be inefficient, or to be open to forms of corruption that are intrinsic to their dependence on trust and mutuality; they unblushingly acknowledge that they probably share some of the worst and best features of their local circumstances, with at least some of the contradictions that go with that fact. They hope they make room for different voices, to offer many entry points for learning. They want to be aware of other possibilities, to be respectful of differences and thus open to change. They see in such openness the best guarantee of uncovering error, and thus of getting closer to truth.

At the Central Park East schools, the play between the parties—parents, kids, teachers, and "administrator"—was always unsettled and open to negotiation. That arrangement was an intentional part of our teaching and learning experience. We never expected to finally get it just right or to get others to follow our recipe. Our schools were always works in progress.

Still, within 10 years, the original Central Park East School became a network of four similar small schools in East Harlem, which soon created a different possibility for many more inner-city public schools. Its story spread widely, and other parents and teachers demanded the right to imitate us. The Central Park East network of four schools helped create more than a hundred other schools that spread progressive ideas, each in quite different ways, throughout the city. Even the three original Central Park East schools began to look more and more different from one another—not better or worse—just different.

These kinds of progressive schools required special people, not necessarily great educators or finer human beings, but unusually tenacious political actors, who also had a stubborn and very particular educational vision. Such people were always embattled, continually being put into awkward positions, straddling fences, making compromises that undermined some of their own work, and making deals that undermined other people's work. They were always looking for a safe niche, a friendly godfather, or an ace in the hole in stressful times. They fought constantly to keep the schools small—very small—although the schools were rarely allowed to stay as small as their advocates believed they should be, which was small enough for all the adults to sit around one table and have it out as well as work it out.

These schools required faculty members who would willingly take on all roles, who imagined themselves as principal, teacher, and student, all at the same time. They looked for support from teacher unions able to see such teacher empowerment as the goal, not the enemy, of teacher unionism. Progressive schools needed families who liked the qualities that made these schools different, felt empowered by their choice, and who struggled over how much they could or should be equal partners with educators in the schools' work.

Each of these qualities ran into some no-no, sometimes a management or union rule, sometimes just accustomed practice. For every ally progressive educators made in traditional schools, they made two enemies. Other teachers and principals both envied the apparent freedom of such schools and also resented it. They would say, "Oh, I could get the same results you do if I had the same . . ." but then deny it would be a good idea to be like progressive educators.

We received both high-level support from the teacher union and petty sabotage from some local leaders who viewed the teachers in these schools as rule-breakers, class collaborators, or just plain suckers. Parents were increasingly loyal and trusting, but often annoyed at feeling left out of decisions made by empowered teachers. School districts flirted with the idea of progressive reform, tried it on a small scale, and then backed away before it became too contagious. Still, by the 1990s, the genie was out of the bottle and hard to put back in again.

BOSTON'S EXPERIMENT WITH PILOT SCHOOLS

As small schools of choice became an attractive option for strong-minded maverick teachers and parents, school systems began making provisions for them. In New York City, several different and sometimes competing networks of small schools of choice were begun by individual local districts and the high school division, aided by a substantial grant from the Annenbergs to support small school development. In Chicago, a network of small progressive schools was organized with support from Bill Ayers and Michael Klonsky's Small Schools Workshop. And in 1995, the Boston Teachers Union (BTU) negotiated an extraordinary deal with the Boston Public Schools (BPS). The Boston pilot schools committed themselves to inventing a system that would operate within the same budget and fiscal restraints (including salary schedule) as the regular school system, but with few other BPS/BTU contractual or managerial constraints. Over a three-year period, 10 Boston schools opted to explore what such freedom and flexibility would allow them to do, and how this idea could be spread to other schools. Although most of the 10 were progressive in the Deweyan sense, this perspective was not a prerequisite.

The 10 have flourished, although the documentation is not yet sufficient to demonstrate a positive correlation between their success and their freedoms. What's hardly surprising is that the BPS and BTU have been far more interested in developing a standards-driven system, which has been ratcheting up the pressure on principals, teachers, and students to produce higher test scores. The BPS and BTU saw the pilots mostly as labs in which this or that best practice might be identified and shipped out to the rest of the system. They haven't reneged on their agreement, but they haven't invested much energy in achieving the freedoms and flexibilities they originally proposed—many of which turned out to be hard to enact. Meanwhile, as the number of pilots has remained stagnant, charters in Massachusetts have become increasingly popular, and vouchers are picking up political steam.

219

THE HARD WORK OF SELF-GOVERNANCE

As the founder of one of the new pilots—Mission Hill School—I am often reminded of why the idea that propels it is powerful. Asked by a colleague from another school, "What's it like to work for Deborah Meier?" a new teacher replied that in fact she wasn't working *for* Deborah Meier but *with* her. Naturally, I enjoyed the story, even though I knew it was far too early for this notion to be truly internalized. It would take years of testing—and I would not always pass the test. But I knew by the tone of the teacher's voice what energy had been released by the mere idea behind her answer.

The "best and brightest" aptly describes people attracted to the idea of governing their own professional lives. Self-governance is even more important than higher wages, both in its attraction and its purpose. When means (self-governance) and ends (schooling for democracy) join together so neatly, hopes may become a reality. The purpose of such schools is to pass on the capacity for self-governance to its students—and such a purpose can be achieved only by adults who live it themselves.

Figuring out what the decision-making power of faculty, parents, and students ought to be in a small self-governing school is not easy. The answer is always particular to the school's mission, its particular location, the age group it serves, and more. Nineteenth century New England town meetings, after all, were rife with class biases (not to mention race and gender biases) and served some interests better than others. A school that serves the public should be responsive not only to its own students and parents but also to the public. Being a school of choice doesn't relieve it of public responsibility. For us at Mission Hill School, the problems of defining who the staff was that "governed" the school's educational decisions, and clarifying the relationships among that staff, the broader parent body (i.e., the Governing Board), and the Boston Public Schools, remain unresolved and full of potential for conflict.

We decided to forgo some of the individual classroom freedom we celebrated at the Central Park East schools. We saw this departure as a way to force us to engage in more collegiality and in more rigorous examination of our ideas and practices. We decided, for example, on the unorthodox idea of having everyone—from 5-year-olds to 14-year-olds—study the same major topics each year. This idea in turn led to greater opportunities for families and students to collaborate across age levels. But it also had its drawbacks and continues to present new challenges.

The advantage of the formal nature of the task presented to us as pilot schools in Boston, compared to the informal way we resolved such problems as merely maverick schools in New York City, is that the more formal environment forces us to confront these issues publicly. It means we can learn from them more easily and also spread the word about what we are learning, although I doubt we will learn that a single size fits all.

No Single Definition for "Well Educated"

The notion that "well educated" can and should have a single definition, or that a democratic institution can only be governed one way, is attractive to many people. It must be attractive, or so many wouldn't be supporting the latest standards-driven reforms. But such single-minded thinking has downsides that have been curiously ignored by too many people. For one thing, there actually happens to be more than one valid view of the well-educated person (as there is more than one valid definition of a good democracy). To ignore this fact means only that we are deceiving ourselves, for which we will later pay a price. Permitting any central body to do all the defining lessens the power of local communities to decide important things, leaving them with power only over trivial things, which reduces both communal and professional responsibility. Finally, it leads to hiding rather than high-lighting differences. Mission Hill School, for example, has much to learn from Central Park East School (and vice versa) because we have not followed the same route on issues of governance or curriculum.

The idea that "well educated" has only one definition is not only essentially false, but also easily leads to the corollary notion that if one can define it, one can measure it. Such thinking in turn leads to cen-trally designed and scored instruments. Teachers and students can thus be centrally monitored, kept to task. Such tests, proponents hope, will not merely sort and differentiate (although they inevitably will do that, too), but also motivate through a system of rewards and punishments. Fearful that teachers will "corrupt" the standards because they know their students well and are subjectively concerned for their future, testing advocates promise a high degree of objective and mechanical precision. They promise to substitute for the judgment of those closest and most involved the judgments of those who don't know the kids at all. Fallible and corruptible human judgment is thus increasingly replaced by the expertise of committees of nameless experts shaped by centralized hired hands (e.g., testing organizations and curriculum designers), with tight rubrics that eliminate the potential for scorer bias (or experience). In the name of test reliability, we reduce scorers to the status of machines. In the name of equality and fairness, we remove the human touch entirely. But think of what has been lost! Just imagine the real-life reliability of a movie rating system that demanded psychometric reliability—where all critics must agree on a common rubric and arrive at a common judgment.

No Substitute for Democracy

Are small schools The Answer, then? That depends. Small schools are attractive for varied reasons. For some, the schools' capacity to use their collective internal intelligence, or to develop their own schemes and designs, or to understand the minds of their students and their communities, draws people. For others, though, the appeal is different. Some see small schools merely as better ways to collectively implement centralized directives and designs. Still others like the idea of close-knit, segregated enclaves. After all, the small town is as likely to squeeze out dissent, stifle growth, and compel conformity as it is to encourage growth and treasure diversity.

If the organizing intelligence always comes from afar, and if the small community serves only as a locus for compliance, small size is of limited value. As long as a mentality of disrespect for ordinary teachers and families exists, and as long as children are viewed mostly as products ready to be filled and shaped by others, resisting the attraction of a central system will be hard. In the absence of respect for the people closest to the children, one could logically suggest that what's needed are teacher-proof programs backed by teacher-proof rewards and sanctions.

SCIENCE IN DEWEY'S DAY AND IN OURS

It's a long leap from such standardized, teacher-proof schools to the Dewey School and other famous progressive schools of the past century. In their thoughtful book about the Dewey School, the Mayhews (Mayhew & Edwards, 1936) worried whether such a school required too much of its adults—in terms of expertise, thoughtfulness, and collaboration. The Dewey School had, of course, the good fortune to be located in the middle of a great educational institution, the University of Chicago. But with all their resources, Dewey and his colleagues were dismayed at the vastness of the task. They wondered if a normal day had enough hours to construct together the kind of community that children needed to be properly educated to become citizens of a complex modern state. They just didn't see an alternative. They thought all schools should be organized to make more time and experts available. The Dewey School was not merely a collection of individuals or even classrooms, but a vibrant community of young and old engaged in an intellectually exciting project that required constant vision and revision. Steeped in a conception of science that was always experimental and tentative, Dewey's form of progressivism involved tinkering, rejecting either/ors. It was hard to capture in a recipe, hard to "prove."

Unfortunately, in current educational research, the dominant notion of science is not Dewey's. We are confronted instead by a science that seeks to reduce complicated ideas to formats that can be measured and controlled in pseudoscientific experiments. This version of science, with its pre- and post-tests of effectiveness, can at best produce citizens who cope with newness and complexity by similar reductionism; they seek sequential before-after causal coherence that papers over the bewildering varieties of experience that real children, real teachers, and in the end, real citizens could bring to solving real problems. By pretending to be able to reduce the causes of the Civil War to three, the advance of civilization to a single time line, and the complexity of all the "we's" and "they's" who inhabit our diverse communities to a watered-down commonality, such a simplistic approach only adds to ignorance, confusion, and finally indifference.

Finding Time for Democracy

We adults at Mission Hill School disagree about many things: what's age appropriate, which books all students should read, and how to word our topics of study. These serious disagreements reflect not only political and religious differences but also our different experiences, expressed in language that betrays our class and racial backgrounds. We want the disagreements to surface, because having access to this broader view makes us better teachers. We become more aware of how certain stories might be heard by others and how our experiences may not mirror those of all our students and their families. That the staff be "diverse" is insufficient—or that we hear from the even greater diversity of our families. What is more critical is that we explore that diversity and help it work in our favor as good educators. Such exploration is tricky because it's likely to lead to serious misunderstandings. Mentioning each other's race or religion can seem enlightened or insulting, respectful or condescending. Even the terms we use—Jew or Hebrew; black, African American, or colored—can lead to offense. Jokes or particular words (e.g., "niggardly") can have unexpected and unsuspected consequences. Dislodging assumptions of racism that stem from such well-intended dialogue is hard. It has to be slow and steady, not done in a rush. It needs to take place around that one table I referred to earlier, where no one can hide and everyone is heard. Of course, this work makes such school-family conversations difficult and time-consuming.

But who has enough time? Our type of democracy takes more time, as the Mayhews reported 50 years ago, than we think we have! At Mission Hill School, we thought we could manage time; all the teachers who applied agreed to commit five extra hours a week, when kids would not be at school, for collective talk—above and beyond the time needed for marking children's papers, fixing up the classroom, and calling families at home. They also agreed to give several weeks during the summer and at least one winter retreat. But even that commitment isn't enough, and not because the faculty isn't willing to give more. The problem is that each day has only 24 hours. Some tasks are not collective, and some ideas take a long, long time to work through. And we have personal lives as well; we belong to other communities. Without these other ties, we wouldn't be as useful to kids.

So we struggle with the time we have. We refuse to give up in favor of more standardized solutions. Experience and study reinforce our belief that the more we standardize our forms of schooling and ways of assessing our work, the more the results will be stark and class-ridden, imbedding existing rank-order inequities deeper into our culture.

MEASURING SUCCESS

We have given up—reluctantly—the notion that we can romantically just let freedom ring. In short, there's a case to be made for state intervention, for outsiders demanding that we defend our practice publicly with strong documentation and credible evidence. We ask only that public officials allow for differing values, give room for our students' special gifts, and remember that their lives are far longer than even our now-prolonged school year. The trajectory of their lives requires forms of perseverance, internal drive, energy, and conviction—plus luck—before we can know where the arrow will land. This approach suggests forms of documentation and evidence gathering that follow the life and work of students over time. We recognize that such evidence is complicated to gather and hard to communicate to the public; it doesn't fit neatly into charts, graphs, and numerical rankings.

Using this long-range version of accountability has enabled schools like Central Park East to better assess their impact on young people's lives. These schools have gathered longitudinal data—both statistical and anecdotal—that provide a way of demonstrating success that test scores can never give us. The gathered evidence demonstrates that these schools have had a particularly positive effect on the least likely candidates, dramatically reducing, if not closing, the gap between rich and poor. In the crassest statistical and fiscal terms, such schools are not only successful, but they have also saved taxpayers' money. But the proof comes from a different kind of evidence—counting cost per graduate (not cost per student), college and career success, and surveys and interviews with students and their families 10 years or more later regarding other quality-of-life issues.

Two factors that made an obvious difference were size and scale. Remember that multi-age schools with fewer than 50 pupils were once the norm; at our schools, we were lucky to stay under 400. We learned that small schools could be located economically within other institutions (e.g., museums, libraries, town halls, and zoos); that we could develop student and family-driven choice between small nearby schools, thus reducing the cost of travel; and that all these could be entirely public.

We showed that schools—ordinary, regular public schools—could be trusted to exercise greater power over their own resources. They could select teachers committed to the school ideals and create assistant teaching and apprenticeship positions for people entering the profession. With a fairer distribution of resources, they could create summer experiences, Saturday schools, and other expensive supplementary programs that play such a prominent role in the lives of the well-to-do.

We also discovered that greater public and parent accessibility to schools was possible under the most adverse circumstances. Even in the South Bronx, the new small schools have astounding parent participation. In all our schools, we developed ways for families, staff, and the public to offer second opinions about the school's work and its students. Experts in many fields, as well as family members, were invited to participate in such evaluations.

Nurturing Democracy

If we are to make use of what was known in Dewey's day and what we know even better today about how the human species best learns, we will have to throw away the mistaken notion of the ant colony—the smoothly functioning factory where everything is done according to plan. We need to replace it with the ideal of a messy, rambunctious community, with multiple demands and complicated trade-offs. Such a school will have to be capable of remaking itself almost daily and still provide for sufficient stability, routine, ritual, and shared ethos. Impossible? Of course. It will veer too far one way or the other at different times in its history and have to shift focus and find a new balance. Camps for more order and others for more messiness will form. Endlessly. Which, if they are not merely being reactive, will take time to right themselves. If we aren't all required to follow the same fads, we will probably learn more from our differences than we learned in the past, when schools thoughtlessly adopted and later threw out innovations to conform to the latest wave.

I am convinced that small, democratic schools are the best way to nurture two indispensable traits of a democratic society: a high degree of tolerance for others—in fact more than tolerance, genuine empathy—and a high degree of tolerance for uncertainty, ambiguity, and puzzlement—indeed, enjoyment of them. Not quite a family, but closer to our definition of family than factory, such schools will demand much of their members, have a sustaining and relentless sense of purpose and coherence, and also be ready to reconsider even their own core beliefs. These schools will exhaust us but never burn us out.

Our schools must belong to their "publics." In the 1920s, the United States had over 200,000 school boards, with a million and a half school board members. Each board member knew intimately the small schools he oversaw. Schools, which were then less important in most citizens' lives, were nevertheless everyone's business. Today, with a citizenry nearly twice as large, with far higher percentages of our youth attending school for longer hours and years, and with schools playing a far larger role in determining students' future lives, less than 20,000 school boards exist, with only a few hundred thousand school board members. Each board member would be hard pressed to claim she had even been inside all the schools she superintends, much less to know the parents and children in her schools. The Central Park East and Mission Hill schools, in contrast, have their own school boards, although not always with any real legal powers, who are responsible to their own constituencies.

We need to rebuild publics for our schools, and they should consist of more than just the families of those who attend them. Whatever is done to increase participation will strengthen the ideal of democracy, without which our far-from-ideal democracy cannot survive. Surely, a democracy in which less than half its members see themselves as making enough difference to bother to vote is endangered. That lack of belief in one's capacity to influence the world—not our economic ups and downs—is what should propel us school people to accept some responsibility in the next century. That's what 30 years of working in small powerful schools has shown me: We can make a difference; we can alter the odds.

No Alternative to Democracy

Democracy in schooling, as in other aspects of life, is imperfect. To decide matters of judicial life and death, we rely—sometimes uneasily—upon the judgment of a jury of our peers. For matters of political life and death, we defer to our fellow voters, misinformed and miseducated though they may be. We accept this process not because we are naively trusting but because, like Winston Churchill, we know that however flawed democratic institutions may be in both theory and practice, the alternatives are worse. Self-governance is not bound to turn out well. But governance without it is bound to turn out badly.

References

Foner, E. (1998). *The story of American freedom*. New York: W. W. Norton.

Mayhew, K. C., & Edwards, A. C. (1936). *The Dewey School*. New York, London: D. Appleton-Century.

About the Editor

Ron Brandt is an author and consultant on education. He was formerly Executive Editor of *Educational Leadership* and other publications of the Association for Supervision and Curriculum Development. He is a commentator on school improvement and reform, and is especially interested in the use of knowledge from cognitive research and neuroscience to improve school learning. His most recent books are *Powerful Learning* and *Assessing Student Learning: New Rules, New Realities.* Brandt writes a monthly column for *Leadership News,* published by the American Association of School Administrators. In 1996, he was named to the EdPress Hall of Fame for his contributions to education publishing. In 1997, he was honored by the National Staff Development Council for lifetime contributions to staff development. Address: 1104 Woodcliff Drive, Alexandria, VA 22308-1058. Phone: 703-765-4779. Fax: 703-765-8038. E-mail: ronbrandt@erols.com

About the Authors

Elliott Asp is Director of Assessment for Douglas County Schools in Castle Rock, Colorado. He has been a classroom teacher, curriculum developer, university professor, and an administrator at the building and district levels. He has contributed to books and professional journals on a wide variety of subjects. Asp is currently a member of the Standards and Assessment Development and Implementation Council and the Commissioner of Education's Assessment Management Team. He was formerly Curriculum and Assessment Specialist with Littleton Public Schools in Colorado and has also served as Director of the Colorado Assessment Consortium. Address: Douglas County Schools,

620 Wilcox Street, Castle Rock, CO 80104. Phone: 303-814-5278. Fax: 303-814-5309. E-mail: Elliott_Asp@ceo. cudenver.edu

James A. Banks is Professor and Director of the Center for Multicultural Education at the University of Washington, Seattle. He is a past President of the American Educational Research Association and a past President of the National Council for the Social Studies. Banks is a specialist in social studies education and in multicultural education, and has written many articles and books in these fields. His books include *Teaching Strategies for Ethnic Studies* and *Multiethnic Education: Theory and Practice.* He is the editor of the *Handbook of Research on Multicultural Education* and the Multicultural Education Series of books published by Teachers College Press. Address: Center for Multicultural Education, University of Washington, Box 353600, Seattle, WA 98195-3600. Phone: 206-543-3386. Fax: 206-543-8439. E-mail: jbanks@u.washington.edu

Allan Glatthorn is Distinguished Research Professor in Education at East Carolina University, North Carolina, where he teaches graduate courses in curriculum and supervision. The author of 25 books in those fields, he has consulted with 100 or more school systems, helping them design curriculums. He began his teaching career in 1947 and has experienced all the curriculum trends about which he writes. Address: Speight Building, East Carolina University, Greenville, NC 27858. Phone: 252-328-6961. Fax: 252-328-4062. E-mail: aglatthorn@aol.com

Jerry Jailall is an education consultant in the Office of Education Reform for the North Carolina Department of Public Instruction. He administers the state's School Improvement Grants program, and he shares responsibility for the Comprehensive School Reform Demonstration grants program. Jailall has taught at schools in Guyana, the Bahamas, and North Carolina. He was a former tutor-lecturer at the University of Guyana. Address: Public Schools of North Carolina, State Board of Education, Department of Public Instruction, Office of Education Reform, 301 N. Wilmington Street, Raleigh, NC 27601-2825. Phone: 919-715-1821. Fax: 919-715-3539. E-mail: jjailall@dpi.state.nc.us

Ann Lieberman is Emeritus Professor from Teachers College, Columbia University. She is currently a Senior Scholar at the Carnegie Foundation for the Advancement of Teaching and a Visiting Professor at Stanford University. She served as President of the American Educational Research Association in 1992 and works in the areas of teacher leadership and development, collaborative research, networks and school-university partnerships, and the problem and prospects of creating learner-centered schools. Lieberman has written numerous books, articles, and chapters on teacher development and school change. She has coauthored several books with Lynne Miller, including *Teachers: Transforming Their World and Their Work*. Address: Carnegie Foundation for the Advancement of Teaching, 555 Middlefield Rd., Menlo Park, CA 94025. Phone: 650-566-5141. Fax: 650-494-7912. E-mail: lieberman@ carnegiefoundation.org

Robert Marzano is a Senior Fellow at Mid-continent Research for Education and Learning in Aurora, Colorado. He has developed numerous programs for K–12 education, including Dimensions of Learning and Literacy Plus. He has worked extensively in the area of standards-based education, and has coauthored a number of works on that topic, including *A Comprehensive Guide to Designing Standards-Based Districts, Schools, and Classrooms* and *Essential Knowledge: The Debate over What American Students Should Know*. Marzano has authored or coauthored numerous books, articles, and chapters on such diverse topics as reading and writing instruction, thinking skills, school effectiveness, restructuring, standards, cognition, and classroom grading. Address: McREL, 2550 S. Parker Road, Suite 500, Aurora, CO 80014. Phone: 303-632-5534. Fax: 303-337-3005. E-mail: bmarzano@mcrel.org

Barbara Means is Codirector of SRI International's Center for Technology in Learning. Her research deals with the development, implementation, and assessment of technology-enabled strategies for addressing critical issues in school reform. Her current projects include studies of technology use in urban high schools and of GLOBE, a worldwide network-based environmental science and education project. Means coleads with John Bransford the assessment research team of the Center for Innovative Learning Technologies. She recently served on the

National Academy of Sciences' Committee on Developments in the Science of Learning and is currently a member of the Academy's Board on Testing and Assessment. Address: Center for Technology in Learning, SRI International, 333 Ravenswood Avenue, Menlo Park, CA 94025. Phone: 650-859-4004. Fax: 650-859-4605. E-mail: barbara.means@sri.com

Deborah Meier is currently Principal of a new public school in Boston. Originally a kindergarten teacher, she was the founder of a network of public schools in East Harlem—the Central Park East schools, vice-chair of the Coalition of Essential Schools, and the author of *The Power of Their Ideas*. She was the recipient of a MacArthur award for her work in East Harlem, and served for three years as an Annenberg Fellow in an effort to expand the role of small, self-governing schools of choice in New York City and other urban communities. Address: Mission Hill School, 67 Alleghany Street, Roxbury, MA 02120. Phone: 617-635-6384. Fax: 617-635-6419. E-mail: dmeier@essentialschools.org

Lynne Miller is Professor of Education and Director of the Southern Maine Partnership at the University of Southern Maine. The partnership seeks to combine teacher development and school development through opportunities for conversation, action, and reflection among university and school-based educators. She was a member of the National Commission on Teaching and America's Future and is active in state and local policy discussions about teaching, learning, and assessment. Miller is author of numerous articles and chapters on teacher development and school reform, and with Ann Lieberman, has coauthored several books, including *Teachers: Their World and Their Work*. Address: College of Education and Human Development, University of Southern Maine, Bailey 221, Gorham, ME 04038. Phone: 207-780-5479. Fax: 207-228-8209. E-mail: lynnem@usm.maine.edu

David Perkins, Codirector of Harvard Project Zero, is a Senior Research Associate at the Harvard Graduate School of Education. He is the author of several books, including *Smart Schools: From Training Memories to Educating Minds* and *Outsmarting IQ: The New Science of Learnable Intelligence*. He has helped develop instructional programs and approaches for teaching understanding and thinking, including initiatives in South Africa, Israel, and Latin America. He is a former Guggenheim Fellow. Address: Project Zero, Harvard Graduate School of Education, 323 Longfellow Hall, 13 Apian Way, Cambridge, MA 02138. Phone: 617-495-4342. Fax: 617-496-4288. E-mail: David_Perkins @pz.harvard.edu

Chris Pipho is Division Director, State Relations/Clearinghouse, for the Education Commission of the States (ECS). ECS, an interstate compact headquartered in Denver, Colorado, helps state leaders improve the quality of education. Pipho began his career in education as a junior high and high school history and music teacher. He served as the curriculum coordinator for a Colorado public school district and as a high school administrator. Before joining ECS, Pipho also worked in various capacities for the Colorado Department of Education. As a nationally recognized authority on state education policy, Pipho is a frequent author and speaker on education issues. He was a major contributor to two books on school reform, " . . . *The Best of Educations*": *Reforming America's Public Schools in the 1980s* and *School Reform in 10 States*. He writes the "Stateline" column on current education issues for *Phi Delta Kappan* magazine and is a regular contributor to *Agenda* magazine. Phone: 303-299-3600. E-mail: rpipho@jeffco.k12.co.us

ASCD 1999–00
Board of Directors

Elected Members as of November 1, 1999

Executive Council

President: Joanna Choi Kalbus, Lecturer in Education, University of California at Riverside, Redlands, California

President-Elect: LeRoy Hay, Assistant Superintendent for Instruction, Wallingford Public Schools, Wallingford, Connecticut

Immediate Past President: Thomas J. Budnik, School Improvement Coordinator, Heartland Area Education Agency, Johnston, Iowa

Bettye Bobroff, Executive Director, New Mexico ASCD, Albuquerque, New Mexico

Martha Bruckner, Chair and Associate Professor, Department of Educational Administration and Supervision, University of Nebraska at Omaha, Nebraska

John Cooper, Assistant Superintendent for Instruction, Canandaigua City School District, Canandaigua, New York

Michael Dzwiniel, Teacher, Edmonton Public Schools, Alberta, Canada

Sharon Lease, Deputy State Superintendent for Public Instruction, Oklahoma State Department of Education, Oklahoma City, Oklahoma

Leon Levesque, Superintendent, Lewiston School District, Lewiston, Maine

Francine Mayfield, Director, Elementary School-Based Special Education Programs, Seigle Diagnostic Center, Las Vegas, Nevada

Andrew Tolbert, Assistant Superintendent, Pine Bluff School District, Pine Bluff, Arkansas

Robert L. Watson, High School Principal, Spearfish 40-2, Spearfish, South Dakota

Sandra K. Wegner, Associate Dean, College of Education, Southwest Missouri State University, Springfield, Missouri

Peyton Williams Jr., Deputy State Superintendent, Georgia State Department of Education, Atlanta, Georgia

Donald Young, Professor, Curriculum Research and Development Group, University of Hawaii, Honolulu, Hawaii

Members at Large

Patricia Ashcraft, Chimneyrock Elementary School, Cordova, Tennessee
Judith Dorsch Backes, Macomb Intermediate SD, Clinton Township, Michigan
Gerald L. Brown, Educational Equity Center, Region VIII, Denver, Colorado
Joanne Brunetti, Dilworth Elementary School, Salt Lake City, Utah
Cathy Bryce, Weatherford, Texas
Evelyn Chatmon, Baltimore County Public Schools, Maryland
Susan H. Copley, Peterborough Elementary School, New Hampshire
Ronald Costello, Noblesville Schools, Indiana
Francis M. Duffy, Gallaudet University, Washington, D.C.
Carol Foster, Las Vegas, Nevada
Kolene Granger, Washington County Schools, St. George, Utah
Linda A. Hoover, Shippensburg University, Pennsylvania
Lou Howell, Urbandale Community School District, Iowa
Donald Kachur, Illinois State University, Normal, Illinois
Carol Mackey, Evergreen School District, Vancouver, Washington
Patricia H. Marshall, Gheens Academy, Louisville, Kentucky
Joann Mychals, Olympia, Washington
Joanne P. Newcombe, Bridgewater State College, Massachusetts
Donna Pagé, Sandy Hook Elementary School, Connecticut
Carol Renner, Kearney Public Schools, Nebraska
Mary Ann Reynolds, Saint James, Houston, Texas
Sarah Booth Riss, Riverview Gardens School District, St. Louis, Missouri
Yvonne Ryans, Marysville School District, Washington
Lucia V. Sebastian, Williamsburg, Virginia
Wayne Starnes, Dayton Independent Schools, Kentucky
Deborah Hasselo Steller, Ellenville, New York
Barbara Warner-Tracy, Susan B. Anthony School, Sacramento, California
Edward Weber, Campbell County School District, Gillette, Wyoming
Craig M. Welle, Spring Branch ISD Music Office, Houston, Texas

Affiliate Presidents

Alabama: Tillie D. Parks, Alexander County Board of Education, Alexander City
Alaska: Ernest B. Manzie, Fairbanks North Star Borough School District

Alberta: Jim Latimer, Calgary Board of Education

Arizona: Suzanne K. Ashby, Rincon High School, Tucson

Arkansas: Thomas L. Gathen, Eudora School District

British Columbia: Marilynn Leskun, McMillan Elementary School, Abbotsford

California: Mary Ann Sanders, Orchard Elementary School, Modesto

Connecticut: Alida D. Begina, Hamden Public School

Curacao: Paul R. de Rooy, Department van Onderwijs

Delaware: Terry Bayard Joyner, Colonial School District, New Castle

District of Columbia: James Amick

Florida: May D. Gamble, Pahokee High School

Georgia: Connie Hoyle, Meadow Creek Elementary School, Norcross

Germany: A. Elizabeth Rowe

Hawaii: Karen H. Hill, Red Hill Elementary School, Honolulu

Idaho: Bonnie A. Farmin, Idaho School District 391, Kellogg

Illinois: Anne Noland, Forest Ridge School District 142, Oak Forest

Indiana: Roger Fisher, Paoli Community Schools

Iowa: Pam Johnson, Valley Southwoods High School, West Des Moines

Japan: Esther M. Golde

Kansas: John Heim, Emporia School District

Kentucky: Carmen Rader-Bowles, Fayette County School District, Lexington

Louisiana: Don Mercer, East Baton Rouge Parish School Board

Maine: Betty Johanson, Lincoln School, Augusta

Manitoba: Diane Phillips, Transcona Springfield School District 12, Winnipeg

Maryland: Gary E. Dunkleberger, North Carroll High School, Hampstead

Massachusetts: Joseph C. Walsh, Tewksbury Public Schools

Michigan: Roberta E. Glaser, St. Johns Public School

Minnesota: Joe F. Wemette, School District 622, Maplewood

Mississippi: Elaine Venable, Charleston Elementary School

Missouri: Arnold Lindaman, Northwest Missouri State University, Maryville

Montana: Bill McCaw, University of Montana, Columbia Falls

Nebraska: Don Fritz, Educational Services Unit 6, Milford

Nevada: Michael Wilson, R. E. Tobler Elementary School, Las Vegas

New Hampshire: Jane M. Lacasse, Boscawen Elementary School, Penacock

New Jersey: Bonnie Weiskittel, Delran Middle School

New Mexico: Elwyn Carl Hulett, Center for Teaching Excellence, Portales

New York: Mary Ellen Freeley, Carle Place Union Free School District

North Carolina: Jean Bullock-Steverson, Rockingham County Schools, Eden

North Dakota: Clarke Ranum, Scranton Public Schools

Northwest Territories: Gordon Miller, Harry Camsell School, Hay River

Ohio: Richard W. Evans, Albion Elementary School, North Royalton

Oklahoma: Peggy G. Matlock, Moore Public Schools

Ontario: Roland D. Kay, Madawaska Valley District High School, Barry's Bay

Oregon: Colin Cameron, McMinnville School District

Pennsylvania: Linda Bigos, East Pennsboro Area School District, Enola

Puerto Rico: Adela de Coro, Ponce

Rhode Island: Kenneth R. DiPietro, Cumberland School District

Singapore: Kwang Yap Tan, Ministry of Education

South Carolina: Judy Lehr, Furman University, Greenville

South Dakota: Merry L. Bleeker, Mitchell School District 17-2

Spain: Julianne Stall, American School of Valencia

St. Maarten: Juliana Hodge-Shipley, Methodist Agogic Center

Tennessee: Sue W. Boyer, Knox County Schools, Knoxville

Texas: Yolanda M. Rey, El Paso Independent School District

Trinidad & Tobago: Jennifer Doyle, Ministry of Education

United Kingdom: Jennie Thomas, Maplesden Noakes School

Utah: Patricia Hunter Rowse, Tintic School District, Eureka

Vermont: Patricia Halloran, Calais Elementary School, Plainfield

Virginia: Peggy B. McMaster, Magruder School, Williamsburg

Washington: Gayle Northcutt, E. Wanatchee School District

West Virginia: Meri Cummings, Wheeling Jesuit University

Wisconsin: Sue Alberti, Ashwaubenon School District, Green Bay

Wyoming: Cathy Hemker, Washington Elementary School, Green River

ASCD REVIEW COUNCIL

Chair: Arthur Stellar, Kingston City School District, New York

Marge Chow, City University, Renton, Washington

Quincy Harrigan, Insular Department of Education, St. Maarten

Corrine Hill, Salt Lake City, Utah

Nancy Oelklaus, Texas ASCD, Austin

ASCD HEADQUARTERS STAFF

Gene R. Carter, *Executive Director*
Diane Berreth, *Deputy Executive Director*
Frank Betts, *Deputy Executive Director, Operations*
Melody Ridgeway, *Assistant Executive Director, Information Systems and Services*
Douglas Soffer, *Assistant Executive Director, Constituent Relations*
Mikki Terry, *Associate Executive Director, Program Development*

Holly Abrams	Joan Halford	Margaret Oosterman
Diana Allen	Deborah Hall	Diane Parker
Barry Amis	Vicki Hancock	Kelvin Parnell
Joanne Arnold	Nancy Harrell	Margini Patel
Holly Cutting Baker	Leon Hayes	Elisa Perodin
Kathy Baker	John Henderson	Carolyn Pool
Monica Barnette	Davene Holland	Ruby Powell
Kimberly Bell	Julie Houtz	Tina Prack
Shannon Bethea	Angela Howard	Pam Price
Gary Bloom	Debbie Howerton	Gena Randall
Cecilia Boamah	Tonya Huntley	Karen Rasmussen
Meltonya Booze	Todd Johnson	Dan Ratner
Maritza Bourque	Jo Ann Jones	Tisha Reed
Susan Bowser	Mary Jones	Christine Richards
Joan Brandt	Teola Jones	Judy Rixey
Dorothy Brown	Pamela Karwasinski	Rita Roberts
Beverly Buckner	Diane Kelly	Carly Rothman
Colette Burgess	Hughie Kelly	Jeff Rupp
Simon Cable	Laura Kelly	Darcie Russell
Angela Caesar	Leslie Kiernan	Jamie Sawatzky
Roger Campbell	Crystal Knight-Lee	Josh Scheers-Masters
Sally Chapman	Tammy Larson	Marge Scherer
John Checkley	Kimberly Lau	Jan Schmidt
Kathy Checkley	Betsy Lindeman	Beth Schweinefuss
Raiza Chernault	Gabe Lynch	Timothy Scott
Sandra Claxton	John Mackie	Bob Shannon
Judi Connelly	Indu Madan	Lisa Shannon
Andrea Corsillo	Larry Mann	Katherine Sibert
Agnes Crawford	Toby Mauldin	Ed Silverman
Marcia D'Arcangelo	Michael Maxwell	Tracey Smith
Jay DeFranco	J'ana McCaleb	Valerie Sprague
Keith Demmons	Jan McCool	Karen Steirer
Becky DeRigge	Georgia McDonald	Brian Sullivan
Clare Driscoll	Robin McDougall	Michelle Tarr
Stephanie Dunn	Michelle McKinley	Beth Taylor
Shiela Ellison	Clara Meredith	Carol Tell
Don Ernst	Ron Miletta	Jocelyn Thomas
Honor Fede	Frances Mindel	Frank Wald
Gillian Fitzpatrick	Nancy Modrak	Mia Wallace
Randi Forster	Kenny Moir	Judy Walter
John Franklin	Karen Monaco	Ingrid West
Julie Garity	Jackie Morrison	Vivian West
Michael Gitau	Margaret Murphy	Bernita Whitaker
Barbara Gleason	Dina Murray	Kay Whittington
Josh Goldfein	Charwin Nah	Linda Wilkey
Troy Gooden	Mary Beth Nielsen	Scott Willis
Yolanda Greene	KayLani Noble	Carolyn Wojcik
Nora Gyuk	John O'Neil	Donna Wright

Index